CLYMER®

HONDA
VT500 • 1983-1988

The world's finest publisher of mechanical how-to manuals

P.O. Box 12901, Overland Park, Kansas 66282-2901

Copyright ©1994 Penton Business Media, Inc.

FIRST EDITION
First Printing May, 1985
Second Printing December, 1985
Third Printing November, 1988
Fourth Printing June, 1990
Fifth Printing December, 1991

SECOND EDITION
First Printing February, 1993

THIRD EDITION
First Printing July, 1994
Second Printing January, 1996
Third Printing November, 1997
Fourth Printing September, 1999
Fifth Printing September, 2001
Sixth Printing June, 2003
Seventh Printing April, 2005
Eighth Printing May, 2008

Printed in U.S.A.

CLYMER and colophon are registered trademarks of Penton Business Media, Inc.

ISBN-10: 0-89287-632-8

ISBN-13: 978-0-89287-632-7

Library of Congress: 94-77635

MEMBER

MOTORCYCLE
INDUSTRY
COUNCIL, INC.

TOOLS AND EQUIPMENT: K and L Supply at www.klsupply.com.

COVER: 1984 VT500FT Ascot owned and photographed by Matthew Busby, Manhattan, KS.

CLYMER®

Publisher Shawn Etheridge

EDITORIAL

Managing Editor
James Grooms

Editor
Steven Thomas

Associate Editor
Rick Arens

Authors
Jay Bogart
Michael Morlan
George Parise
Mark Rolling
Ed Scott
Ron Wright

Technical Illustrators
Steve Amos
Errol McCarthy
Mitzi McCarthy
Bob Meyer

Group Production Manager
Dylan Goodwin

Production Manager
Greg Araujo

Senior Production Editor
Darin Watson

Production Editors
Holly McComas
Adriane Roberts
Taylor Wright

Production Designer
Jason Hale

MARKETING/SALES AND ADMINISTRATION

Sales Managers
Justin Henton
Matt Tusken

Marketing and Sales Representative
Erin Gribbin

Director, Operations–Books
Ron Rogers

Customer Service Manager
Terri Cannon

Customer Service Account Specialist
Courtney Hollars

Customer Service Representatives
Dinah Bunnell
April LeBlond

Warehouse & Inventory Manager
Leah Hicks

Penton Media

P.O. Box 12901, Overland Park, KS 66282-2901 • 800-262-1954 • 913-967-1719

More information available at *clymer.com*

CONTENTS

QUICK REFERENCE DATA

MOTORCYCLE INFORMATION

MODEL:_____ YEAR:_____

VIN NUMBER:_____

ENGINE SERIAL NUMBER:_____

CARBURETOR SERIAL NUMBER OR I.D. MARK:_____

TUNE-UP SPECIFICATIONS

Valve clearance (cold)	
Intake	0.10 mm (0.004 in.)
Exhaust	0.10 mm (0.004 in.)
Compression pressure (at sea level)	12.0 2.0 kg.cm^2 (171 ± 28 psi)
Spark plug type	
Standard heat rang	ND X24EPR-U9 or NGK DPR8EA-9
Cold weather*	ND X22EPR-U9 or NGK DPR7EA-9
Extended high-speed	ND X27EPR-UP or NGK DPR9EA-9
Spark plug gap	0.8-0.9 mm (0.031-0.035 in.)
Ignition timing	"F" mark @ 1,100 ± 100 rpm
Idle speed	1,100 ± 100 rpm

*Cold weather climate—below 41° F (5° C).

COOLING SYSTEM SPECIFICATIONS

Coolant capacity	
Total system	
VT500C	
1983-1984	1.7 liters (1.8 U.S. qt.)
1985-1986	2.0 liters (2.1 U.S. qt.)
VT500FT	1.7 liters (1.8 U.S. qt.)
VT500E	2.0 liters (1.76 Imp. qt.)
Radiator and engine	
VT500C	
1983-1984	1.2 liters (1.3 U.S. qt.)
1985-1986	1.55 lliters (1.64 U.S. qt.)
VT500FT	1.2 liters (1.3 U.S. qt.)
VT500E	1.55 liters (1.36 Imp. qt.)
Reserve tank	
VT500C	
1983-1984	0.5 liters (0.5 U.S. qt.)
1985-1986	0.45 liters (0.47 U.S. qt.)
VT500FT	0.5 liters (0.5 U.S. qt.)
VT500E	0.45 liters (0.4 Imp. qt.)
Radiator cap relief pressure	0.75-1.05 kg/cm^2 (10.7-14.9 psi)
Thermostat	
Begins to open	80-84° C (176-183° F)
Valve lift	Minimum of 8 mm @ 95° C (203° F)
Boiling point (50:50 mixture)	
Unpressurized	107.7° C (226° F)
Pressureized (cap on)	125.6° C (258° F)
Freezing point (hydrometer test)	
55:45 water:antifreeze	−32° C (−25° F)
50:50 water:antifireeze	−37° C (−34° F)
45:55 water:antifreeze	−45.5° C (−48° F)

FLUID CAPACITIES

Fuel
VT500C
   1983-1984   12.0 liters (3.1 U.S. gal., 2.64 Imp. gal.)
   1985-1986   11.5 liters (3.0 U.S. gal., 2.5 Imp. gal.)
VT500FT   9.5 liters (2.51 U.S. gal., 2.09 Imp. gal.)
VT500E   12.0 liters (3.1 U.S. gal., 2.64 Imp. gal.)
Engine oil
  Oil and filter change   2.5 liters (2.6 U.S. qt., 2.2 Imp. qt.)
  At overhaul   3.0 liters (3.2 U.S. qt., 2.6 Imp. qt.)
Coolant (total)
VT500C
   1983-1984   1.7 liters (1.8 U.S. qt.)
   1985-1986   2.0 liters (2.1 U.S. qt.)
VT500FT   1.7 liters (1.8 U.S. qt.)
VT500E   2.0 liters (1.76 Imp. qt.)
Final drive unit (oil change)   120 cc (4.1 oz.)

FORK OIL CAPACITY

VT500FT Ascot*   390 cc (13.2 U.S. fl. oz.)
VT500C Shadow
1983-1984
   Right-hand leg   440 cc (14.9 U.S. fl. oz.)
   Left-hand leg   455 cc (15.4 U.S. fl. oz.)
1985-1986
   Left- and right-hand leg 442 cc (15.0 U.S. fl. oz.)
VT500E Euro Sport*   360 cc (12.7 Imp. fl. oz.)

*Capacity for each fork leg.

REPLACEMENT BULBS

| Item | Wattage | | Number |
	VT500C and FT	VT500E	U.S.
Headlight (quartz bulb)	12 V 60/55W	12 V 60/55W	H4
Tail/brakelight	12 V 8/27W	12 V 21/5W	SAE No. 1157
Turn signals			
Front	12 V 23/8W	12 V 21W	SAE No. 1034
Rear	12 V 23W	12 V 21W	SAE No. 1073
Instrument lights	12 V 3W	12 V 3W	—
Indicator lights	12 V 3W	12 V 3W	—
High beam indicator	12 V 3W	12 V 3W	—
Oil pressure warning	12 V 3W	12 V 3W	—
Neutral indicator	12 V 3W	12 V 3W	—
Position light	12 V 8W	12 V 4W	SAE No. 1034

FRONT FORK AIR PRESSURE

Normal	Maximum*
0-6 psi (0-0.4 kg/cm^2)	43 psi (4 kg/cm^2)

*Do not exceed the maximum air pressure or internal parts of the fork will be damaged.

TIRE INFLATION PRESSURE (COLD)

Tire size	Air pressure	
	Up to 200 lb. (890 kg)	Maximum load limit*
Front 3.50S-18	28 psi (2.00 kg/cm^2)	28 psi (2.00 kg/cm^2)
Rear 130/90-16	28 psi (2.00 kg/cm^2)	36 psi (2.50 kg/cm^2)

*Maximum load limit includes total weight of motorcycle with accessories, rider(s) and luggage.

CHAPTER ONE

GENERAL INFORMATION

This detailed, comprehensive manual covers the Honda 500 cc water-cooled V-twins from 1983-1988. The expert text gives complete information on maintenance, tune-up, repair and overhaul. Hundreds of photos and drawings guide you through every step. The book includes all you need to know to keep your Honda running right.

A shop manual is a reference. You want to be able to find information fast. As in all Clymer books, this one is designed with you in mind. All chapters are thumb tabbed. Important items are extensively indexed at the rear of the book. All procedures, tables, photos, etc., in this manual are for the reader who may be working on the bike or using this manual for the first time. All the most frequently used specifications and capacities are summarized on the *Quick Reference Data* pages at the front of the book.

Keep the book handy in your tool box. It will help you to better understand how the bike runs, lower repair and maintenance costs and generally improve your satisfaction with the bike.

Table 1 is at the end of this chapter.

MANUAL ORGANIZATION

All dimensions and capacities are expressed in English units familiar to U.S. mechanics as well as in metric units.

This chapter provides general information and discusses equipment and tools useful both for preventive maintenance and troubleshooting.

Chapter Two provides methods and suggestions for quick and accurate diagnosis and repair of problems. Troubleshooting procedures discuss typical symptoms and logical methods to pinpoint the trouble.

Chapter Three explains all periodic lubrication and routine maintenance necessary to keep the Honda running well. Chapter Three also includes recommended tune-up procedures, eliminating the need to constantly consult chapters on the various assemblies.

Subsequent chapters describe specific systems such as the engine, clutch, transmission, fuel, exhaust, cooling, suspension and brakes. Each chapter provides disassembly, repair and assembly procedures in simple step-by-step form. If a repair is impractical for a home mechanic, it is so indicated. It is usually faster and less expensive to take such repairs to a dealer or competent repair shop. Specifications concerning a particular system are included at the end of the appropriate chapter.

Some of the procedures in this manual specify special tools. In most cases, the tool is illustrated either in actual use or alone. Well-equipped mechanics may find they can substitute similar tools already on hand or can fabricate their own.

The terms NOTE, CAUTION and WARNING have a specific meaning in this manual. A NOTE provides additional information to make a step or procedure easier or clearer. Disregarding a NOTE could cause inconvenience, but would not cause equipment damage or personal injury.

A CAUTION emphasizes areas where equipment damage could result. Disregarding a CAUTION could cause permanent mechanical damage; however, personal injury is unlikely.

A WARNING emphasizes areas where personal injury or even death could result from negligence. Mechanical damage may also occur. WARNINGS *are to be taken seriously.* In some cases, serious injury or death has resulted from disregarding similar warnings.

Throughout this manual keep in mind 2 conventions. "Front" refers to the front of the bike. The front of any component, such as the engine, is the end which faces toward the front of the bike. The "left-" and "right-hand" sides refer to the position of the parts as viewed by a rider sitting on the seat facing forward. For example, the throttle control is on the right-hand side and the clutch lever is on the left-hand side. These rules are simple, but even experienced mechanics occasionally become disoriented.

SERVICE HINTS

Most of the service procedures covered are straightforward and can be performed by anyone reasonably handy with tools. It is suggested, however, that you consider your own capabilities carefully before attempting any operation involving major disassembly of the engine.

Some operations, for example, require the use of a press. It would be wiser to have these performed by a shop equipped for such work, rather than trying to do the job yourself with makeshift equipment. Other procedures require precise measurements. Unless you have the skills and equipment required, it would be better to have a qualified repair shop make the measurements for you.

There are many items available that can be used on your hands before and after working on your bike. A little preparation prior to getting "all greased up" will help when cleaning up later.

Before starting out, work Vaseline, soap or a product such as Pro-Tek (**Figure 1**) onto your forearms, into your hands and under your fingernails and cuticles. This will make cleanup a lot easier.

For cleanup, use a waterless hand soap such as Sta-Lube and then finish up with powdered Boraxo and a fingernail brush.

Repairs go much faster and easier if the bike is clean before you begin work. There are special cleaners, such as Gunk or Bel-Ray Degreaser, for washing the engine and related parts. Just spray or brush on the cleaning solution, let it stand, then

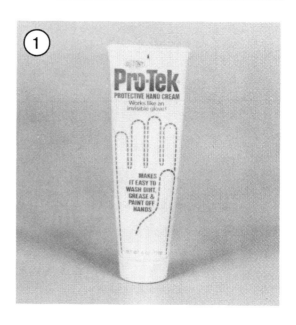

rinse it away with a garden hose. Clean all oily or greasy parts with cleaning solvent as you remove them.

> *WARNING*
> *Never use gasoline as a cleaning agent. It presents an extreme fire hazard. Be sure to work in a well-ventilated area when using cleaning solvent. Keep a fire extinguisher, rated for gasoline fires, handy in any case.*

Special tools are required for some repair procedures. These may be purchased from a dealer or motorcycle shop, rented from a tool rental dealer or fabricated by a mechanic or machinist (often at a considerable savings).

Much of the labor charged for repairs made by mechanics are for the removal and disassembly of other parts to reach the defective unit. It is usually possible to perform the preliminary operations yourself and then take the defective unit in to the dealer for repair.

Once you have decided to tackle the job yourself, read the entire section in this manual which pertains to it, making sure you have identified the proper one. Study the illustrations and text until you have a good idea of what is involved in completing the job satisfactorily. If special tools or replacement parts are required, make arrangements to get them before you start. It is frustrating and time-consuming to get partly into a job and then be unable to complete it.

Simple wiring checks can be easily made at home, but knowledge of electronics is almost a necessity for performing tests with complicated electronic testing gear.

During disassembly of parts keep a few general cautions in mind. Force is rarely needed to get things apart. If parts are a tight fit, such as a bearing in a case, there is usually a tool designed to separate them. Never use a screwdriver to pry parts with machined surfaces such as crankcase halves. You will mar the surfaces and end up with leaks.

Make diagrams (or take a Polaroid picture) wherever similar-appearing parts are found. For instance, crankcase bolts are often not the same length. You may think you can remember where everything came from, but mistakes are costly. There is also the possibility you may be sidetracked and not return to work for days or even weeks, in which interval carefully laid out parts may have become disturbed.

Tag all similar internal parts for location and mark all mating parts for position. Record number and thickness of any shims as they are removed. Small parts such as bolts can be identified by placing them in plastic sandwich bags. Seal and label them with masking tape.

Wiring should be tagged with masking tape and marked as each wire is removed. Again, do not rely on memory alone.

Protect finished surfaces from physical damage or corrosion. Keep gasoline and hydraulic fluid off painted surfaces.

Frozen or very tight bolts and screws can often be loosened by soaking with penetrating oil, such as WD-40 or Liquid Wrench, then sharply striking the bolt head a few times with a hammer and punch (or screwdriver for screws). Avoid heat unless absolutely necessary, since it may melt, warp or remove the temper from many parts.

No parts, except those assembled with a press fit, require unusual force during assembly. If a part is hard to remove or install, find out why before proceeding.

Cover all openings after removing parts to keep dirt, small tools, etc., from falling in.

When assembling 2 parts, start all fasteners, then tighten evenly.

Wiring connections and brake components should be kept clean and free of grease and oil.

When assembling parts, be sure all shims and washers are installed exactly as they came out.

Whenever a rotating part butts against a stationary part, look for a shim or washer. Use new gaskets if there is any doubt about the condition of the old ones. A thin coat of oil on gaskets may help them seal effectively.

Heavy grease can be used to hold small parts in place if they tend to fall out during assembly.

However, keep grease and oil away from electrical and brake components.

High spots may be sanded off a piston with sandpaper, but fine emery cloth and oil will do a much more professional job.

Carbon can be removed from the head, the piston crowns and the exhaust ports with a dull screwdriver. *Do not* scratch machined surfaces. Wipe off the surface with a clean cloth when finished.

The carburetors are best cleaned by disassembling them and soaking the parts in a commercial carburetor cleaner. Never soak gaskets and rubber parts in these cleaners. Never use wire to clean out jets and air passages; they are easily damaged. Use compressed air to blow out the carburetor *after* the float has been removed.

A baby bottle makes a good measuring device for adding oil to the final drive and front forks. Get one that is graduated in fluid ounces and cubic centimeters. After it has been used for this purpose, do not let a small child drink out of it as there will always be an oil residue in it.

Take your time and do the job right. Do not forget that a newly rebuilt engine must be broken in the same as a new one. Keep the rpm within the limits given in your owner's manual when you get back on the road.

TORQUE SPECIFICATIONS

Torque specifications throughout this manual are given in Newton meters (N•m) and foot pounds (ft.-lb.). Newton meters have been adopted in place of meter kilograms (mkg) in accordance with the International Modernized Metric System. Tool manufacturers offer torque wrenches calibrated in Newton meters and Sears has a Craftsman line calibrated in both values.

Existing torque wrenches calibrated in meter kilograms can be used by performing a simple conversion. All you have to do is move the decimal point one place to the right; for example, 4.7 mkg = 47 N•m. This conversion is accurate enough for mechanical work even though the exact mathematical conversion is 3.5 mkg = 34.3 N•m.

SAFETY FIRST

Professional mechanics can work for years and never sustain a serious injury. If you observe a few rules of common sense and safety, you can enjoy many hours servicing your own machine. If you ignore these rules you can hurt yourself or damage the bike.

1. Never use gasoline as a cleaning solvent.

2. Never smoke or use a torch in the vicinity of flammable liquids such as cleaning solvent in open containers.

3. If welding or brazing is required on the machine, remove the fuel tank to a safe distance, at least 50 feet away.

4. Use the proper sized wrenches to avoid damage to nuts and injury to yourself.

5. When loosening a tight or stuck nut, think about what would happen if the wrench should slip. Be careful; protect yourself accordingly.

6. Keep your work area clean and uncluttered.

7. Wear safety goggles during all operations involving drilling, grinding or the use of a cold chisel.

8. Never use worn tools.

9. Keep a fire extinguisher handy and be sure it is rated for gasoline and electrical fires.

SPECIAL TIPS

Because of the extreme demands placed on a bike several points should be kept in mind when performing service and repair. The following items are general suggestions that may improve the overall life of the machine and help avoid costly failures.

1. Use a locking compound such as Loctite Lock N' Seal No. 2114 (blue Loctite) on all bolts and nuts, even if they are secured with lockwashers. This type of Loctite does not harden completely and allows easy removal of the bolt or nut. A screw or bolt lost from an engine cover or bearing retainer could easily cause serious and expensive damage before its loss is noticed.

When applying Loctite, use a small amount. If too much is used, it can work its way down the threads and stick parts together not meant to be stuck.

Keep a tube of Loctite in your tool box; when used properly it is cheap insurance.

2. Use a hammer-driven impact tool to remove and install all bolts, particularly engine cover screws. These tools help prevent the rounding off of bolt heads and ensure a tight installation.

3. When replacing missing or broken fasteners (bolts, nuts and screws), especially on the engine or frame components, always use Honda replacement parts. They are specially hardened for each application. The wrong 50-cent bolt could easily cause serious and expensive damage, not to mention rider injury.

4. When installing gaskets in the engine, always use Honda replacement gaskets *without* sealer, unless designated. These gaskets are designed to swell when they come in contact with oil. Gasket sealer will prevent the gaskets from swelling as intended, which can result in oil leaks. These Honda gaskets are cut from material of the precise thickness needed. Installation of a too thick or too thin gasket in a critical area could cause engine damage.

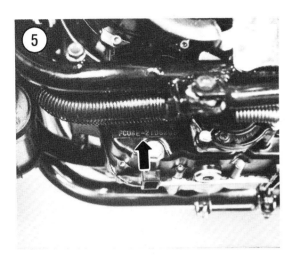

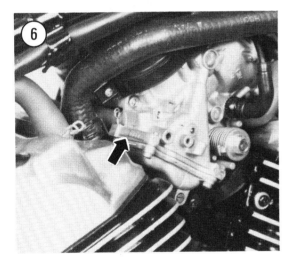

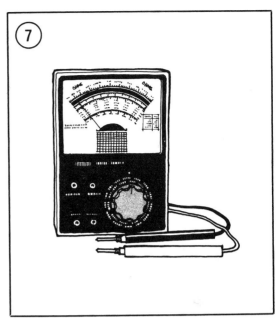

SERIAL NUMBERS

You must know the model serial number and VIN number for registration purposes and when ordering replacement parts.

The frame serial number is stamped on the right-hand side of the steering head (**Figure 3**). The vehicle identification number (VIN) is on the left-hand side of the steering head (**Figure 4**). The engine serial number is located on the lower left-hand side of the crankcase above the oil drain plug (**Figure 5**). The carburetor identification number is located on the rear of the carburetor body above the float bowl on the intake side as shown in **Figure 6**.

TUNE-UP AND TROUBLESHOOTING TOOLS

Multimeter or Volt-ohm Meter

This instrument (**Figure 7**) is invaluable for electrical system troubleshooting and service. A few of its functions may be duplicated by homemade test equipment, but for the serious mechanic it is a must. Its uses are described in the applicable sections of the book.

Strobe Timing Light

This instrument is necessary for tuning. By flashing a light at the precise instant the spark plug fires, the position of the timing mark can be seen. Marks on the alternator flywheel line up with the stationary mark on the crankcase while the engine is running.

EXPENDABLE SUPPLIES

Certain expendable supplies are required during maintenance and repair work. These include grease, oil, gasket cement, wiping rags and cleaning solvent. Ask your dealer for the special locking compounds, silicone lubricants and other products (**Figure 2**) which make vehicle maintenance simpler and easier. Cleaning solvent or kerosene is available at some service stations or hardware stores.

PARTS REPLACEMENT

Honda makes frequent changes during a model year—some minor, some relatively major. When you order parts from the dealer or other parts distributor, always order by engine and frame number. Write the numbers down and carry them with you. Compare new parts to old before purchasing them. If they are not alike, have the parts manager explain the difference to you.

Suitable lights range from inexpensive neon bulb types to powerful xenon strobe lights. See **Figure 8**. Neon timing lights are difficult to see and must be used in dimly lit areas. Xenon strobe timing lights can be used outside in bright sunlight. Both types work on the bike; use according to the manufacturer's instructions.

Portable Tachometer

A portable tachometer is necessary for tuning. See **Figure 9**. Ignition timing and carburetor adjustments must be performed at the specified idle speed. The best instrument for this purpose is one with a low range of 0-1,000 or 0-2,000 rpm and a high range of 0-4,000 rpm. Extended range (0-6,000 or 0-8,000 rpm) instruments lack accuracy at lower speeds. The instrument should be capable of detecting changes of 25 rpm on the low range.

Compression Gauge

A compression gauge measures the engine compression (**Figure 10**). They are available from motorcycle or auto supply stores and mail order outlets.

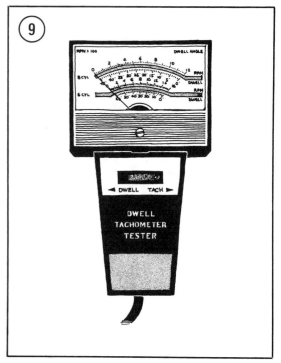

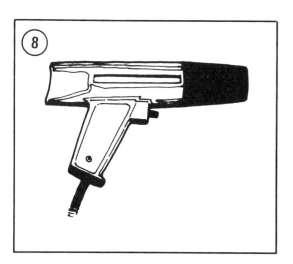

Table 1 HOME WORKSHOP TOOLS

Tool	Size or Specification
Screwdrivers	
Slot	5/16×8 in. blade
Slot	3/8×12 in. blade
Phillips	Size 2 tip, 6 in. blade
Pliers	
Gas pliers	6 in. overall
Vise grips®	10 in. overall
Needlenose	6 in. overall
Channel Lock	12 in. overall
Snap ring	–
Wrenches	
Box-end set	10-17, 20, 32 mm
Open-end set	10-17, 20, 32 mm
Crescent (adjustable)	6 and 12 in. overall
Socket set	1/2 in. drive ratchet with 10-17, 20, 32 mm sockets
Allen set	2-10 mm
Cone wrenches	–
Spoke wrench	–
Other Special Tools	
Impact driver	1/2 in. drive with ass't tips
Torque wrench	1/2 in. drive—0-100 ft.-lb.
Tire levers	For moped or motorcycle tires

CHAPTER TWO

TROUBLESHOOTING

Diagnosing mechanical problems is relatively simple if you use orderly procedures and keep a few basic principles in mind.

The troubleshooting procedures in this chapter analyze typical symptoms and show logical methods of isolating causes. These are not the only methods. There may be several ways to solve a problem, but only a systematic, methodical approach can guarantee success.

Never assume anything. Do not overlook the obvious. If you are riding along and the engine suddenly quits, check the easiest, most accessible problems first. Is there gasoline in the tank? Is the fuel shutoff valve in the ON position? Has a spark plug wire fallen off?

If nothing obvious turns up in a quick check, look a little further. Learning to recognize and describe symptoms will make repairs easier for you or a mechanic at the shop. Describe problems accurately and fully. Saying that "it won't run" isn't the same as saying "it quit at high speed and won't start" or that it "sat in my garage for 3 months and then wouldn't start."

Gather as many symptoms together as possible to aid in diagnosis. Note whether the engine lost power gradually or all at once. Remember that the more complicated a machine is, the easier it is to troubleshoot because symptoms point to specific problems.

After the symptoms are defined, areas which could cause the problems are tested and analyzed.

Guessing at the cause of a problem may provide the solution, but it can easily lead to frustration, wasted time and a series of expensive, unnecessary parts replacements.

You do not need fancy equipment or complicated test gear to determine whether repairs can be attempted at home. A few simple checks could save a large repair bill and time lost while the bike sits in a dealer's service department. On the other hand, be realistic and don't attempt repairs beyond your abilities. Service departments tend to charge a lot for putting together a disassembled engine that may have been abused. Some dealers won't even take on such a job—so use common sense and don't get in over your head.

OPERATING REQUIREMENTS

An engine needs 3 basics to run properly: correct fuel-air mixture, compression and a spark at the correct time. If one or more are missing, the engine just won't run. The electrical system is the weakest link of the 3. More problems result from electrical breakdowns than from any other source. Keep that in mind before you begin tampering with carburetor adjustments and the like.

If the bike has been sitting for any length of time and refuses to start, check and clean the spark plugs and then look to the gasoline delivery system. This includes the fuel tank, fuel shutoff valve and the fuel line to the carburetors. Gasoline deposits may have formed and gummed up the carburetor jets and air

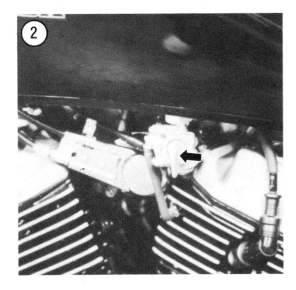

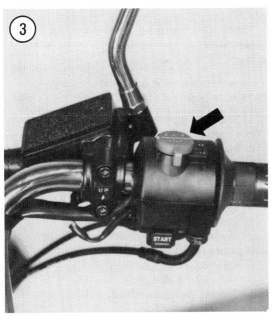

passages. Gasoline tends to lose its potency after standing for long periods. Condensation may contaminate the fuel with water. Drain the old fuel and try starting with a fresh tankful.

EMERGENCY TROUBLESHOOTING

When the bike is difficult to start or won't start at all, it does not help to wear down the battery using the starter. Check for obvious problems even before getting out your tools. Go down the following list step by step. Do each one; you may be embarrassed to find your kill switch is stuck in the OFF position, but that is better than wearing down the battery. If it still will not start, refer to the appropriate troubleshooting procedure which follows in this chapter.

1. Is there fuel in the tank? Open the filler cap (**Figure 1**) and rock the bike. Listen for fuel sloshing around.

> *WARNING*
> *Do not use an open flame to check in the tank. A serious explosion is certain to result.*

2. Is the fuel shutoff valve (**Figure 2**) in the ON position?
3. Make sure the kill switch (**Figure 3**) is not stuck in the OFF position.
4. Are all 4 spark plug wires on tight? Make sure to check the spark plug wire that is buried in the deep well at each end of the cylinder head. Push all of them on and slightly rotate them to clean the electrical connection between the plug and the connector.
5. Is the choke lever (**Figure 4**) in the right position? The lever should be moved *up* for a cold engine and *down* for a warm engine.

ENGINE STARTING

An engine that refuses to start or is difficult to start is very frustrating. More often than not, the problem is very minor and can be found with a simple and logical troubleshooting approach.

The following items show a beginning point from which to isolate engine starting problems.

Engine Fails to Start

Perform the following spark test to determine if the ignition system is operating properly.

1. Remove one of the spark plugs from one of the cylinders.
2. Connect the spark plug wire and connector to each of the spark plugs and touch the spark plug's base to a good ground like the engine cylinder head. Position the spark plugs so you can see the electrode (**Figure 5**).
3. Crank the engine over with the starter. A fat blue spark should be evident across each spark plug electrode.

> *WARNING*
> *If it is necessary to hold the high voltage lead, do so with an insulated pair of pliers. The high voltage generated by the CDI could produce serious or fatal shocks.*

4. If the spark is good, check for one or more of the following possible malfunctions:
   a. Obstructed fuel line.
   b. Leaking head gasket(s).
   c. Low compression.
5. If spark is not good, check for one or more of the following:
   a. Weak ignition coil(s).
   b. Weak CDI pulse generator(s).
   c. Weak spark unit(s).
   d. Broken or shorted high tension lead to the spark plug.
   e. Loose electrical connections.
   f. Loose or broken ignition coil ground wire.

Engine Is Difficult to Start

Check for one or more of the following possible malfunctions:
   a. Fouled spark plug(s).
   b. Improperly adjusted choke.
   c. Contaminated fuel system.
   d. Improperly adjusted carburetors.
   e. Weak ignition coil(s).
   f. Weak CDI pulse generator(s).
   g. Weak spark unit(s).

   h. Incorrect type ignition coil(s).
   i. Poor compression.

Engine Will Not Crank

Check for one or more of the following possible malfunctions:
   a. Discharged battery.
   b. Defective starter solenoid or starter motor.
   c. Seized piston(s).
   d. Seized crankshaft bearings.
   e. Broken connecting rod(s).
   f. Locked-up transmission or clutch assembly.

ENGINE PERFORMANCE

In the following check list, it is assumed that the engine runs, but is not operating at peak performance. This will serve as a starting point from which to isolate a performance malfunction.

The possible causes for each malfunction are listed in a logical sequence and in order of probability.

Engine Will Not Start or
Is Hard to Start

   a. Fuel tank empty.
   b. Obstructed fuel line or fuel shutoff valve.
   c. Sticking float valve in carburetor(s).
   d. Carburetor(s) incorrectly adjusted.
   e. Improper choke operation.
   f. Fouled or improperly gapped spark plug(s).
   g. Ignition timing incorrect.
   h. Broken or shorted ignition coil(s).
   i. Weak or faulty spark unit(s) or pulse generator(s).
   j. Valve clearance incorrect.
   k. Improper valve timing.
   l. Clogged air filter element.
   m. Contaminated fuel.

Engine Will Not Idle

a. Carburetor(s) incorrectly adjusted.
b. Fouled or improperly gapped spark plug(s).
c. Leaking head gasket(s).
d. Ignition timing incorrect.
e. Weak or faulty spark unit(s) or pulse generator(s).
f. Valve clearance incorrect.
g. Improper valve timing.
h. Obstructed fuel line or fuel shutoff valve.

Engine Misses at High Speed

a. Fouled or improperly gapped spark plugs.
b. Improper ignition timing.
c. Improper valve clearance.
d. Improper carburetor main jet selection.
e. Clogged jets in the carburetors.
f. Weak ignition coil.
g. Weak or faulty spark unit(s) or pulse generator(s).
h. Improper valve timing.
i. Obstructed fuel line or fuel shutoff valve.

Engine Overheating

a. Coolant level low.
b. Faulty temperature gauge or gauge sensor.
c. Thermostat stuck in the closed position.
d. Faulty radiator cap.
e. Passages blocked in the radiator, hoses or water jackets in the engine.
f. Fan blades cracked or missing.
g. Faulty fan motor.
h. Improper ignition timing.
i. Improper spark plug heat range.

Smoky Exhaust and Engine Runs Roughly

a. Carburetor mixture too rich.
b. Choke not operating correctly.
c. Water or other contaminants in fuel.
d. Clogged fuel line.
e. Clogged air filter element.

Engine Loses Power

a. Carburetor(s) incorrectly adjusted.
b. Engine overheating.
c. Improper ignition timing.
d. Incorrectly gapped spark plugs.
e. Weak ignition coil(s).
f. Weak spark unit(s).
g. Weak CDI pulse generator(s).

h. Obstructed muffler(s).
i. Dragging brake(s).

Engine Lacks Acceleration

a. Carburetor(s) mixture too lean.
b. Clogged fuel line.
c. Improper ignition timing.
d. Improper valve clearance.
e. Dragging brake(s).

ENGINE NOISES

1. *Knocking or pinging during acceleration—* Caused by using a lower octane fuel than recommended. May also be caused by poor fuel. Pinging can also be caused by spark plugs of the wrong heat range. Refer to *Spark Plug Selection* in Chapter Three.

2. *Slapping or rattling noises at low speed or during acceleration—* May be caused by piston slap (excessive piston to cylinder wall clearance).

3. *Knocking or rapping while decelerating—* Usually caused by excessive rod bearing clearance.

4. *Persistent knocking and vibration—* Usually caused by excessive main bearing clearance.

5. *Rapid on-off squeal—* Compression leak around cylinder head gasket(s) or spark plugs.

EXCESSIVE VIBRATION

This can be difficult to find without disassembling the engine. Usually this is caused by loose engine mounting hardware.

FRONT SUSPENSION AND STEERING

Poor handling may be caused by improper tire pressure, a damaged or bent frame or front steering components, a worn front fork assembly, worn wheel bearings or dragging brakes.

BRAKE PROBLEMS

Sticking disc brakes may be caused by a stuck piston(s) in a caliper assembly or warped pad shim(s).

A sticking drum brake may be caused by worn or weak return springs, dry pivot and cam bushings or improper adjustment. Grabbing brakes may be caused by greasy linings which must be replaced. Brake grab may also be due to an out-of-round drum. Glazed linings will cause loss of stopping power.

LUBRICATION, MAINTENANCE AND TUNE-UP

A motorcycle, even in normal use, is subjected to tremendous heat, stress and vibration. When neglected, any bike becomes unreliable and actually dangerous to ride.

To gain the utmost in safety, performance and useful life from the Honda V-twins it is necessary to make periodic inspections and adjustments. Frequently, minor problems are found during these inspections that are simple and inexpensive to correct at the time. If they are not found and corrected at this time they could lead to major and more expensive problems later on.

Start out by doing simple tune-up, lubrication and maintenance. Tackle more involved jobs as you become more acquainted with the bike.

This chapter explains lubrication, maintenance and tune-up procedures required for the Honda 500 cc V-twins.

Table 1 is a suggested factory maintenance schedule. **Tables 1-8** are located at the end of this chapter.

ROUTINE CHECKS

The following simple checks should be performed at each stop at a service station for gas.

Engine Oil Level

Refer to *Engine Oil Level Check* under *Periodic Lubrication* in this chapter.

Coolant Level

Check the coolant level when the engine has warmed up to normal operating temperature.

Check the level in the coolant reserve tank. The level should be between the "UPPER" and "LOWER" marks (A, **Figure 1**). If necessary, add coolant to the reserve tank (not the radiator filler cap) through the fill cap (B, **Figure 1**) until the level is to the "UPPER" mark.

General Inspection

1. Quickly inspect the engine for signs of oil, fuel or coolant leakage.

2. Check the tires for embedded stones. Pry them out with your ignition key.

3. Make sure all lights work.

NOTE
At least check the brake light. It can burn out at any time. Motorists cannot stop as quickly as you and need all the warning you can give.

Tire Pressure

Tire pressure must be checked with the tires cold. Correct tire pressure varies with the load you are carrying. See **Table 2**.

Battery

Remove the left-hand side cover and check the battery electrolyte level. The level must be between the upper and lower level marks on the case (**Figure 2**).

For complete details see *Battery Removal, Installation and Electrolyte Level Check* in this chapter.

Check the level more frequently in hot weather; electrolyte will evaporate rapidly as heat increases.

Lights and Horn

With the engine running, check the following.

1. Pull the front brake lever on and check that the brake light comes on.

2. Push the rear brake pedal down and check that the brake light comes on soon after you have begun depressing the pedal.

3. Move the headlight dimmer switch to both the HI and LO positions and check to see that both headlight elements are working.

4. Turn the turn signal switch to the left and right positions and check that all 4 turn signals are working.

5. Push the horn button and make sure that the horn blows loudly.

6. If the horn or any of the lights failed to operate properly, refer to Chapter Seven.

PRE-CHECKS

The following checks should be performed prior to the first ride of the day.

1. Inspect all fuel lines and fittings for wetness.

2. Make sure the fuel tank is full of fresh gasoline.

3. Make sure the engine oil level is correct.

4. Inspect the coolant level in the coolant reserve tank.

5. Inspect the oil level in the final drive unit.

6. Check the operation of the clutch and adjust if necessary.

7. Check the operation of the front brake. Add hydraulic fluid to the brake master cylinder if necessary.

8. Check the throttle and the rear brake pedal. Make sure they operate properly with no binding.

9. Inspect the front and rear suspension; make sure it has a good solid feel with no looseness.

10. Check tire pressure. Refer to **Table 2**.

11. Check the air pressure in the front forks. Refer to **Table 3**.

12. Check the exhaust system for damage.

13 Check the tightness of all fasteners, especially engine mounting hardware.

SERVICE INTERVALS

The services and intervals shown in **Table 1** are recommended by the factory. Strict adherence to these recommendations will ensure long service from the Honda. If the bike is run in an area of high humidity, the lubrication services must be done more frequently to prevent possible rust damage.

For convenience when maintaining your motorcycle, most of the services shown in the table are described in this chapter. However, some procedures which require more than minor disassembly or adjustment are covered elsewhere in the appropriate chapter.

TIRES AND WHEELS

Tire Pressure

Tire pressure should be checked and adjusted to maintain the smoothness of the tire, good traction and handling and to get the maximum life out of the tire. A simple, accurate gauge (**Figure 3**) can be purchased for a few dollars and should be carried in your motorcycle tool kit. The appropriate tire pressures are shown in **Table 2**.

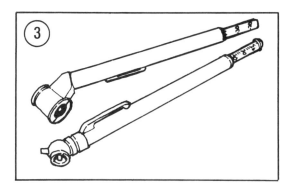

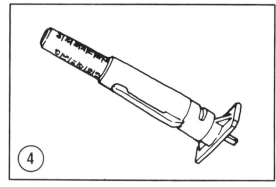

Tire Inspection

The tires take a lot of punishment so inspect them periodically for excessive wear, cuts, abrasions, etc. If you find a nail or other object in the tire, mark its location with a light crayon prior to removing it. This will help locate the hole for repair. Refer to Chapter Nine for tire changing and repair information.

Check local traffic regulations concerning minimum tread depth. Measure the tread depth at the center of the tire tread using a tread depth gauge (**Figure 4**) or small ruler. Honda recommends that original equipment tires be replaced when the front tire tread depth is 1.5 mm (1/16 in.) or less, when the rear tread depth is 2.0 mm (3/32 in.) or less or when tread wear indicators appear across the tire indicating the minimum tread depth.

Rim Inspection

Frequently inspect the wheel rims. If a rim has been damaged it might have been enough to knock it out of alignment. Improper wheel alignment can cause severe vibration and result in an unsafe riding condition. If the rim portion of the alloy wheel is damaged the wheel must be replaced as it cannot be repaired.

CRANKCASE BREATHER HOSE (U.S. MODELS ONLY)

Remove both side covers, seat and fuel tank. Inspect the breather hoses for cracks and deterioration. Make sure that all hose clamps are tight (**Figure 5**).

EVAPORATION EMISSION CONTROL (1984 CALIFORNIA MODELS ONLY)

Inspect the hoses for cracks, kinks and deterioration. Make sure that all hoses are tight where they attach to the various components. For correct hose routing, refer to Chapter Six.

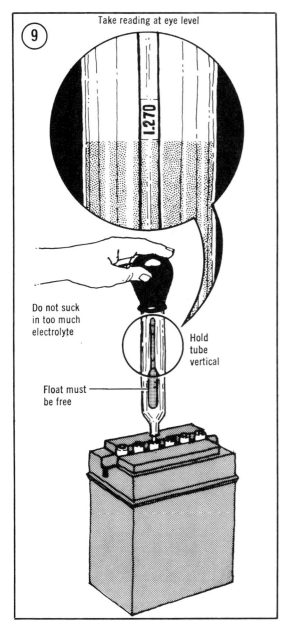

Take reading at eye level

1.270

Do not suck
in too much
electrolyte

Hold
tube
vertical

Float must
be free

BATTERY

Removal, Installation and Electrolyte Level Check

The battery is the heart of the electrical system. It should be checked and serviced as indicated in **Table 1**. The majority of electrical system troubles can be attributed to neglect of this vital component.

The electrolyte level should be maintained between the 2 marks on the battery case (**Figure 2**). If the electrolyte level is low, remove the battery from the bike so it can be thoroughly serviced and checked.

1. Remove the left-hand side cover and the seat.
2. Disconnect the electrical connector going to the voltage regulator (**Figure 6**).
3. Remove the nut (**Figure 7**) securing the battery holder plate and swing the holder plate out of the way.
4. Disconnect the battery negative (–) lead and then the positive (+) lead from the battery (A, **Figure 8**).
5. Unhook the battery vent tube (B, **Figure 8**) from the battery. Leave it routed through the bike's frame.
6. Slide the battery out of the frame.
7. Wipe off any of the highly corrosive residue that may have dripped from the battery during removal.

> *WARNING*
> *Protect your eyes, skin and clothing. If electrolyte gets into your eyes, flush your eyes thoroughly with clean water and get prompt medical attention.*

> *CAUTION*
> *Be careful not to spill battery electrolyte on painted or polished surfaces. The liquid contains sulphuric acid that is highly corrosive and will damage the finish. If it is spilled, wash it off immediately with soapy water and thoroughly rinse with clean water.*

8. Remove the caps from the battery cells and add distilled water to correct the fluid level. Never add electrolyte (acid) to correct the level.

> *NOTE*
> *If distilled water has been added, reinstall the battery caps and gently shake the battery for several minutes to mix the existing electrolyte with the new water.*

9. After the fluid level has been corrected and the battery allowed to stand a few minutes, remove the battery caps and check the specific gravity of the electrolyte in each cell with a hydrometer (**Figure 9**). See *Battery Testing* in this chapter.

10. After the battery has been refilled, recharged or replaced, install it by reversing these removal steps.

> *CAUTION*
> *If you removed the breather tube from the frame, be sure to route it so that residue will not drain onto any part of the bike's frame. The tube must be free of bends or twists as any restriction may pressurize the battery and damage it.*

Testing

Hydrometer testing is the best way to check battery condition. Use a hydrometer with numbered graduations from 1.100 to 1.300 rather than one with color-coded bands. To use the hydrometer, squeeze the rubber ball, insert the tip into the cell and release the pressure on the ball. Draw enough electrolyte to float the weighted float inside the hydrometer. Note the number in line with the surface of the electrolyte; this is the specific gravity for this cell (**Figure 10**). Squeeze the rubber ball again and return the electrolyte to the cell from which it came.

The specific gravity of the electrolyte in each battery cell is an excellent indication of that cell's condition. A fully charged cell will read from 1.260-1.280, while a cell in good condition reads from 1.230-1.260 and anything below 1.140 is discharged.

Specific gravity varies with temperature. For each 10° the electrolyte temperature exceeds 27° C (80° F), add 0.004 to readings indicated on the hydrometer. Subtract 0.004 for each 10° below 27° C (80° F).

If the cells test in the poor range, the battery requires recharging. The hydrometer is useful for checking the progress of the charging operation. **Table 4** shows approximate state of charge.

Charging

> *WARNING*
> *During the charging process, highly explosive hydrogen gas is released from the battery. The battery should be charged only in a well-ventilated area away from any open flames (including pilot lights on home gas appliances). Do not allow any smoking in the area. Never check the charge of the battery by arcing across the terminals; the resulting spark can ignite the hydrogen gas.*

> *CAUTION*
> *Always remove the battery from the bike before connecting the battery*

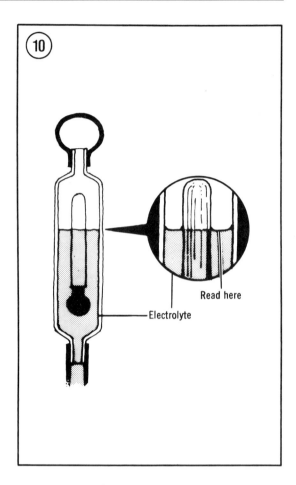

charger. Never recharge a battery in the bike's frame; the corrosive mist that is emitted during the charging process will corrode the surface.

1. Connect the positive (+) charger lead to the positive (+) battery terminal (or lead) and the negative (–) charger lead to the negative (–) battery terminal (or lead).

2. Remove all vent caps from the battery, set the charger at 12 volts and switch the charger on. If the output of the charger is variable, it is best to select a low setting–1 1/2 to 2 amps.

> *CAUTION*
> *The electrolyte level must be maintained at the upper level during the charging cycle; check and refill as necessary.*

3. After the battery has been charged for about 8 hours, turn the charger off, disconnect the leads and check the specific gravity. It should be within the limits specified in **Table 4**. If it is, and remains stable for 1 hour, the battery is considered charged.

4. Clean the battery terminals, electrical cable connectors and surrounding case and reinstall them

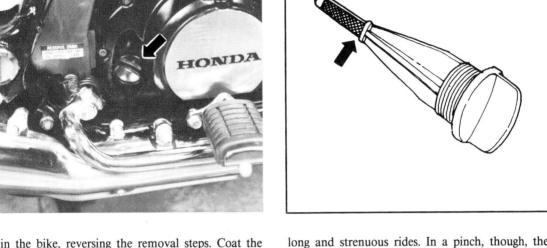

in the bike, reversing the removal steps. Coat the battery terminals with Vaseline or silicone spray to retard corrosion and decomposition of the terminals.

> *CAUTION*
> *Route the breather tube so that it does not drain onto any part of the bike's frame. The tube must be free of bends or twists as any restriction may pressurize the battery and damage it.*

New Battery Installation

When replacing the old battery with a new one, be sure to charge it completely (specific gravity 1.260-1.280) before installing it in the bike. Failure to do so or using the battery with a low electrolyte level will permanently damage the new battery.

PERIODIC LUBRICATION

Oil

Oil is graded according to its viscosity, which is an indication of how thick it is. The Society of Automotive Engineers (SAE) system distinguishes oil viscosity by numbers. Thick oils have higher viscosity numbers than thin oils. For example, an SAE 5 oil is a thin oil while an SAE 90 oil is relatively thick.

Grease

A good quality grease (preferably waterproof) should be used. Water does not wash grease off parts as easily as it washes oil off. In addition, grease maintains its lubricating qualities better than oil on

long and strenuous rides. In a pinch, though, the wrong lubricant is better than none at all. Correct the situation as soon as possible.

Engine Oil Level Check

Engine oil level is checked with the dipstick located at the rear of the right-hand crankcase/clutch cover (**Figure 11**).
1. Place the bike on level ground and on the centerstand.
2. Start the engine and let it idle for 2-3 minutes.
3. Shut off the engine and let the oil settle.
4. Unscrew the dipstick and wipe it clean. Reinsert the dipstick onto the threads in the hole; do not screw it in.
5. Remove the dipstick and check the oil level.
6. The level should be between the 2 lines (**Figure 12**) and not above the upper one. If the level is below the lower line, add the recommended type engine oil to correct the level.

Engine Oil and Filter Change

The factory-recommended oil and filter change interval is listed in **Table 1**. This assumes that the motorcycle is operated in moderate climates. In extreme climates, oil should be changed every 30 days. The time interval is more important than the mileage interval because acids formed by combustion blow-by will contaminate the oil even if the motorcycle is not run for several months. If the motorcycle is operated under dusty conditions, the oil will get dirty more quickly and should be changed more frequently than recommended.

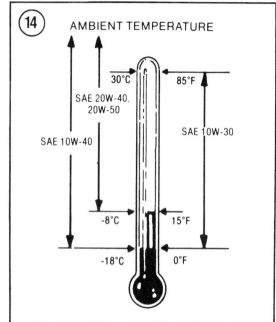

AMBIENT TEMPERATURE

Use only a high-quality detergent motor oil with an API classification of SE or SF. The classification is stamped or printed on top of the can (**Figure 13**). Try to use the same brand of oil at each change. Use of oil additives is not recommended as it may cause clutch slippage. Refer to **Figure 14** for correct oil viscosity to use under anticipated ambient temperatures (not engine oil temperature).

To change the engine oil and filter you will need the following:

   a. Drain pan.
   b. Funnel.
   c. Can opener or pour spout.
   d. 17 mm wrench (drain plug).
   e. Strap wrench for the oil filter.
   f. 3 quarts of oil.
   g. New oil filter.

There a number of ways to discard the old oil safely. Some service stations and oil retailers will accept your used oil for recycling, some may even give you money for it. Never drain the oil onto the ground.

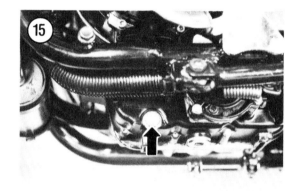

> *NOTE*
> *Never dispose of motor oil in the trash, on the ground, or down a storm drain. Many service stations accept used motor oil and waste haulers provide curbside used motor oil collection. Do not combine other fluids with motor oil to be recycled. To locate a recycler, contact the American Petroleum Institute (API) at www.recycleoil.org.*

1. Start the engine and let it reach operating temperature; 15-20 minutes of stop-and-go riding is usually sufficient.

2. Turn the engine off and place the bike on the centerstand.

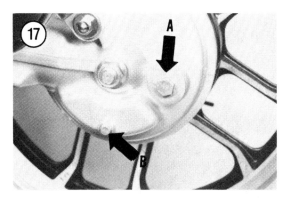

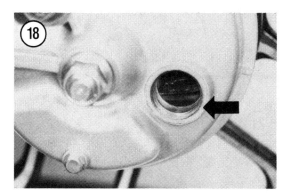

3. Place a drain pan under the engine. Place the drain pan so it is under the crankcase drain plug and the oil filter.

4. Remove the oil pan drain plug (**Figure 15**). Using a hammer and nail, carefully punch a hole in the bottom of the oil filter and allow the oil to drain out of the oil filter. Remove the oil filler cap (**Figure 11**); this will speed up the flow of oil.

5. Let it drain for at least 15-20 minutes. During this time, push the starter button a couple of times to help drain any remaining oil.

CAUTION
Do not let the engine start and run without oil in the crankcase.

6. Inspect the sealing washer on the crankcase drain plug. Replace if its condition is in doubt.

7. Install the oil pan drain plug and tighten to 35-40 N•m (25-29 ft.-lb.).

NOTE
Before removing the oil filter, thoroughly clean off all road dirt and oil around it.

8. Use a strap wrench and unscrew the oil filter from the crankcase (**Figure 16**).

NOTE
Prior to installing the oil filter, clean off the mating surface of the crankcase—do not allow any road dirt to enter into the oil system.

9. Apply a light coat of new engine oil to the rubber seal on the new oil filter and screw on the oil filter. Tighten the oil filter to approximately 18 N•m (12 ft.-lb.).

10. Insert a funnel into the oil fill hole and fill the engine with the recommended viscosity and quantity of oil. Refer to **Table 5**.

11. Screw in the oil filler cap securely.

12. Start the engine, let it run at moderate speed and check for leaks.

13. Turn the engine off and check for correct oil level; adjust as necessary.

Final Drive Oil Level Check

The final drive case should be cool. If the bike has been run, allow it to cool down (minimum of 10 minutes), then check the oil level. When checking or changing the final drive oil, do not allow any dirt or foreign matter to enter the case opening.

1. Place the bike on the centerstand on a level surface.

2. Wipe the area around the oil filler cap clean and unscrew the oil filler cap (A, **Figure 17**).

3. The oil level is correct if the oil is up to the lower edge of the filler cap hole (**Figure 18**). If the oil level is low, add hypoid gear oil API GL-5 until the oil level is correct.

NOTE
Use SAE 90 for ambient temperatures above 5° C (41° F) or SAE 80 for ambient temperatures below 5° C (41° F).

4. Inspect the O-ring seal (**Figure 19**) on the oil filler cap. If it is deteriorated or starting to harden it must be replaced.

5. Install the oil filler cap.

Final Drive Oil Change

The factory-recommended oil change interval is listed in **Table 1**.

To drain the oil you will need the following:

a. Drain pan.

b. Funnel.

c. Approximately 120-150 cc (4.1-5.1 oz.) of hypoid gear oil.

Discard old oil as outlined under *Engine Oil and Filter Change* in this chapter.

1. Ride the bike until normal operating temperature is obtained. Usually 15-20 minutes of stop-and-go riding is sufficient.

2. Place the bike on the centerstand.

3. Place a drain pan under the drain plug.

4. Remove the oil filler cap (A, **Figure 17**) and the drain plug (B, **Figure 17**).

5. Let the oil drain for at least 15-20 minutes to ensure that the majority of the oil has drained out.

6. Inspect the sealing washer on the drain plug; replace the sealing washer if necessary.

7. Install the drain plug and tighten it securely.

8. Insert a funnel into the oil filler cap hole.

9. Add approximately 120 cc (4.1 oz.) of hypoid gear oil. If you are filling the final drive unit after an overhaul, the capacity is 150 cc (5.1 oz.). Remove the funnel and make sure the oil level is correct.

NOTE
In order to measure the correct amount of fluid, use a plastic baby bottle. These have measurements in cubic centimeters (cc) and fluid ounces (oz.) on the side.

10. Install the oil filler cap.

11. Test ride the bike and check for oil leaks. After the test ride recheck the oil level as described in this chapter and readjust if necessary.

Front Fork Oil Change

There is no factory-recommended fork oil change interval but it's a good practice to change the oil every 12,800 km (8,000 miles) or when it becomes contaminated.

1. Remove each fork top cover and bleed off *all* air pressure from each fork by depressing the valve stem (A, **Figure 20**).

WARNING
Always bleed off all air pressure; failure to do so may cause personal injury when disassembling the fork.

NOTE
Release the air pressure gradually. If released too fast, fork oil will spurt out with the air. Protect your eyes and clothing accordingly.

2. Place wood block(s) under the engine to support it securely with the front wheel off the ground.

3. Unscrew the fork top cap (B, **Figure 20**) slowly as it is under spring pressure from the fork spring.

4. Place a drain pan under the drain screw and remove the drain screw (**Figure 21**). Allow the oil to drain for at least 5 minutes. *Never* reuse the oil.

CAUTION
Do not allow the fork oil to come into contact with any of the brake components.

5. Inspect the gasket on the drain screw; replace it if necessary. Install the drain screw.

6. Repeat Steps 3-5 for the other fork.

7. Refill each fork leg with the specified quantity of DEXRON automatic transmission fluid or 10W fork oil. Refer to **Table 6** for specified quantity.

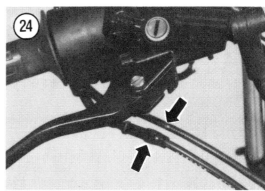

3

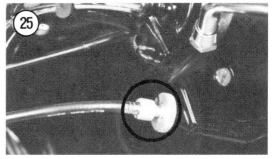

NOTE
In order to measure the correct amount of fluid, use a plastic baby bottle. These have measurements in cubic centimeters (cc) and fluid ounces (oz.) on the side.

8. Inspect the O-ring seal (**Figure 22**) on the fork top cap; replace if necessary.

9. Install the fork top cap while pushing down on the spring. Start the fork top cap slowly; don't cross thread it. Tighten fork top cap to 15-30 N•m (11-22 ft.-lb.).

10. Inflate the front forks to 0-40 kPa (0-6 psi). Do not use compressed air; only use a small hand-operated air pump as shown in **Figure 23**.

WARNING
Never use any type of compressed gas as an explosion may be lethal. Never heat the fork assembly with a torch or place it near an open flame or extreme heat as this will also result in an explosion.

11. Install the fork top cover on each fork leg.
12. Road test the bike and check for leaks.

Control Cable Lubrication

The throttle and clutch control cables should be lubricated at the interval indicated in **Table 1**. They should also be inspected at this time for fraying and the cable sheath should be checked for chafing. The cables are relatively inexpensive and should be replaced when found to be faulty.

The throttle control and clutch cables can be lubricated either with oil or with any of the popular cable lubricants and a cable lubricator. The first method requires more time and complete lubrication of the entire cable is less certain.

Examine the exposed end of the inner cable. If it is dirty or the cable feels gritty when moved up and down in its housing, first spray it with a lubricant/solvent such as LPS-25 or WD-40. Let this solvent drain out, then proceed with the following steps.

Oil method

1. Remove the screws that clamp the throttle control/switch housing together to gain access to the cable ends. Disconnect the cables from the throttle grip assembly (**Figure 24**).

2. Remove the clutch cable (**Figure 25**) from the clutch lever.

3. Make a cone of stiff paper and tape it to the end of the cable sheath (**Figure 26**).

4. Hold the cable upright and pour a small amount of thin oil (SAE 10W-30) into the cone. Work the cable in and out of the sheath for several minutes to help the oil work its way down to the end of the cable.

NOTE
To avoid a mess, place a shop cloth at the end of the cable to catch the oil as it runs out.

5. Remove the cone, reconnect the cables and adjust the cable(s) as described in this chapter.

Lubricator method

1. Remove the screws that clamp the throttle control/switch housing together to gain access to the cable ends. Disconnect the cables from the throttle grip assembly (**Figure 24**).

2. Remove the clutch cable (**Figure 25**) from the clutch lever.

3. Attach a lubricator following the manufacturer's instructions.

4. Insert the nozzle of the lubricant can in the lubricator, press the button on the can and hold it down until the lubricant begins to flow out of the other end of the cable.

NOTE
Place a shop cloth at the end of the cable(s) to catch all excess lubricant that will flow out.

5. Remove the lubricator, reconnect the cable(s) and adjust the cable(s) as described in this chapter.

Speedometer and Tachometer
Cable Lubrication

Lubricate the cables every year or whenever needle operation is erratic. The procedure is the same for both instruments.

1. Unscrew the retaining collar and remove the cable from the instrument (**Figure 27**).

2. Pull the cable from the cable sheath.

3. If the grease on the cable is contaminated, thoroughly clean off all old grease.

4. Thoroughly coat the cable with a good grade multipurpose grease and reinstall into the sheath.

5. Make sure the speedometer cable is correctly seated into the drive unit at the wheel.

6. Make sure the tachometer cable is correctly seated in the drive gear in the front cylinder head.

7. Insert the cable into the instrument and screw the retaining collar on securely.

PERIODIC MAINTENANCE

Disc Brake Fluid Level

The fluid level in the front brake reservoir should be up to the upper mark within the reservoir. This upper level mark is only visible when the master cylinder top cover is removed. If the brake fluid level reaches the lower level mark (**Figure 28**), visible through the viewing port on the side of the

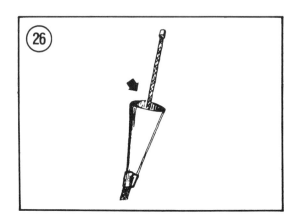

master cylinder reservoir, the fluid level must be corrected by adding fresh brake fluid.

1. Place the bike on level ground and position the handlebars so the master cylinder reservoir is level.
2. Clean any dirt from the area around the top cover prior to removing the cover.
3. Remove the top cover (**Figure 29**) and the diaphragm. Add brake fluid until the level is to the

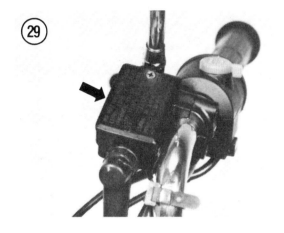

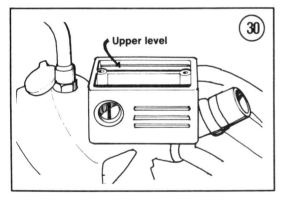

upper level line (**Figure 30**) within the master cylinder body. Use fresh brake fluid from a sealed brake fluid container.

> *WARNING*
> *Only use brake fluid from a sealed container clearly marked DOT 3 (specified for disc brakes). Others may vaporize and cause brake failure. Do not intermix different brands or types of brake fluid as they may not be compatible. Do not intermix a silicone based (DOT 5) brake fluid as it can cause brake component damage leading to brake system failure.*

> *CAUTION*
> *Be careful when handling brake fluid. Do not spill it on painted or plated surfaces as it will destroy the surface. Wash the area immediately with soapy water and thoroughly rinse it off.*

4. Reinstall the diaphragm and the top cover. Tighten the screws securely.

Disc Brake Lines

Check brake lines between the master cylinder and the brake caliper. If there is any leakage, tighten the connections and bleed the brakes as described in Chapter Eleven. If this does not stop the leak or if a brake line is obviously damaged, cracked or chafed, replace the brake line and bleed the system.

Disc Brake Pad Wear

Inspect the brake pads for excessive or uneven wear, scoring and oil or grease on the friction surface. Look at the pads from the top of the caliper assembly (**Figure 31**). Replace the pads if the wear line on the pads reaches the brake disc.

> *NOTE*
> *Always replace all pads at the same time.*

If any of these conditions exist, replace the pads as described in Chapter Eleven.

Disc Brake Fluid Change

Every time the reservoir cap is removed, a small amount of dirt and moisture enters the brake fluid. The same thing happens if a leak occurs or any part of the hydraulic system is loosened or disconnected. Dirt can clog the system and cause unnecessary wear. Water in the brake fluid vaporizes at high temperature, impairing the hydraulic action and reducing the brake's stopping ability.

To maintain peak performance, change the brake fluid as indicated in **Table 1**. To change brake fluid, follow the *Bleeding the Brake System* procedure in Chapter Eleven. Continue adding new fluid to the master cylinder and bleeding out at the caliper(s) until the fluid leaving the caliper(s) is clean and free of contaminants.

> *WARNING*
> *Only use brake fluid from a sealed container clearly marked DOT 3 (specified for disc brakes). Others may vaporize and cause brake failure. Do not intermix different brands or types of brake fluid as they may not be compatable. Do not intermix a silicone-based (DOT 5) brake fluid as it can cause brake component damage leading to brake system failure.*

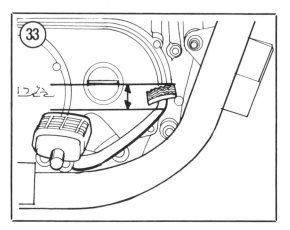

Rear Drum Brake Lining

Check the rear brake linings for wear. If the arrow on the brake arm aligns with the raised index mark on the brake backing plate (**Figure 32**) when the brake pedal is applied, the brake linings require replacement.

If replacement is necessary, refer to Chapter Eleven.

Rear Brake Pedal
Height Adjustment

The rear brake pedal should be adjusted as indicated in **Table 1**.

1. Place the bike on the centerstand.
2. Check that the brake pedal is in the at-rest position.
3. Adjust the pedal height so the brake pedal is 25 mm (1 in.) above the top surface of the front footpeg (**Figure 33**).

4A. *1983-1984*—To change height position perform the following:
   a. Remove the coolant reserve tank cover.
   b. Loosen the locknut and turn the adjuster bolt (**Figure 34**).
   c. Tighten the locknut.
   d. Install the coolant reserve tank cover.

> *NOTE*
> *Figure 34 is shown with the brake pedal removed for clarity.*

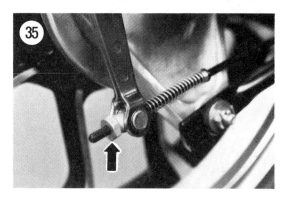

4B. *1985-1986*—To change pedal height position, loosen the stopper bolt locknut on the bottom side of the footpeg then rotate the stopper bolt to obtain the desired setting. Retighten the locknut.

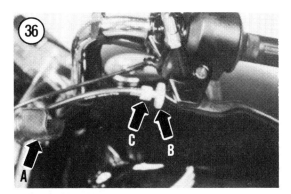

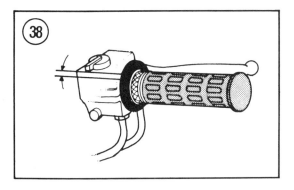

Rear Brake Pedal Free Play

Free play is the distance the rear brake pedal travels from the at-rest position to the applied position when the pedal is depressed by hand.
1. Place the bike on the centerstand with the rear wheel off the ground.
2. Adjust the brake pedal to the correct height as described in this chapter.
3. Turn the adjust nut on the end of the brake rod (**Figure 35**) until the pedal has 20-30 mm (3/4-1 1/4 in.) free play.
4. Rotate the rear wheel and check for brake drag.
5. Operate the brake pedal several times to make sure the pedal returns to the at-rest position immediately after release.

Clutch Adjustment

Adjust the clutch at the interval indicated in **Table 1**. For the clutch to fully engage and disengage there must be 10-20 mm (3/8-3/4 in.) of free play at the tip of the clutch lever.

If the proper amount of free play cannot be achieved by using this procedure, the clutch cable has stretched to the point that it needs to be replaced. Refer to Chapter Five.
1. Minor adjustments can be made at the upper adjuster at the hand lever as follows:
   a. Pull back the rubber boot (A, **Figure 36**).
   b. Loosen the locknut (B, **Figure 36**) and turn the adjuster barrel (C, **Figure 36**) in or out to achieve the correct amount of free play. Tighten the locknut.

NOTE
If the proper amount of free play cannot be achieved at the hand lever, additional adjustment can be made next to the clutch actuating lever on the right-hand crankcase cover as described in Step 2 and Step 3.

2. At the hand lever, loosen the locknut and turn the adjuster barrel all the way in forward the hand lever. Tighten the locknut.
3. At the clutch actuating lever on the right-hand crankcase, loosen the locknut (A, **Figure 37**) and turn the adjuster barrel (B, **Figure 37**) in or out to achieve the correct amount of free play. Tighten the locknut.
4. If necessary, repeat Step 1 for fine adjustment.
5. After adjustment is complete, check that the locknuts are tight both at the hand lever and the clutch actuating lever on the crankcase.
6. Test ride the bike and make sure the clutch is operating correctly.

Throttle Adjustment and Operation

The throttle grip should have 2-6 mm (1/8-1/4 in.) rotational free play (**Figure 38**). If adjustment is necessary, loosen the locknut and turn the adjuster (**Figure 39**) at the throttle grip in or out to achieve proper free play rotation. Tighten the locknut.

NOTE
*Minor adjustments can be made at the throttle grip. Major adjustments can be made where the throttle cables attach to the carburetor assembly (**Figure 40**).*

Check the throttle cables from grip to carburetor. Make sure they are not kinked or chafed. Replace as necessary.

Make sure the throttle grip rotates freely from a fully closed to fully open position. Check with the handlebar at center, at full right and at full left. If necessary, remove the throttle grip and apply a lithium base grease to it.

Air Filter Element Cleaning

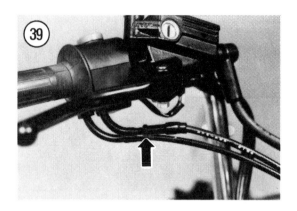

NOTE
A paper air filter element is used on 1985-1986 models. Filter must be replaced if contamination is noted. Follow Steps 1-4 to remove the element and Steps 10-13 to install the element.

The air filter element should be removed and cleaned as indicated in **Table 1**.

The air filter removes dust and abrasive particles from the air before the air enters the carburetors and engine. Without the air filter, very fine particles could enter into the engine and cause rapid wear of the piston rings, cylinder and bearings and might clog small passages in the carburetors. Never run the bike without the air filter element installed.

Proper air filter servicing can do more to ensure long service from your engine than almost any other single item.

1. Remove the right-hand side cover.
2. Remove the screws securing the air filter cover (**Figure 41**).
3. Remove the air filter element holder and the air filter element (**Figure 42**).
4. Wipe out the interior of the air box with a shop rag dampened with cleaning solvent. Remove any foreign matter that may have passed through a broken element.

5. Slide the outer holder off of the element (**Figure 43**) then slide the element off of the inner holder (**Figure 44**).
6. Clean the outer and inner holders in cleaning solvent. Make sure all of the openings are clean and free from dirt to allow maximum air flow. Thoroughly dry both holders with compressed air.
7. Clean the element gently in cleaning solvent until all dirt is removed. Thoroughly dry the element in a clean shop cloth until all solvent residue is removed. Let it dry for about one hour.

NOTE
Inspect the element; if it is torn or broken in any area it should be replaced. Do not run with a damaged element as it may allow dirt to enter the engine.

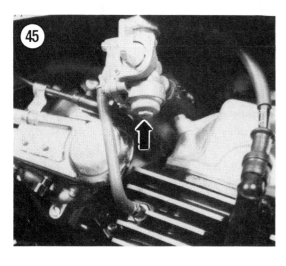

8. Pour a small amount of SAE 80 gear oil or foam air filter oil onto the air filter element and work it into the porous foam material. Do not oversaturate the element as too much oil will restrict air flow. The element will be discolored by the oil and should have an even color indicating that the oil is distributed evenly. If foam air filter oil was used, let the element dry for another hour prior to installation. If installed too soon, the chemical carrier in the foam air filter oil will be drawn into the engine and may cause damage.

9. Install the air filter element onto the inner holder then install this assembly into the outer holder.

10. Install the air filter element assembly into the air box.

11. Inspect the gasket on the air filter cover. If it is damaged in any way, replace the gasket.

12. Install the air filter cover and secure it with the screws.

13. Install the right-hand side cover.

Fuel Strainer Cleaning

1. Turn the fuel shutoff valve to the OFF position.

2. Remove the fuel cup, O-ring seal and filter screen from the bottom of the fuel shutoff valve (**Figure 45**).

3. Clean the screen with a medium soft toothbrush and blow out with compresed air. Replace the screen if it is broken in any area.

4. Wash the fuel cup in solvent to remove any residue or foreign matter. Throughly dry with compressed air.

5. Align the index marks on the filter screen and the fuel shutoff valve body (**Figure 46**).

6. Install the O-ring and screw on the fuel cup.

7. Hand-tighten the fuel cup and then tighten to a final torque of 3-5 N•m (2-4 ft.-lb.). Do not overtighten the fuel cup as it may be damaged.

8. Turn the fuel shutoff valve to the ON position and check for leaks.

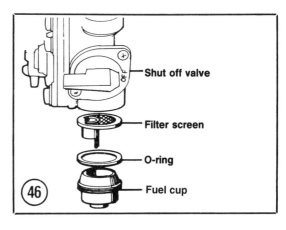

Shut off valve

Filter screen

O-ring

Fuel cup

Fuel Line Inspection

Inspect the fuel lines from the fuel tank to the carburetor. If any are cracked or starting to deteriorate they must be replaced. Make sure the small hose clamps are in place and holding securely.

WARNING
A damaged or deteriorated fuel line presents a very dangerous fire hazard to both the rider and the bike if fuel should spill onto a hot engine or exhaust pipe.

Cooling System Inspection

At the interval indicated in **Table 1**, the following items should be checked. If you do not have the test equipment, the tests can be done by a Honda dealer, automobile dealer, radiator shop or service station.

1. Have the radiator cap pressure tested (**Figure 47**). The specified radiator cap relief pressure is 0.75-1.05 kg/cm² (10.7-14.9 psi). The cap must be able to sustain this pressure for 6 seconds. Replace the radiator cap if it does not hold pressure or if the relief pressure is too high or too low.

2. Leave the radiator cap off and have the entire cooling system pressure tested (**Figure 48**). The entire cooling system should be pressurized up to, but not exceeding, 1.05 kg/cm² (14.9 psi). The system must be able to sustain this pressure for 6 seconds. Replace or repair any components that fail this test.

CAUTION
If test pressure exceeds the specifications the radiator may be damaged.

3. Test the specific gravity of the coolant with an antifreeze tester (**Figure 49**) to ensure adequate temperature and corrosion protection. The system must have at least a 50/50 mixture of antifreeze and distilled water. Never let the mixture become less than 40% antifreeze or corrosion protection will be impaired.

4. Check all cooling system hoses for damage or deterioration. Replace any hose that is questionable. Make sure all hose clamps are tight.

5. Carefully clean any road dirt, bugs, mud, etc. from the radiator core. Use a whisk broom, compressed air or low-pressure water. If the radiator has been hit by a small rock or other item, *carefully* straighten out the fins with a screwdriver.

NOTE
If the radiator has been damaged across approximately 20% or more of the frontal area, the radiator should be recored or replaced.

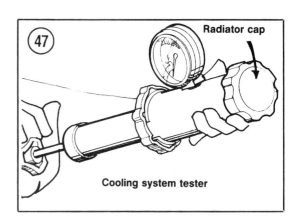

Radiator cap

Cooling system tester

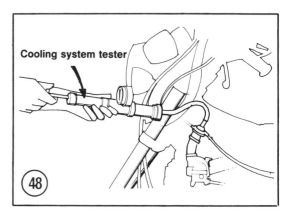

Cooling system tester

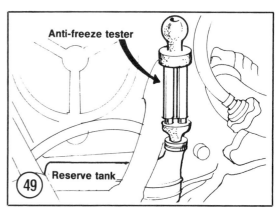

Anti-freeze tester

Reserve tank

Coolant Change

The cooling system should be completely drained and refilled at the interval indicated in **Table 1**.

CAUTION
Use only a high quality ethylene glycol antifreeze specifically labeled for use with aluminum engines. Do not use an alcohol-based antifreeze.

In areas where freezing temperatures occur, add a higher percentage of antifreeze to protect the system

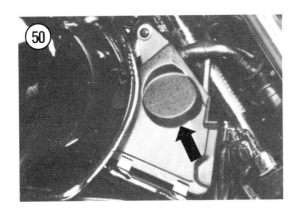

3. Remove the screw and remove the right-hand plastic cover (**Figure 50**) next to the steering head.

4. Remove the radiator cap (**Figure 51**). This will speed up the draining process.

5. Place a drain pan under the frame on the left-hand side of the bike under the water pump. Remove the drain screw and sealing washer on the water pump cover (**Figure 52**).

6. Take the bike off the centerstand and tip the bike from side to side to drain any residual coolant from the cooling system. Place the bike back onto the centerstand.

7. Install the drain screw and sealing washer on the water pump cover.

8. Refill the cooling system. Add the coolant through the radiator filler neck, not the reserve tank. Use the recommended mixture of antifreeze and distilled water; see **Table 7**. Do not install the radiator cap at this time.

9. Start the engine and let it run at idle speed until the engine reaches normal operating temperature. Make sure there are no air bubbles in the coolant and that the coolant level stabilizes at the correct level. Add coolant as necessary.

10. Install the radiator cap and the plastic cover next to the steering head.

11. Add coolant to the reserve tank to the correct level.

12. Test ride the bike and readjust the coolant level in the reserve tank if necessary.

Wheel Bearings

There is no factory-recommended mileage interval for cleaning and repacking the wheel bearings. They should be serviced whenever they are removed from the wheel hub or whenever there is the likelihood of water contamination. The correct service procedures are covered in Chapter Nine and Chapter Ten.

Steering Head Adjustment Check

The steering head is fitted with assembled bearings. It should be checked as indicated in **Table 1**.

Place the bike up on wood block(s) so that the front wheel is off the ground. Hold onto the front fork tubes and gently rock the fork assembly back and forth. If you can feel looseness, the steering stem must be disassembled and adjusted; refer to Chapter Nine.

Front Suspension Check

1. Apply the front brake and pump the forks up and down as vigorously as possible. Check for smooth operation and check for any oil leaks.

to temperatures far below those likely to occur. **Table 7** lists the recommended amount of antifreeze for protection at various ambient temperatures. The following procedure must be performed when the engine is cool.

CAUTION
Be careful not to spill antifreeze on painted surfaces as it will destroy the surface. Wash immediately with soapy water and rinse thoroughly with clean water.

1. Place the bike on the centerstand.
2. Remove the seat and both side covers.

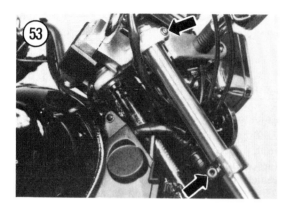

2. Make sure the upper and lower fork bridge bolts are tight (**Figure 53**).

3. Make sure the bolts securing the handlebar holders (**Figure 54**) are tight and that the handlebar is secure.

4. Make sure the front axle and axle pinch bolt are tight (**Figure 55**).

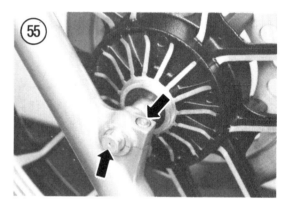

> *CAUTION*
> *If any of the previously mentioned bolts and nuts are loose, refer to Chapter Nine for correct proceures and torque specifications.*

Rear Suspension Check

1. Place the bike on the centerstand.

2. Push hard on the rear wheel (sideways) to check for side play in the rear swing arm bushings.

3. Check the tightness of the upper and lower shock absorber mounting bolts and nuts (**Figure 56**) on each shock absorber.

4. Make sure the rear axle nut is tight (**Figure 57**).

5. Check the tightness of the rear brake torque arm bolt (**Figure 58**).

> *CAUTION*
> *If any of the previously mentioned bolts and nuts are loose, refer to Chapter Ten for correct procedures and torque specifications.*

Nuts, Bolts and Other Fasteners

Constant vibration can loosen many of the fasteners on the motorcycle. Check the tightness of all fasteners, especially those on:

    a. Engine mounting hardware.
    b. Engine crankcase covers.
    c. Handlebar and front forks.
    d. Gearshift lever.
    e. Brake pedal and lever.
    f. Exhaust system.

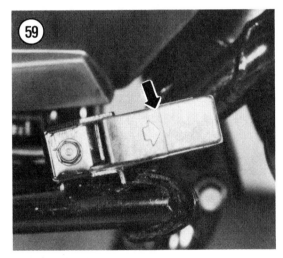

3

Sidestand Rubber

The rubber pad on the sidestand kicks the sidestand up if you should forget. If it wears down to the molded line (**Figure 59**), it will no longer be effective and must be replaced.

Remove the bolt and replace the rubber pad with a new one. Be sure the new rubber pad is marked "Over 260 lbs. Only."

Crankcase Breather
(U.S. Models Only)

At the interval indicated in **Table 1** or sooner if a considerable amount of riding is done at full throttle or in the rain, the residue in the breather drain tube should be drained.

Remove the drain plug (**Figure 60**) and drain out all residue. Install the cap; make sure the clamp is tight.

Refer to Chapter Six for complete details on the breather system.

TUNE-UP

A complete tune-up should be performed at the interval indicated in **Table 1** for normal riding. More frequent tune-ups may be required if the bike is ridden primarily in stop-and-go traffic. The purpose of the tune-up is to restore the performance lost due to normal wear and deterioration of parts.

Table 8 summarizes tune-up specifications.

The spark plugs should be routinely replaced at every tune-up. In addition, this is a good time to clean the air filter element. Have the new parts on hand before you begin.

The cam chain tensioners are completely automatic and do not require any periodic adjustment. There are no provisions for tensioner adjustment on the engine.

Because different systems in an engine interact, the procedure should be done in the following order:

  a. Clean or replace the air filter element.
  b. Adjust the valve clearances.
  c. Run a compression test.
  d. Check or replace the spark plugs.
  e. Check the ignition timing.
  f. Adjust the carburetor idle speed.
  g. Synchronize the carburetors.

To perform a tune-up on your Honda, you will need the following tools:

  a. 18 mm spark plug wrench.
  b. Socket wrench and assorted sockets.
  c. Flat feeler gauges.
  d. Compression gauge.
  e. Spark plug wire feeler gauge and gapper tool.

f. Ignition timing light.

g. Tune-up tachometer.

h. Manometer (carburetor synchronization tool).

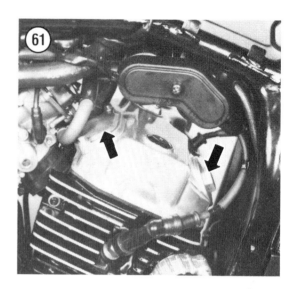

Air Filter Element Cleaning

The air filter element should be cleaned or replaced prior to doing other tune-up procedures, as described in this chapter.

Valve Clearance Adjustment

Valve clearance must be measured with the engine cool, at room temperature (95° F/35° C). The correct valve clearance is 0.10 mm (0.004 in.) for both the intake and exhaust valves.

There are 2 intake valves and 1 exhaust valve in each cylinder.

1. Place the bike on the centerstand.

2. Remove the seat.

3. Remove the right- and left-hand side covers.

4. Remove the fuel tank as described in Chapter Six.

5. Disconnect the spark plug caps and leads and tie them up out of the way.

6. Remove one of the 2 spark plugs from each cylinder (this will make it easier to turn the engine over by hand).

7. Remove the valve adjuster covers and caps (**Figure 61**).

8. Remove the timing cap (**Figure 62**) on the left-hand crankcase cover.

9. The correct valve clearance for both the intake and exhaust valves is 0.10 mm (0.004 in.).

> *NOTE*
> *The intake valves are located toward the center "V" of the engine (next to the carburetors) and the exhaust valves are located at the front and rear of the engine (next to the exhaust pipes).*

10. To adjust the front cylinder valves, perform the following:

   a. Rotate the crankshaft by turning the bolt (**Figure 63**) on the primary drive gear with a 17 mm wrench (**Figure 64**).

   b. Rotate the crankshaft *clockwise* (as viewed from the right-hand side) until the "FT" mark on the pulse generator plate aligns with the crankcase index mark (**Figure 65**).

   c. The front cylinder must be at top dead center (TDC) on the compression stroke. Check and record the clearances on the intake valve and both exhaust valves on the No. 1 cylinder.

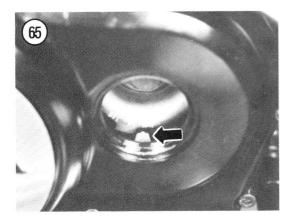

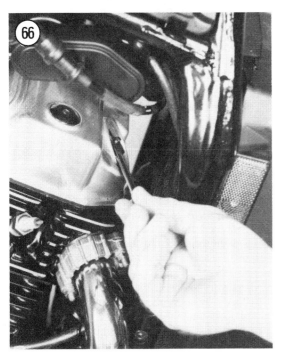

NOTE
A cylinder at TDC of its compression stroke will have free play in all of its rocker arms, indicating that both the intake and exhaust valves are closed.

11. To measure the clearance, insert a flat feeler gauge (**Figure 66**) between the valve stem and the valve adjuster. The clearance is measured correctly when there is a slight drag on the feeler gauge when it is inserted and withdrawn.

NOTE
Be sure to check and adjust both intake valves.

12. To correct the clearance (if necessary), use a box end wrench and back off the locknut. Screw the adjuster in or out so there is a slight resistance felt on the feeler gauge. Hold the adjuster and tighten the locknut to 23 N•m (17 ft.-lb.). Then recheck the clearance to make sure the adjuster did not slip when the locknut was tightened. Readjust if necessary.

CAUTION
Be sure to tighten the locknut to the specified torque value. Failure to do so may result in the adjuster locknuts working loose and allowing incorrect valve clearances.

13. To adjust the rear cylinder valves, perform the following:
   a. Rotate the crankshaft by turning the 17 mm bolt (**Figure 63**) on the primary drive gear with a wrench (**Figure 64**).
   b. Rotate the crankshaft *clockwise* (as viewed from the right-hand side) until the "RT" mark on the pulse generator plate aligns with the crankcase index mark (**Figure 67**).

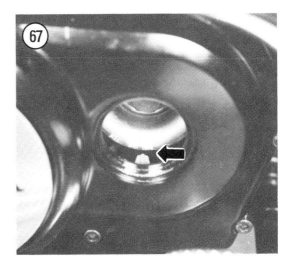

c. The rear cylinder must be at top dead center (TDC) on the compression stroke. Check and record the clearances on both intake valves and both exhaust valves on the No. 1 cylinder.

NOTE
A cylinder at TDC of its compression stroke will have free play in all of its rocker arms, indicating that both the intake and exhaust valves are closed.

14. With the rear cylinder at this position repeat Step 11 and Step 12 to check the clearance for the valves of the rear cylinder.

15. Inspect the the rubber gasket on each valve adjuster cover and cap. Replace any that have started to deteriorate or harden; replace as a set even if only one is bad.

16. Install the timing cover on the right-hand crankcase cover.

17. Install the spark plugs that were removed and install the spark plug caps and leads.

18. Install the fuel tank as described in Chapter Six.

19. Install the right- and left-hand side covers and the seat.

Compression Test

At every other tune-up check cylinder compression. Record the results and compare them at the next tune-up. A running record will show trends in deterioration so that corrective action can be taken before complete failure.

The results, when properly interpreted, can indicate general cylinder, piston ring and valve condition.

1. Warm the engine to normal operating temperature. Shut off the engine. Make sure that the choke valve and throttle valve are completely open.

2. Place the bike on the centerstand.

3. Disconnect the spark plug wires from all spark plugs.

4. Remove only one of the spark plugs from each cylinder. Remove the one next to the exhaust pipe outlet as it will be easier to connect a tester to that hole. Leave the other spark plug in place as it is necessary to seal off the cylinder.

5. Connect the compression tester to one cylinder following manufacturer's instructions.

6. Using the starter, crank the engine over until there is no further rise in pressure. Maximum pressure is usually reached within 4-7 seconds of engine cranking.

NOTE
Do not turn the engine over more than absolutely necessary. When spark plug

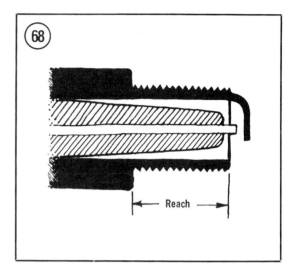

leads are disconnected, the electronic ignition will produce the highest voltage possible and the coils may overheat and be damaged.

7. Remove the tester and record the reading.

8. Repeat Step 5 and Step 6 for the other cylinder.

When interpreting the results, actual readings are not as important as the difference between the readings. Readings should be about 10-14 kg/cm^2 (143-199 psi). A maximum difference of 4 kg/cm^2 (57 psi) between the 2 cylinders is acceptable. Greater differences indicate worn or broken rings, leaking or sticking valves, a blown head gasket(s) or a combination of all.

If compression readings do not differ between the 2 cylinders by more than 10 psi, the rings and valves are in good condition.

If a low reading (10% or more) is obtained on one of the cylinders, it indicates valve or ring trouble. To

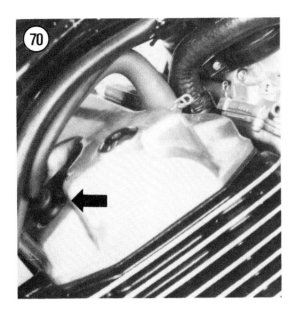

determine which, insert a small funnel into the spark plug hole and pour about a teaspoon of engine oil through it onto the top of the piston. Turn the engine over once to distribute the oil, then take another compression test and record the reading. If the compression increases significantly, the valves are good but the rings are defective on that cylinder. If compression does not increase, the valves require servicing. A valve could be hanging open or a piece of carbon could be on a valve seat.

Spark Plug Selection

Spark plugs are available in various heat ranges, hotter or colder than plugs originally installed at the factory.

Select plugs of a heat range designed for the loads and temperature conditions under which the bike will be run. The use of incorrect heat ranges can cause seized pistons, scored cylinder walls or damaged piston crowns.

In general, use a hot plug for low speeds, low engine loads and low temperatures. Use a cold plug for high speeds, high engine loads and high temperatures. The plug should operate hot enough to burn off unwanted deposits, but not so hot that it is damaged or causes preignition. A spark plug of the correct heat range will show a light tan color on the portion of the insulator within the cylinder after the plug has been in service.

In areas where seasonal temperature variations are great, the factory recommends a "2-plug system"–cold plugs for hard summer riding and hot plugs for slower winter operation.

The reach (length) of a plug is also important. A longer than normal plug could interfere with the valves and pistons, causing permanent and severe damage. Refer to **Figure 68**. The recommended spark plugs are listed in **Table 8**.

Spark Plug Removal/Cleaning

There are 2 spark plugs per cylinder and 2 of the spark plugs are not easy to see. These hidden spark plugs are located at the front of the front cylinder (**Figure 69**) and at the rear of the rear cylinder (**Figure 70**).

Be sure to use a spark plug wrench with a rubber insert that grabs onto the spark plug. Do not use a deep socket as it will be difficult to remove and install the spark plugs in the deep wells.

1. Grasp the spark plug lead (**Figure 71**) as near to the plug as possible and pull it off the plug. If the boot is stuck to the plug, twist it slightly to break it loose.
2. Blow away any dirt that has accumulated in the spark plug wells. This is especially true for the spark plugs that are buried deep in the cylinder head.

CAUTION
The dirt could fall into the cylinders when the plugs are removed, causing serious engine damage.

3. Remove spark plug with an 18 mm spark plug wrench.

NOTE
If plugs are difficult to remove, apply penetrating oil around base of plugs and let it soak in about 10-20 minutes.

4. Inspect spark plug carefully. Look for a plug with broken center porcelain, excessively eroded electrodes and excessive carbon or oil fouling. Replace such plugs. If deposits are light, the plug may be cleaned in solvent with a wire brush or in a special spark plug sandblast cleaner. Regap the plug as explained in this chapter.

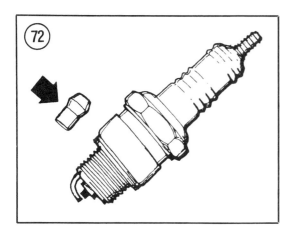

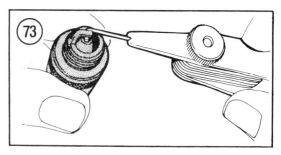

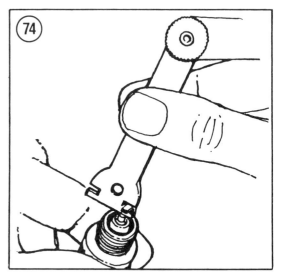

Spark Plug Gapping and Installation

New plugs should be carefully gapped to ensure a reliable, consistent spark. You must use a special spark plug gapping tool with a wire feeler gauge.

Be sure to replace all 4 spark plugs at the same time; all 4 plugs must be of the same heat range.

1. Remove the new plugs from the box. Do *not* screw in the small piece that is loose in each box (**Figure 72**); it is not used.

2. Insert a wire feeler gauge between the center and the side electrode of each plug (**Figure 73**). The correct gap is 0.8-0.9 mm (0.031-0.035 in.). If the gap is correct, you will feel a slight drag as you pull the wire through. If there is no drag or the gauge won't pass through, bend the side electrode *with the gapping tool* (**Figure 74**) to set the proper gap.

3. Put a *small* drop of oil or aluminum anti-seize compound on the threads of each spark plug.

NOTE
On spark plugs that are buried in a deep well, make sure that the gasket is firmly attached to the spark plug so it will not fall off in the well. If installing a used gasket that will not stay on the spark plug, apply a light coat of cold grease to the gasket and install it on the spark plug.

4. Install the spark plug into a spark plug wrench (and extension for the hidden plugs).

5. Screw each spark plug in by hand until it seats. Very little effort is required. If force is necessary, you have a plug cross-threaded; unscrew it and try again.

6. Tighten the spark plugs an additional 1/2 turn after the gasket has made contact with the head. If you are reinstalling old, regapped plugs and are reusing the old gasket, only tighten an additional 1/4 turn.

NOTE
Do not overtighten. This will only squash the gasket and destroy its sealing ability.

7. Install each spark plug lead; make sure the lead is on tight.

8. On spark plugs that are buried deep in the cylinder head, make sure that the rubber boot surrounding the spark plug lead is seated correctly (**Figure 69**). The boots are designed to keep out moisture and dirt.

Reading Spark Plugs

Much information about engine and spark plug performance can be determined by careful examination of the spark plugs. This information is more valid after performing the following steps.

1. Ride the bike a short distance at full throttle in any gear.

2. Turn the engine kill switch to the OFF position before closing the throttle and simultaneously pull in the clutch or shift to NEUTRAL; coast and brake to a stop.

3. Remove all spark plugs and examine them. Compare them to **Figure 75**. If the insulator is white

SPARK PLUG CONDITION

(75)

3

NORMAL

- Identified by light tan or gray deposits on the firing tip.
- Can be cleaned.

GAP BRIDGED

- Identified by deposit buildup closing gap between electrodes.
- Caused by oil or carbon fouling. If deposits are not excessive, the plug can be cleaned.

OIL FOULED

- Identified by wet black deposits on the insulator shell bore and electrodes.
- Caused by excessive oil entering combustion chamber through worn rings and pistons, excessive clearance between valve guides and stems, or worn or loose bearings. Can be cleaned. If engine is not repaired, use a hotter plug.

CARBON FOULED

- Identified by black, dry fluffy carbon deposits on insulator tips, exposed shell surfaces and electrodes.
- Caused by too cold a plug, weak ignition, dirty air cleaner, too rich a fuel mixture, or excessive idling. Can be cleaned.

LEAD FOULED

- Identified by dark gray, black, yellow, or tan deposits or a fused glazed coating on the insulator tip.
- Caused by highly leaded gasoline. Can be cleaned.

WORN

- Identified by severely eroded or worn electrodes.
- Caused by normal wear. Should be replaced.

FUSED SPOT DEPOSIT

- Identified by melted or spotty deposits resembling bubbles or blisters.
- Caused by sudden acceleration. Can be cleaned.

OVERHEATING

- Identified by a white or light gray insulator with small black or gray brown spots and with bluish-burnt appearance of electrodes.
- Caused by engine overheating, wrong type of fuel, loose spark plugs, too hot a plug, or incorrect ignition timing. Replace the plug.

PREIGNITION

- Identified by melted electrodes and possibly blistered insulator. Metallic deposits on insulator indicate engine damage.
- Caused by wrong type of fuel, incorrect ignition timing or advance, too hot a plug, burned valves, or engine overheating. Replace the plug.

or burned, the plug is too hot and should be replaced with a colder one.

A too-cold plug will have sooty or oily deposits ranging in color from dark brown to black. Replace with a hotter plug and check for too-rich carburetion or evidence of oil blow-by at the piston rings.

If the plug has a light tan or gray colored deposit and no abnormal gap wear or electrode erosion is evident, the plug and the engine are running properly.

If the plug exhibits a black insulator tip, a damp and oily film over the firing end and a carbon layer over the entire nose, it is oil fouled. An oil fouled plug can be cleaned, but it is better to replace it.

If any one plug is found unsatisfactory, discard and replace all plugs.

Ignition Timing

The Honda V-twins are equipped with a capacitor discharge ignition (CDI) system. This system uses no breaker points and is non-adjustable. The timing should be checked to make sure all ignition components are operating correctly.

Incorrect ignition timing can cause a drastic loss of engine performance and efficiency. It may also cause overheating.

Before starting on this procedure, check all electrical connections related to the ignition system. Make sure all connections are tight and free of corrosion and that all ground connections are tight.

1. Start the engine and let it reach normal operating temperature. Shut the engine off.
2. Place the bike on the centerstand.
3. Remove the timing cover on the right-hand rear crankcase cover (**Figure 62**).
4. Connect a portable tachometer following the manufacturer's instructions. The bike's tachometer is not accurate enough in the low rpm range for this adjustment.
5. Connect a timing light to one of the spark plugs on the front cylinder following the manufacturer's instructions.
6. Fill in the timing marks on the pulse generator rotor with white grease pencil or typewriter white correction fluid. This will make the marks more visible.
7. Start the engine and let it idle at the idle speed listed in **Table 8**.
8. Aim the timing light at the timing hole in the crankcase cover and pull the trigger. If the timing mark "F" aligns with the fixed pointer on the crankcase cover (**Figure 76**), the timing is correct.
9. If the timing is incorrect, refer to Chapter Seven and check the spark units and the pulse generators.

There is no method for adjusting ignition timing.
10. Shut off the engine and disconnect the timing light and portable tachometer. Install the timing cover.

Carburetor Idle Mixture

The idle mixture (pilot screw) is preset at the factory and is *not* to be reset. Do not adjust the pilot screws unless the carburetors have been overhauled; refer to Chapter Six.

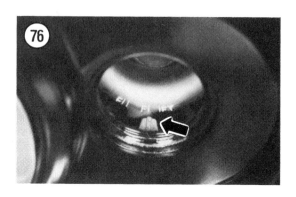

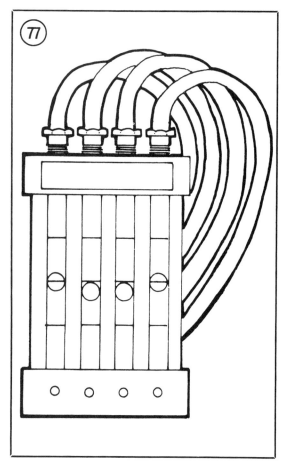

Carburetor Synchronization

When the carburetors are properly synchronized the engine will warm up faster and there will be an improvement in throttle response, performance and mileage.

Prior to synchronizing the carburetors, the air filter element must be clean and valve clearances must be properly adjusted. The ignition timing must also be checked to make sure all components are operating correctly.

This procedure requires special tools. You will need a mercury manometer (carb-sync tool). This is a tool that measures the manifold vacuum for both cylinders simultaneously. A carb-sync tool (**Figure 77**) can be purchased from a Honda dealer, motorcycle supply store or mail order firm.

NOTE
When purchasing this tool, check that it is equipped with restrictors. These

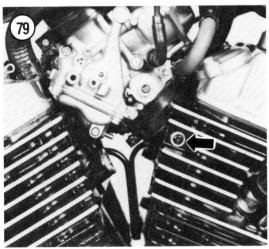

restrictors keep the mercury from being drawn into the engine when engine rpm is increased during the adjustment procedure. If the mercury is drawn into the engine the tool will have to be replaced.

1. Start the engine and let it warm up to normal operating temperature. Ten minutes of stop-and-go riding is usually sufficient. Shut off the engine.
2. Place the bike on the centerstand.
3. Remove both side covers and the seat.
4. Remove the fuel tank as described in Chapter Six. There should be enough fuel left in the float bowls to run the bike for this procedure.

WARNING
*Do **not** rig up a temporary fuel supply as this presents a real fire danger. If you start to run out of fuel during the test, shut off the engine and momentarily install the fuel tank to refill the carburetor float bowls, then proceed with the test.*

5. The rear cylinder is fitted with a vacuum fitting (**Figure 78**) for the vacuum operated fuel shutoff valve. If the hose on the carb-synch tool will not fit onto this fitting, remove the fitting from the cylinder head and attach the tool to the hole.
6. On the front cylinder, remove the vacuum plug (consisting of a screw and flat washer) from the cylinder head (**Figure 79**).
7. Install the vacuum line adaptors into the vacuum hole in each cylinder head.

NOTE
Most carb-synch tools are made for 4-cylinder engines. Use the vacuum lines for No. 1 (front cylinder) and No. 2 (rear cylinder).

8. Connect the vacuum lines from the carb-sync tool, following the manufacturer's instructions. Be sure to route the vacuum lines to the correct cylinder. Most carb-sync tools have the cylinder number indicated on them adjacent to each tube containing mercury.

NOTE
The left-hand carburetor has no synchronization screw; the right-hand carburetor must be synchronized to it. The left-hand side refers to a rider sitting on the seat facing forward.

9. Start the engine and let it idle at the idle speed listed in **Table 8**.
10. If the difference in gauge readings is 50 mm Hg (2.0 in. Hg) or less between the 2 cylinders, the

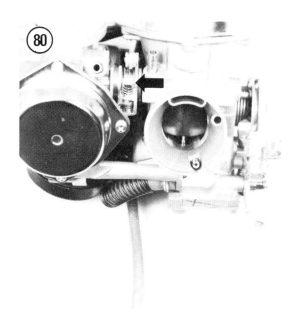

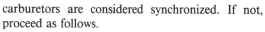

carburetors are considered synchronized. If not, proceed as follows.

11. Turn the synchronization adjusting screw on the right-hand carburetor (**Figure 80**). Turn the adjusting screw until the reading is the same as that on the left-hand carburetor. Open the throttle a little and close it back down after each adjustment.

NOTE
Figure 80 is shown with the carburetor assembly removed for clarity. Do not remove the carburetor assembly for this procedure.

CAUTION
If your carb-sync tool is not equipped with restrictors, open and close the throttle very gently to avoid sucking mercury into the engine. If this happens, it will not harm the engine but will render the tool useless.

NOTE
To gain the utmost in performance and efficiency from the engine, adjust the carburetors so that the gauge readings are as close to each other as possible.

12. Shut off the engine and remove the vacuum lines and adaptors. Install the screw and washer into the vacuum port in the front cylinder head. Make sure it is in tight to prevent a vacuum leak.
13. If removed, install the vacuum fitting to the rear cylinder.
14. Install the fuel tank.
15. Install the seat and the side covers.
16. Restart the engine and readjust the idle speed if necessary as described in this chapter.

Idle Speed Adjustment

Before making this adjustment, the air filter element must be clean, the carburetors must be synchronized and the engine must have adequate compression. Otherwise, this procedure cannot be done properly.

1. Attach a portable tachometer following the manufacturer's instructions.

NOTE
The bike's tachometer is not accurate enough in the low rpm range for this adjustment.

2. Start the engine and let it warm up to normal operating temperature.
3. Set the idle speed by turning the large black plastic idle speed stop screw (**Figure 81**) in to increase or out to decrease idle speed. The correct idle speed is listed in **Table 8**.
4. Open and close the throttle a couple of times; check for variations in idle speed. Readjust if necessary.

WARNING
*With the engine idling, move the handlebar from side to side. If idle speed increases during this movement, the throttle cables may need adjusting or they may be incorrectly routed through the frame. Correct this problem immediately. Do **not** ride the bike in this unsafe condition.*

5. Shut off the engine and disconnect the portable tachometer.

Table 1 SERVICE INTERVALS*

Every 600 miles (1,000 km) or 6 months	•Check engine oil level •Check battery specific gravity and electrolyte level •Check hydraulic fluid level in brake master cylinder •Lubricate rear brake pedal and shift lever •Lubricate side and centerstand pivot points •Inspect front steering for looseness •Check wheel bearings for smooth operation •Check wheel runout
Every 4,000 miles (6,400 km)	•Clean air filter element (1983-1984) •Inspect air filter element (1985-1986) •Replace spark plugs •Check and adjust throttle operation and free play •Adjust rear brake pedal height and free play •Clean fuel shutoff valve and filter •Check hydraulic fluid level in brake master cylinder •Inspect brake pads and linings for wear •Inspect crankcase breather hose for cracks or loose hose clamps; drain out all residue •Inspect fuel line for chafed, cracked or swollen ends •Check engine mounting bolts for tightness •Check all suspension components
Every 8,000 miles (12,800 km)	•Check and adjust valve clearance •Check ignition timing •Check and adjust the carburetors •Check and synchronize the carburetors •Check and adjust the choke •Run a compression test •Change engine oil and filter •Inspect fuel lines for wetness or damage •Inspect the radiator for damage or leakage •Inspect entire brake system for leaks or damage •Check and adjust clutch •Change front fork oil •Inspect oil level in final drive unit •Inspect wheel bearings •Inspect and repack the steering head bearings •Lubricate the speedometer drive cable •Lubricate final drive splines •Check and adjust headlight aim
Every 24,000 miles (38,000 km)	•Change oil in final drive unit •Change hydraulic fluid in brake master cylinder •Change coolant
Every 4 years	•Replace the hydraulic brake hoses

*This Honda factory maintenance schedule should be considered as a guide to general maintenance and lubrication intervals. Harder than normal use and exposure to mud, water, sand, high humidity, etc., will naturally dictate more frequent attention to most maintenance items.

3

Table 2 TIRE INFLATION PRESSURE (COLD)

Tire size	Air pressure	
	Up to 200 lb. (890 kg)	Maximum load limit*
Front 3.50S-18	28 psi (2.00 kg/cm^2)	28 psi (2.00 kg/cm^2)
Rear 130/19-16	28 psi (2.00 kg/cm^2)	36 psi (2.50 kg/cm^2)
*Maximum load limit includes total weight of motorcycle with accessories, rider(s) and luggage.		

Table 3 FRONT FORK AIR PRESSURE

Normal	Maximum*
0-6 psi (0-0.4 kg/cm^2)	43 psi (4 kg/cm^2)
*Do not exceed the maximum air pressure or internal parts of the fork will be damaged.	

Table 4 STATE OF CHARGE

Specific gravity	State of charge
1.110-1.130	Discharged
1.140-1.160	Almost discharged
1.170-1.190	One-quarter charged
1.200-1.220	One-half charged
1.230-1.250	Three-quarters charged
1.260-1.280	Fully charged

Table 5 ENGINE OIL CAPACITY

Oil and filter change	2.5 liters (2.6 U.S. qt., 2.2 Imp. qt.)
At overhaul	3.0 liters (3.2 U.S. qt., 2.6 Imp. qt.)

Table 6 FRONT FORK OIL CAPACITY*

VT500FT Ascot* VT500C Shadow	390 cc (13.2 U.S. fl. oz.)
1983-1984	
Right-hand leg	440 cc (14.9 U.S. fl. oz.)
Left-hand leg	455 cc (15.4 U.S. fl. oz.)
1985-1986	
Left- and right-hand leg	442 cc (15.0 U.S. fl. oz.)
VT500E Euro Sport*	360 cc (12.7 Imp. fl. oz.)
*Capacity for each fork leg.	

Table 7 ANTIFREEZE PROTECTION AND CAPACITY

Temperature	Antifreeze-to-water ratio
Above −25° F (−32° C)	45:55
Above −34° F (−37° C)	50:50
Above −48° F (−44.5° C)	55:45
Coolant capacity	
Total system	
VT500C	
1983-1984	1.7 liters (1.8 U.S. qt.)
1985-1986	2.0 liters (2.1 U.S. qt.)
VT500FT	1.7 liters (1.8 U.S. qt.)
VT500E	2.0 liters (1.76 Imp. qt.)
Radiator and engine	
VT500C	
1983-1984	1.2 liters (1.3 U.S. qt.)
1985-1986	1.55 liters (1.64 U.S. qt.)
VT500FT	1.2 liters (1.3 U.S. qt.)
VT500E	1.55 liters (1.36 Imp. qt.)
Reserve tank	
VT500C	
1983-1984	0.5 liters (0.5 U.S. qt.)
1985-1986	0.45 liters (0.47 U.S. qt.)
VT500FT	0.5 liters (0.5 U.S. qt.)
VT500E	0.45 liters (0.4 Imp. qt.)

Table 8 TUNE-UP SPECIFICATIONS

Valve clearance (cold)	
Intake	0.10 mm (0.004 in.)
Exhaust	0.10 mm (0.004 in.)
Compression pressure (at sea level)	12.0 ± 2.0 kg/cm^2 (171 ± 28 psi)
Spark plug type	
Standard heat range	ND X24EPR-U9 or NGK DPR8EA-9
Cold weather*	ND X22EPR-U9 or NGK DPR7EA-9
Extended high-speed	ND X27EPR-U9 or NGK DPR9EA-9
Spark plug gap	0.8-0.9 mm (0.031-0.035 in.)
Ignition timing	"F" mark @ $1,100 \pm 100$ rpm
Idle speed	$1,100 \pm 100$ rpm
*Cold weather climate—below 41° F (5° C).	

CHAPTER FOUR

ENGINE

The engine in the 500 cc V-twin is a water-cooled, 4-stroke engine with a single overhead camshaft per cylinder. The crankshaft is supported by 2 main bearings and the camshafts are chain-driven from sprockets on each end of the crankshaft. The camshafts operate rocker arms above each of the 3 valves per cylinder and each valve has its own adjuster.

Engine lubrication is by wet sump, with the oil supply housed in the crankcase. The chain-driven oil pump supplies oil under pressure throughout the engine.

The starter motor is located just behind the rear cylinder and drives the starter clutch on the alternator side of the engine.

This chapter provides complete service and overhaul procedures for the Honda 500 cc V-twin engine. Although the clutch and the transmission are located within the engine, they are covered separately in Chapter Six to simplify the presentation of this material.

Service procedures for all models are virtually the same. Where differences occur, they are identified.

Table 1 provides complete engine specifications. **Tables 1-6** are located at the end of this chapter.

ENGINE PRINCIPLES

Figure 1 explains how the engine works. This will be helpful when troubleshooting or repairing your engine.

SERVICING ENGINE IN FRAME

The following components can be serviced while the engine is mounted in the frame (the bike's frame is a great holding fixture for breaking loose stubborn bolts and nuts):
  a. Clutch assembly (with sub-frame removed).
  b. Alternator.
  c. Carburetor assembly.
  d. External shift mechanism.

ENGINE REMOVAL/INSTALLATION

WARNING
The engine weighs 64 kg (141 lb.). Due to this weight it is essential that a minimum of 2, preferably 3, people be available for the removal and installation procedure.

1. Place the bike on the centerstand and remove the seat and the side covers.
2. Disconnect the battery negative and positive leads.
3. Remove the fuel tank as described in Chapter Six.
4. Drain the engine oil as described under *Engine Oil and Filter Change* in Chapter Three.
5. Drain the engine coolant as described under *Coolant Change* in Chapter Three.
6. Remove the radiator as described in Chapter Eight.

① **4-STROKE OPERATING PRINCIPLES**

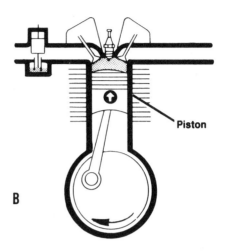

Carburetor

Intake valve

Piston

A

B

As the piston travels downward, the exhaust valve is closed and the intake valve opens, allowing the new air-fuel mixture from the carburetor to be drawn into the cylinder. When the piston reaches the bottom of its travel (BDC), the intake valve closes and remains closed for the next 1 1/2 revolutions of the crankshaft.

While the crankshaft continues to rotate, the piston moves upward, compressing the air-fuel mixture.

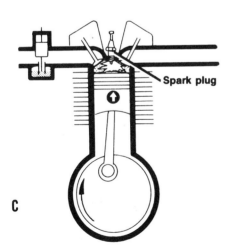

Spark plug

C

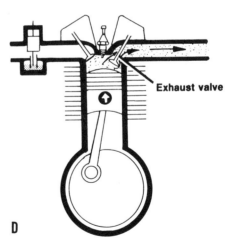

Exhaust valve

D

As the piston almost reaches the top of its travel, the spark plug fires, igniting the compressed air-fuel mixture. The piston continues to top dead center (TDC) and is pushed downward by the expanding gases.

When the piston almost reaches BDC, the exhaust valve opens and remains open until the piston is near TDC. The upward travel of the piston forces the exhaust gases out of the cylinder. After the piston has reached TDC, the exhaust valve closes and the cycle starts all over again.

4

7. Disconnect the spark plug wires and tie them up out of the way.

8. Remove the rear brake pedal as described in Chapter Eleven.

9. Remove the exhaust system as described in Chapter Six.

10. Remove the carburetor assembly as described in Chapter Six. After the carburetor assembly has been removed, insert a clean shop cloth into the intake ports to prevent the entry of foreign matter and coolant.

11. Disconnect the coolant hoses and the engine breather hose from the cylinder head (**Figure 2**).

12. Remove the ignition coils as described in Chapter Eight.

13. Remove the alternator as described in this chapter.

14. Remove the sub-frame and remove the clutch as described in Chapter Six.

15. Remove the external shift mechanism as described in Chapter Six.

16. Remove the starter as described in Chapter Seven.

17. Disconnect the engine ground strap, the thermo sensor wire, the neutral/OD switch wire, the oil pressure sender wire and the pulse generator wire connector.

18. Disconnect the tachometer drive cable (**Figure 3**).

19. Take a final look all over the engine to make sure everything has been disconnected.

20. Loosen, but do not remove, the rear through bolts and nuts.

21. Place two 4×6 and one 2×4 pieces of wood on their sides under the engine as shown in **Figure 4**. This stack-up of wood fits snugly under the crankcase.

> *WARNING*
> *Due to the weight of the engine the following steps must be taken slowly and carefully to avoid dropping the engine out of the frame, causing damage not only to the engine but to yourself and your helpers.*

22. Remove the front through bolts (**Figure 5**). The nuts were removed from these through bolts when the sub-frame was removed.

23. Remove the upper and then the lower rear through bolts (**Figure 6**). The engine should now be resting on the stack-up of wood blocks.

> *CAUTION*
> *The engine assembly is very heavy. This final step requires a minimum of 2, preferably 3, people to safely remove the engine from the frame.*

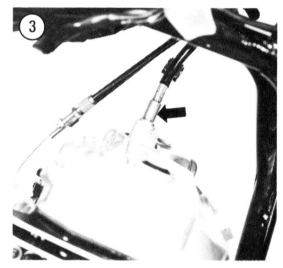

5

6

7

24. Carefully and slowly pivot the engine (on the wood blocks) out of the right-hand side of the frame in order to gain access to all sides. Move it out far enough so that everyone can get a good hand hold on the engine.

25. Slide the engine out of the open frame area on the right-hand side.

26. Place the engine in an engine stand or take it to a work bench for further disassembly.

27. Install by reversing these removal steps, noting the following.

NOTE
Due to the weight of the complete engine assembly, it is suggested that all components removed be left off until the crankcase assembly is reinstalled into the frame. If you choose to install a completed engine assembly, it requires a minimum of 3 people.

28. Install all through bolts in from the left-hand side and tighten the bolts and nuts to the torque specifications listed in **Table 2**.

29. Fill the crankcase with the recommended type and quantity of engine oil and coolant. Refer to Chapter Three.

30. Start the engine and check for leaks.

CYLINDER HEAD COVER AND CAMSHAFT

There are 2 camshafts and 2 cam chains. Each cylinder has one camshaft that operates all 3 valves for that cylinder. There are 2 intake valves and one exhaust valve per cylinder.

There is a cam chain sprocket on the left-hand side of the crankshaft and a separate sprocket that is splined onto the crankshaft on the right-hand side. Both cam chains are the Hy-Vo type and the engine must be removed and disassembled to remove the chains.

Either cylinder head cover and camshaft can be removed without removing these items from the other cylinder.

Front Cylinder Head Cover and Camshaft Removal

1. Remove the ignition timing hole cap (**Figure 7**) on the right-hand crankcase cover.

2. Remove the engine as described in this chapter.

3. Remove the bolts securing the coolant pipes to each cylinder head. Remove the coolant pipes and O-ring seals.

4. Remove the bolts securing the cylinder head covers and remove both covers.

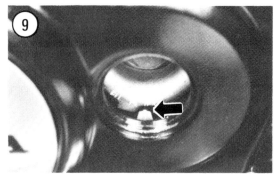

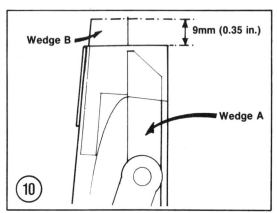

5. Remove all 4 spark plugs. This will make it easier to rotate the engine by hand in the following steps.

6. Using a 17 mm socket, rotate the engine using the primary drive gear bolt (**Figure 8**).

NOTE
Figure 8 *and* ***Figure 9*** *are shown with the engine in the frame.*

7. Rotate the engine *clockwise* until the "F-T" mark (**Figure 9**) aligns with the fixed pointer on the crankcase cover.

8. Prior to removing any parts, perform the following to inspect cam chain length:

   a. Measure the amount that wedge B protrudes above the top surface of the cam chain tensioner (**Figure 10**).

   b. If the dimension exceeds 9.0 mm (0.35 in.) the cam chain has stretched and must be replaced.

9. To achieve the minimum amount of cam chain tension for cam removal and installation perform the following:

   a. Push wedge B down and pull wedge A straight up until the hole in wedge A is exposed.

   b. Install a 2 mm pin or piece of wire in the hole (**Figure 11**) in wedge A. This will hold wedge A in the up position.

10. Loosen all valve adjustment locknuts and loosen all valve adjusters. This will relieve any stress on the rocker arms during removal.

11. Remove the bolts (**Figure 12**) securing the camshaft holder on the chain side. Remove the holder and locating dowels.

12. Remove the bolts and nut (**Figure 13**) securing the camshaft holder and oil passage. Remove the holder, oil passage and locating dowels.

13. Remove the exposed cam sprocket bolt (**Figure 14**).

14. Rotate the engine *clockwise* 360° and remove the other exposed sprocket bolt.

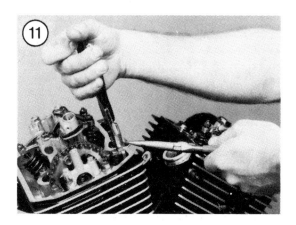

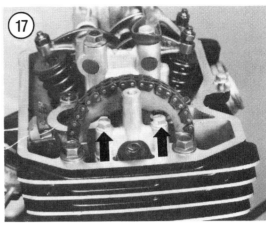

15. Rotate the engine *clockwise* 180°.

16. Slide the cam sprocket and cam chain off the shoulder on the cam.

17. Slide the cam out of the cam sprocket and remove the cam.

18. Remove the cam sprocket and tie a piece of wire to the cam chain. Tie the other end of the wire to an external part of the engine so the cam chain will not fall down into the crankcase.

Rear Cylinder Head Cover and Camshaft Removal

1. Perform Steps 1-6 of *Front Cylinder Head Cover and Camshaft Removal* in this chapter.

2. Rotate the engine *clockwise* until the "R-T" mark (**Figure 15**) aligns with the fixed pointer on the crankcase cover.

3. Prior to removing any parts, perform the following to inspect cam chain length:

   a. Measure the amount that wedge B protrudes above the top surface of the cam chain tensioner (**Figure 10**).

   b. If the dimension exceeds the service limit of 9.0 mm (0.35 in.) the cam chain has stretched and must be replaced.

4. To achieve the minimum amount of cam chain tension for cam removal and installation perform the following:

   a. Push wedge B down and pull wedge A straight up until the hole in wedge A is exposed.

   b. Install a 2 mm pin or piece of wire in the hole (**Figure 16**) in wedge A. This will hold wedge A in the up position.

5. Loosen all valve adjustment locknuts and loosen all valve adjusters. This will relieve stress on the rocker arms during removal.

6. Remove the bolts (**Figure 17**) securing the camshaft holder on the chain side. Remove the holder and locating dowels.

7. Remove the bolts and nut (**Figure 18**) securing the camshaft holder and oil passage. Remove the holder, oil passage and locating dowels.

8. Remove the exposed cam sprocket bolt (**Figure 19**).

> *CAUTION*
> *If the front cylinder head cover and camshaft have been removed, step 9 and Step 10 will require the aid of a helper. When rotating the engine in the following steps, have the helper pull up on the cam chain for the front cylinder and keep it properly meshed with the sprocket on the crankshaft. This is necessary to avoid letting the chain bunch up and damage the crankcase and chain.*

9. Rotate the engine *clockwise* 360° and remove the other exposed sprocket bolt.

10. Rotate the engine *clockwise* 180°.

11. Slide the cam sprocket and cam chain off the shoulder on the cam.

12. Slide the cam out of the cam sprocket and remove the cam.

13. Remove the cam sprocket and tie a piece of wire to the cam chain. Tie the other end of the wire to an external part of the engine so the cam chain will not fall down into the crankcase.

> *CAUTION*
> *If the crankshaft must be rotated when the camshafts are removed, pull up on the cam chains and keep them taut while rotating the crankshaft. Make certain that the chains are positioned onto the crankshaft sprockets. If this is not done, the chains may become kinked and may damage both the chains and the sprockets on the crankshaft.*

Inspection

1. Check the camshaft bearing journals (A, **Figure 20**) for wear and scoring.

2. Even though the camshaft bearing journal surface appears to be satisfactory, with no visible signs of wear, the camshaft bearing journal must be measured with a micrometer as shown in **Figure 21**. Replace the camshaft(s) if worn beyond the service limits listed in **Table 1**.

3. Check the camshaft lobes for wear (B, **Figure 20**). The lobes should not be scored and the edges should be square. Slight damage may be removed with a silicon carbide oilstone. Use No. 100-200 grit initially, then polish with a No. 280-320 grit.

4. Even though the camshaft lobe surface appears to be satisfactory, with no visible signs of wear, the

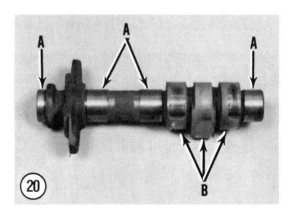

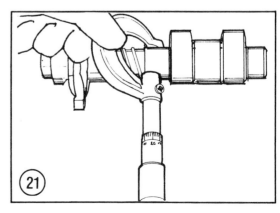

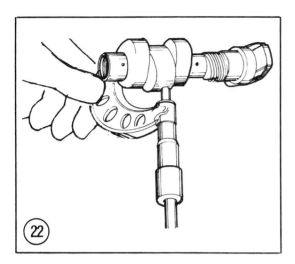

camshaft lobes must be measured with a micrometer as shown in **Figure 22**. Replace the camshaft(s) if worn beyond the service limits listed in **Table 1**.

5. Measure the runout of the camshaft with a dial indicator and V-blocks as shown in **Figure 23**. Use 1/2 of the total runout and compare to the service limits listed in **Table 1**.

6. Check the camshaft bearing journals in the cylinder head (**Figure 24**) and cam holder (**Figure 25**) for wear and scoring. They should not be scored or excessively worn. If necessary, replace the cylinder head and cam holder as a matched pair.

7. Inspect the cam sprockets for wear; replace if necessary.

4

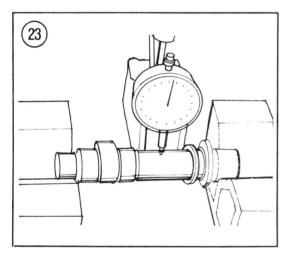

**Camshaft Bearing
Clearance Measurement**

This procedure requires the use of a Plastigage set. The camshaft must be installed into the head. Prior to installation, wipe all oil residue from each cam bearing journal and bearing surface in the head and all camshaft holders.

The front camshaft has the tachometer drive gear on it. Perform this measurement on one cylinder at a time.

1. Install the camshaft into the cylinder head with the lobes facing down.

2. Install all camshaft holder locating dowels into position in the cylinder head.

3. Wipe all oil from cam bearing journals prior to using the Plastigage material.

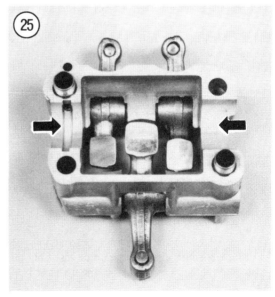

4. Place a strip of Plastigage material on top of each cam bearing journal, parallel to the cam, as shown in **Figure 26**. Place the camshaft holders into their correct position.

5. Install all camshaft holder bolts and nut that hold the camshaft holders in place. Install finger-tight at first, then tighten in a crisscross pattern to the final torque specification listed in **Table 2**.

> *NOTE*
> *Do not rotate either camshaft with the Plastigage material in place.*

6. Gradually remove the bolts and nut in a crisscross pattern. Remove the camshaft holders carefully.

7. Measure the width of the flattened Plastigage according to manufacturer's instructions (**Figure 27**).

8. If the clearance exceeds the wear limit in **Table 1**, measure the camshaft bearing journals with a micrometer and compare to the wear limits in **Table 1**. If the camshaft bearing journal is less than the dimension specified, replace the cam. If the cam is within specifications, the cylinder head and camshaft holders must be replaced as a matched set.

> *CAUTION*
> *Remove all particles of Plastigage material from all camshaft bearing journals and camshaft holders. This material must not be left in the engine as it can plug up a small oil control orifice and cause severe engine damage.*

Front Cylinder Head Cover and Camshaft Installation

If both cylinder head covers and cam shafts have been removed, install the front camshaft and holders first then the rear. The front camshaft has the tachometer drive gear on it.

> *CAUTION*
> *If the rear cylinder head cover and camshaft have been removed, the following steps will require the aid of a helper. When rotating the engine in the following steps, have the helper pull up on the cam chain for the rear cylinder and keep it properly meshed with the sprocket on the crankshaft. This is necessary to avoid letting the chain bunch up and damage the crankcase and chain.*

1. Coat all camshaft lobes and bearing journals with molybdenum disulfide grease or assembly oil. Also coat the bearing surfaces in the cylinder head and camshaft bearing holders.

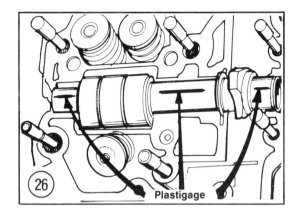

Plastigage

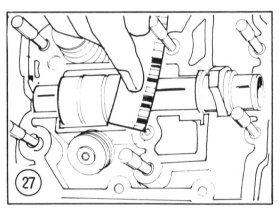

2. Position the cam sprocket so that the index marks face the left-hand side of the engine and are up and down (90° from the top surface of the cylinder head).

3. Temporarily install the cam chain onto the cam sprocket.

4. Install the cam into the sprocket and cam chain and fill the cam lobe oil cavity (**Figure 28**) in the cylinder head with fresh engine oil.

5. Position the cam with the lobes facing down (**Figure 29**).

> *CAUTION*
> *The following steps require the aid of a helper. When rotating the engine in the following steps, have the helper pull up on the rear cam chain and keep it properly meshed with the sprocket on the crankshaft. This is necessary to avoid causing damage to the crankcase and chain.*

6. Using a 17 mm socket, rotate the engine using the primary drive gear bolt (**Figure 8**).

> *NOTE*
> ***Figure 8*** *and* ***Figure 9*** *are shown with the engine in the frame.*

7. Rotate the engine *clockwise* until the "F-T" mark (**Figure 9**) aligns with the fixed pointer on the crankcase cover.

8. Carefully pull the cam chain off of the cam sprocket and rotate the cam sprocket until the index marks are parallel to the top surface of the cylinder head (A, **Figure 30**).

9. Pull the cam chain and sprocket up onto the shoulder on the camshaft. Again check the alignment of the index marks as noted in Step 8. If the alignment is incorrect, correct it at this time.

10. Temporarily install the sprocket bolt into the exposed hole (B, **Figure 30**).

11. Rotate the engine *clockwise* 360° and install the other cam sprocket bolt.

12. Rotate the engine *clockwise* 360° and check for correct cam sprocket alignment as described in Step 7 and Step 8. Readjust if necessary.

> *CAUTION*
> *Very expensive damage could result from improper camshaft and chain alignment. Recheck your work several times to be sure alignment is correct.*

13. Remove the exposed cam sprocket bolt and apply Loctite Lock N' Seal to the bolt threads and to the underside of the bolt head. Install the bolt and tighten to the torque specifications listed in **Table 2**.

14. Rotate the engine *clockwise* one full turn (360°). Remove the exposed cam sprocket bolt and apply Loctite Lock N' Seal to the bolt threads and to the underside of the bolt head. Install this bolt and tighten to the torque specifications listed in **Table 2**.

15. Install the locating dowels (**Figure 31**) and then the camshaft holder on the chain side. Install the 6 mm bolts (**Figure 17**) and tighten to the torque specification listed in **Table 2**.

16. Install the locating dowels, the camshaft holder and the oil passage. Make sure the tachometer driven gear is meshed properly with the drive gear on the camshaft (A, **Figure 32**).

17. Install the 8 mm bolts and 8 mm nut (B, **Figure 32**) and tighten in a crisscross pattern in 2-3 stages to the torque specification listed in **Table 2**.

Rear Cylinder Head Cover and Camshaft Installation

1. Using a 17 mm socket, rotate the engine using the primary drive gear bolt (**Figure 8**). Rotate the engine *clockwise* 232°. Make sure the "R-T" mark (**Figure 15**) aligns with the fixed pointer on the crankcase cover.

NOTE
Figure 8 is shown with the engine in the frame.

2. Coat all camshaft lobes and bearing journals with molybdenum disulfide grease or assembly oil. Also coat the bearing surfaces in the cylinder head and camshaft bearing holders.

3. Position the cam sprocket so that the index marks face the right-hand side of the engine and are up and down (90° from the top surface of the cylinder head).

4. Temporarily install the cam chain onto the cam sprocket.

5. Install the cam into the sprocket and cam chain and fill the cam lobe oil cavity (**Figure 28**) in the cylinder head with fresh engine oil.

6. Position the cam with the lobes facing down (**Figure 29**).

7. Make sure the "R-T" mark (**Figure 15**) still aligns with the fixed pointer on the crankcase cover.

8. Carefully pull the cam chain off of the cam sprocket and rotate the cam sprocket until the index

marks are parallel to the top surface of the cylinder head (A, **Figure 33**).

9. Pull the cam chain and sprocket up onto the shoulder on the camshaft. Again check the alignment of the index marks as noted in Step 8. If the alignment is incorrect, correct it at this time.

10. Temporarily install the sprocket bolt into the exposed hole (B, **Figure 33**).

11. Rotate the engine *clockwise* 360° and install the other cam sprocket bolt.

12. Rotate the engine *clockwise* 360° and check for correct cam sprocket alignment as described in Step 7 and Step 8. Readjust if necessary.

CAUTION
Very expensive damage could result from improper camshaft and chain alignment. Recheck your work several times to be sure alignment is correct.

13. Remove the exposed cam sprocket bolt and apply Loctite Lock N' Seal to the bolt threads and to the underside of the bolt head. Install the bolts and tighten to the torque specifications listed in **Table 2**.

14. Rotate the engine *clockwise* one full turn (360°). Remove the exposed cam sprocket bolt and apply Loctite Lock N' Seal to the bolt threads and to the underside of the bolt head. Install this bolt and tighten to the torque specifications listed in **Table 2**.

15. Install the locating dowels and then the camshaft holder on the chain side. Install the 6 mm bolts (**Figure 17**) and tighten to the torque specification listed in **Table 2**.

16. Install the locating dowels, the camshaft holder and the oil passage.

17. Install the 8 mm bolts and 8 mm nut (**Figure 18**) and tighten in a crisscross pattern in 2-3 stages to the torque specification listed in **Table 2**.

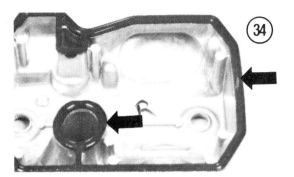

mark (**Figure 15**) aligns with the pointer on the crankcase cover. Make sure the index marks (A, **Figure 33**) on the rear cylinder cam sprocket align with the top surface of the cylinder head.

20. Inspect the rubber gaskets (**Figure 34**) on the cylinder head covers; replace if necessary.

21. Install the cylinder head covers and bolts. Tighten the bolts securely.

22. Install the ignition timing hole cap on the right-hand crankcase cover.

23. Adjust the valve clearances as described in Chapter Three.

24. Install the engine as described in this chapter.

25. Make sure the O-ring seals are in place on the coolant pipes. Install the coolant pipes to each cylinder head as described in Chapter Eight.

CYLINDER HEADS

Removal/Installation

If both cylinder heads are going to be removed, either cylinder head can be removed without first removing the other cylinder head. Either can be removed first. This procedure pertains to either cylinder head.

NOTE
In the next 2 steps, there is a sealing washer on each side of the oil line fitting where the bolt secures the oil line to the engine. Don't lose them.

1. Remove the bolts and sealing washers (**Figure 35**) securing the external oil line to each cylinder head.

2. Remove the union bolt and sealing washers and the Allen bolt (**Figure 36**) securing the external oil line to the lower left-hand side of the engine. Remove the external oil line from the engine.

3. Remove the engine as described in this chapter.

4. Remove the cylinder head cover and camshaft for the specific cylinder as described in this chapter.

5. Remove the bolts (**Figure 37**) securing the cam chain tensioner and pull the cam chain tensioner assembly up out of the cylinder head.

18. Using pliers, remove the 2 mm pin or piece of wire from the cam chain tensioner (**Figure 11**) on both the front and rear cylinders.

19. For a final check, perform the following:
  a. Using the bolt on the primary drive gear, rotate the engine *clockwise* until the "F-T" mark (**Figure 9**) aligns with the pointer on the crankcase cover. Make sure the index marks (A, **Figure 30**) on the front cylinder cam sprocket aligns with the top surface of the cylinder head.

  b. Using the bolt on the primary drive gear, rotate the engine *clockwise* until the "R-T"

6. To prevent warpage of the head, loosen the cylinder head bolts (A, **Figure 38**) and nuts (B, **Figure 38**) 1/2 turn at a time in a crisscross pattern.

7. After all bolts and nuts have been loosened, remove them.

8. Loosen the head by tapping around the perimeter with a rubber or plastic mallet.

> *CAUTION*
> *Remember, the fins on the cylinder head are fragile and may be damaged if tapped or pried too hard. Never use a metal hammer. These fins are more for cosmetic value than cooling. They are not as fragile as those on an air-cooled engine but they still may break.*

9. Untie the wire securing the cam chain and retie it to the cylinder head. Lift the cylinder head straight up and off the crankcase studs. Pull the cam chain and wire through the opening in the cylinder head and retie the cam chain up to one of the crankcase studs.

> *NOTE*
> *If both heads are going to be removed, mark them with an "F" (front cylinder) or "R" (rear cylinder) so they will be reinstalled onto the correct position on the engine. The heads on some models are marked with the engine series number "MF5-3F" or "MF5-3R" (**Figure 39**). The "F" and "R" relate to the front or rear cylinder location.*

10. Remove the head gasket, dowel pins and the cam chain guide.

11. Place a clean shop rag into the cam chain opening in the cylinder to prevent entry of foreign matter.

12. Repeat Steps 4-9 for the other cylinder head if necessary.

13. Install by reversing these removal steps, noting the following.

14. Clean the cylinder head mating surfaces of any gasket material.

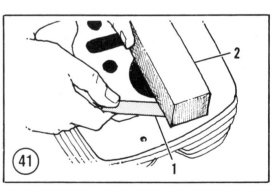

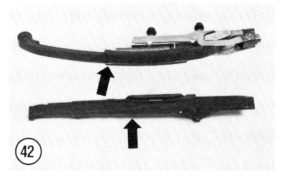

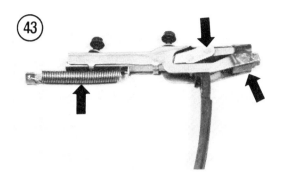

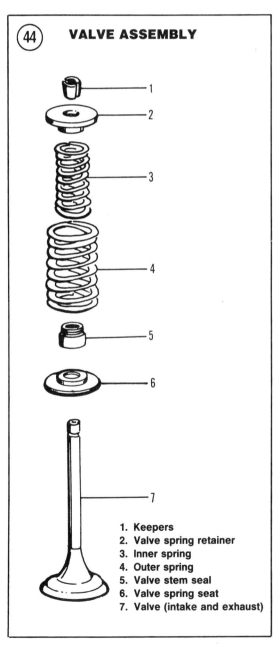

VALVE ASSEMBLY

1. Keepers
2. Valve spring retainer
3. Inner spring
4. Outer spring
5. Valve stem seal
6. Valve spring seat
7. Valve (intake and exhaust)

15. Install a new head gasket (A, **Figure 40**) and locating dowels (B, **Figure 40**).

16. Install the cam chain guide (C, **Figure 40**).

17. Install the bolts (**Figure 37**) securing the cam chain tensioner and tighten the bolts securely.

18. Install the bolt and nuts securing the cylinder head. Tighten the bolts in 2-3 stages in a crisscross pattern to the torque specifications listed in **Table 2**.

19. Repeat Steps 4-18 for the other cylinder head if necessary.

20. After the engine has been installed in the frame, install the oil line assembly. Place a sealing washer on each side of each fitting, then insert the bolts. These washers must be installed as noted to prevent an oil leak. Tighten the bolts to the torque specification listed in **Table 2**.

Inspection

1. Remove all traces of gasket material from the cylinder head and the cylinder mating surface.

2. *Without* removing the valves, remove all carbon deposits from the combustion chambers with a wire brush. A blunt screwdriver or chisel may be used if care is taken not to damage the head, valves and spark plug threads.

3. After all carbon is removed from the combustion chambers and valve intake and exhaust ports, clean the entire head in solvent.

4. Clean away all carbon on the piston crowns. Do not remove the carbon ridge at the top of the cylinder bore.

5. Check for cracks in the combustion chamber and exhaust ports. A cracked head must be replaced.

6. After the head has been thoroughly cleaned, place a straightedge across the gasket surface (**Figure 41**) at several points. Measure warp by inserting a flat feeler gauge between the straightedge and the cylinder head at each location. There should be no warpage; if a small amount is present, the head can be resurfaced by a Honda dealer or qualified machine shop.

7. Check the valves and valve guides as described in this chapter.

8. Inspect the cam chain tensioner and cam chain guide for wear (**Figure 42**).

9. Inspect the spring and all moving parts of the cam chain tensioner assembly (**Figure 43**) for wear or damage. If any parts are worn the assembly must be replaced.

**VALVES AND
VALVE COMPONENTS**

Removal

Refer to **Figure 44** for this procedure.

1. Remove the cylinder head(s) as described in this chapter.

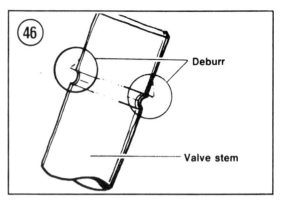

2. Compress springs with a valve spring compressor tool (**Figure 45**). Remove the valve keepers and release compression. Remove the valve compressor tool.

> *CAUTION*
> *To avoid loss of spring tension, do not compress the springs any more than necessary to remove the keepers.*

3. Prior to removing the valves, remove any burrs from the valve stem (**Figure 46**). Otherwise, the valve guides will be damaged.

4. Remove the valve keepers, valve spring retainer and both inner and outer springs (**Figure 47**).

5. Remove the valve seal/ring and the valve spring seat.

Inspection

1. Clean all valves with a wire brush and solvent.

2. Inspect the contact surface of each valve for burning. Minor roughness and pitting can be removed by lapping the valve as described in this chapter. Excessive unevenness of the contact surface is an indication that the valve is not serviceable.

> *NOTE*
> *The contact surface of the valve **cannot** be ground; the valve must be replaced if this area shows more than minor damage.*

3. Measure valve stems for wear (**Figure 48**). Compare with specifications in **Table 1**.

4. Remove all carbon and varnish from the valve guides (**Figure 49**) with a stiff spiral wire brush.

> *NOTE*
> *The next step assumes that all valve stems are within specifications.*

5. Insert each valve in its guide. Hold the valve just slightly off its seat and rock it sideways in 2

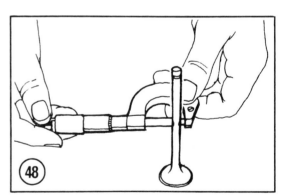

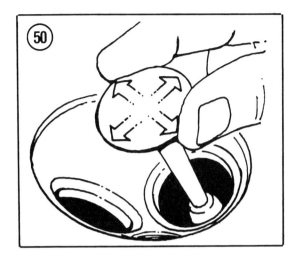

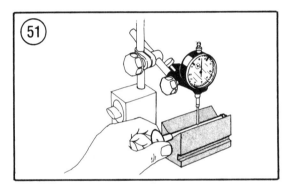

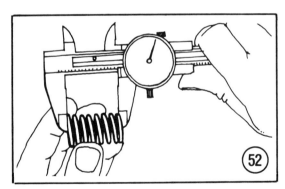

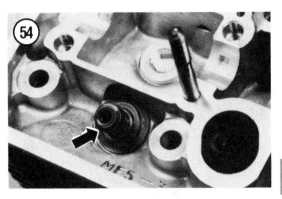

directions (**Figure 50**). If it rocks more than slightly, the guide is probably worn and should be replaced. If a dial indicator is available, a more accurate measurement can be made as shown in **Figure 51**. Replace any guides that exceed the valve stem-to-guide clearance specified in **Table 1**. If the guides must be replaced, take the cylinder head to a dealer or machine shop for guide replacement.

6. Measure the valve spring heights with a vernier caliper (**Figure 52**). All should be the length specified in **Table 1** with no bends or other distortion. Replace defective springs as a set.

7. Check the valve spring retainer and valve keepers. If they are in good condition, they may be reused.

8. Inspect valve seats. If worn or burned, they must be reconditioned. This should be performed by your dealer or a qualified machine shop. Seats and valves in near-perfect condition can be reconditioned by lapping with a fine carborundum paste. Lapping, however, is always inferior to precision grinding.

Installation

1. Install the valve spring seat (**Figure 53**).

2. Remove the ring from the valve seal. This will make valve seal installation much easier.

3. Install a new valve seal (**Figure 54**) and then install the ring (**Figure 55**) onto the valve seal.

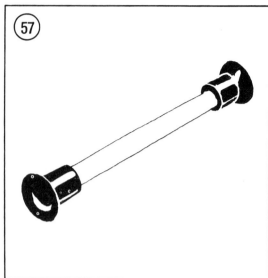

NOTE
The exhaust valves have a stripe of green paint on them.

4. Coat the valve stems with molybdenum disulfide grease. To avoid damage to the valve stem seal, turn the valve slowly while inserting the valve into the cylinder head.

5. Install the valve springs with the narrow pitch end (end with coils closest together) facing the head (**Figure 56**). Install the upper valve spring retainers.

6. Push down on upper valve spring retainers with the valve spring compressor and install valve keepers.

CAUTION
To avoid loss of spring tension, do not compress the springs any more than necessary to install the keepers.

7. After all keepers have been installed, gently tap the valve stems with a plastic mallet to make sure the keepers are properly seated.

Valve Guide Replacement

When guides are worn so that there is excessive stem-to-guide clearance or valve tipping, they must be replaced. Replace all, even if only one is worn. This job should only be done by a dealer, as special tools are required.

Valve Seat Reconditioning

This job is best left to your dealer or local machine shop. They have the special equipment and knowledge for this exacting job. You can still save considerable money by removing the cylinder heads and taking just the heads to the shop.

Valve Lapping

Valve lapping is a simple operation which can restore the valve seal without machining if the amount of wear or distortion is not too great.

CAUTION
Excessive lapping will wear off the special surface coating on the valve face. If this happens the valves will burn prematurely.

1. Coat the valve seating area in the head with a lapping compound such as Carborundum or Clover Brand.

2. Insert the valve into the cylinder head.

3. Wet the suction cup (**Figure 57**) of the lapping stick and stick it onto the head of the valve. Lap the valve to the seat by rotating the lapping stick in both directions. Every 5 to 10 seconds, rotate the valve

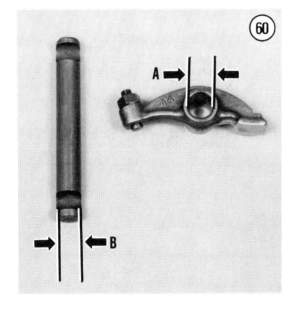

4

180° in the valve seat; continue lapping until the contact surfaces of the valve and the valve seat are a uniform grey. Stop as soon as they are, to avoid removing too much material.

4. Thoroughly clean the valves and cylinder head in solvent to remove all lapping compound. Any compound left on the valves or the cylinder head will end up in the engine and will cause damage.

5. After the lapping has been completed and the valve assemblies have been reinstalled into the head, the valve seal should be tested. Check the seal of each valve by pouring solvent into each of the intake and exhaust ports. The solvent should not flow past the valve seat and the valve head. Perform on all sets of valves. If fluid leaks past any of the seats, disassemble that valve assembly and repeat the lapping procedure until there is no leakage.

ROCKER ARM ASSEMBLIES

The rocker arms for the front and rear cylinders are identical (same Honda part No.) but they will develop different wear patterns during use. It is recommended that the rocker arm assembly from one head be disassembled, inspected and then assembled to avoid the intermixing of parts.

Removal/Inspection/ Installation

1. Remove the camshaft holder as described in this chapter.
2. Using a rubber mallet, tap on the end of the camshaft holder (**Figure 58**). The rocker arms will work their way partially out of the camshaft holder.
3. Withdraw the exhaust rocker arm shaft and remove the rocker arm and the wave washer (**Figure 59**).
4. Wash all parts in cleaning solvent and thoroughly dry.
5. Inspect the rocker arm pad where it rides on the cam lobe and where the adjuster rides on the valve stem. If the pad is scratched or unevenly worn, inspect the cam lobe for scoring, chipping or flat spots. Replace the rocker arm if defective.
6. Measure the inside diameter of the rocker arm (A, **Figure 60**) with an inside micrometer and check against dimensions in **Table 1**. Replace if worn to the service limit or greater.
7. Inspect the rocker arm shaft for signs of wear or scoring. Measure the outside diameter (B, **Figure 60**) with a micrometer and check against dimensions in **Table 1**. Replace if worn to the service limit or less.
8. Coat the rocker arm shaft and rocker arm bore with assembly oil.
9. Partially install the rocker arm shaft and install the wave washer onto the rocker arm shaft (**Figure 61**).
10. Install the rocker arm and push the rocker arm shaft in sufficiently to hold the rocker arm in place.

11. Align the cutout in the rocker arm shaft (A, **Figure 62**) with the bolt hole in the camshaft holder (B, **Figure 62**). Push the rocker arm shaft all the way in.

12. Repeat Steps 3-11 for the intake rocker arm assembly of the same camshaft holder. On the intake valve rocker arm assembly, the wave washer for each rocker arm is located next to the center support of the camshaft holder (**Figure 63**).

13. Using a screwdriver in the slot in the end of each rocker arm shaft (**Figure 64**), align the cutout in the rocker arm shafts with the bolt holes in the camshaft holder.

14. Repeat this procedure for the other cylinder head camshaft holder assembly.

CYLINDER

Removal

1. Remove the cylinder head as described in this chapter.

2. Remove the coolant pipes as described in Chapter Eight.

3. Loosen the cylinder by tapping around the perimeter with a rubber or plastic mallet. If necessary, *gently* pry the cylinder loose with a broad-tipped screwdriver.

4. Pull the cylinder straight out and off of the crankcase studs. Work the cam chain wire through the opening in the cylinder.

5. Remove the cylinder base gasket and discard it. Remove the dowel pins from the crankcase studs.

6. Install a piston holding fixture under the piston (**Figure 65**) to protect the piston skirt from damage. This fixture may be purchased or may be a homemade unit of wood. See **Figure 66** for dimensions.

7. If both cylinders are going to be removed they should be marked with an "F" (front cylinder) or "R" (rear cylinder) as shown in **Figure 67**. This will avoid any mix-up upon installation.

Inspection

The following procedure requires the use of highly specialized and expensive measuring instruments. If such equipment is not readily available, have the measurements performed by a dealer or qualified machine shop.

1. Do not remove or damage the carbon ridge around the top of the cylinder bore. If the cylinders,

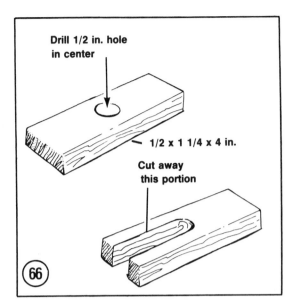

Drill 1/2 in. hole in center

1/2 x 1 1/4 x 4 in.

Cut away this portion

66

67

pistons and rings are found to be dimensionally correct and can be reused, removal of the carbon ridge from the top of the cylinder bores or the ring from the top of pistons will promote excessive oil consumption.

2. Soak with solvent any old cylinder head gasket material on the cylinder. Use a broad-tipped *dull* chisel and gently scrape off all gasket residue. Do not gouge the sealing surface as oil and air leaks will result.

3. Measure the cylinder bore with a cylinder gauge or inside micrometer at the points shown in **Figure 68**. Measure in 2 axes—in line with the piston pin and at 90° to the pin. If the taper or out-of-round is 0.10 mm (0.004 in.) or greater, the cylinder must be rebored to the next oversize and a new piston installed. There are 2 oversize piston sizes available (0.25 mm and 0.50 mm oversize).

NOTE
The new piston should be obtained before the cylinder is rebored so that the piston can be measured; slight manufacturing tolerances must be taken into account to determine the actual size and working clearance.

4. Check the cylinder wall (**Figure 69**) for scratches; if evident, the cylinder should be rebored.

NOTE
*The maximum wear limit on the cylinder is listed in **Table 1**. If the cylinder is worn to this limit, it must be replaced. Never rebore a cylinder if the finished rebore diameter will be this dimension or greater.*

4

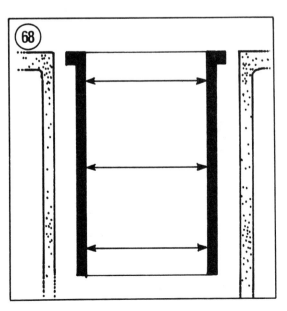

68

69

Installation

1. Check that the top surface of the crankcase and the bottom surface of the cylinder are clean prior to installing a new base gasket.
2. Install a new cylinder base gasket (A, **Figure 70**) and locating dowels (B, **Figure 70**) to either the crankcase or to the base of the cylinder.
3. Make sure the piston holding fixture is still under the piston (**Figure 65**).
4. Make sure the end gaps of the piston rings are *not* lined up with each other—they must be staggered. Lightly oil the piston rings and the inside of the cylinder bores with assembly oil.
5. Install the cylinder and slide it down onto the crankcase studs.
6. Carefully feed the cam chain and wire up through the opening in the cylinder and tie it to the engine.

> *CAUTION*
> *The side rails of the oil ring assembly are very thin. Be very careful that the cylinder does not snag one of these rings, especially the lower one, during installation.*

7. Start the cylinder down over the piston. Compress each piston ring with your fingers as it enters the cylinder.
8. Slide the cylinder down until it bottoms on the piston holding fixture (**Figure 71**).
9. Remove the piston holding fixture and slide the cylinder down into place on the crankcase.
10. Install the cylinder head as described in this chapter.
11. Follow the *Break-in Procedure* in this chapter if the cylinder was rebored or honed or a new piston or piston rings were installed.
12. Repeat this procedure for the other cylinder.
13. Install the coolant pipes as described in Chapter Eight.

PISTON, PISTON PIN AND PISTON RINGS

The piston is made of an aluminum alloy and is fitted with 2 compression rings and one oil control ring.

Piston Removal

1. Remove the cylinder head as described in this chapter.
2. Mark the top of each piston with an "F" (front cylinder) or "R" (rear cylinder) so they will be reinstalled in their correct cylinder. Refer to **Figure 72**.
3. Remove the cylinder as described in this chapter.

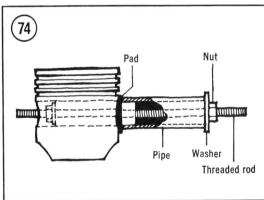

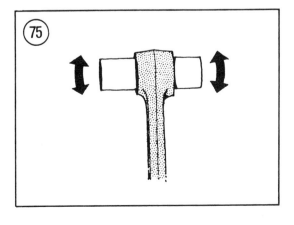

4. Remove the piston rings as described in this chapter.

NOTE
Wrap a clean shop cloth under the piston so the piston pin clip will not fall into the crankcase.

5. Remove the piston pin clips (**Figure 73**) from each side of the piston with a small screwdriver or scribe. Hold your thumb over one edge of the clip when removing it to prevent it from springing out.
6. Use a proper size wooden dowel or socket extension and push out the piston pin.

CAUTION
Be careful when removing the pin to avoid damaging the connecting rod. If it is necessary to gently tap the pin to remove it, be sure that the piston is properly supported.

7. If the piston pin is difficult to remove, heat the piston and pin with a small butane torch. The pin will probably push right out. If not, heat the piston to about 60° C (140° F), i.e., until it is too warm to touch, but not excessively hot. If the pin is still difficult to push out, use a special tool as shown in **Figure 74**.

Piston Inspection

1. Carefully clean the carbon from the piston crown with a chemical remover or with a soft scraper. Do not remove or damage the carbon ridge around the circumference of the piston above the top ring. If the pistons, rings and cylinders are found to be dimensionally correct and can be reused, removal of the carbon ring from the top of pistons or carbon ridge from the top of cylinder bores will promote excessive oil consumption.

CAUTION
Do not wire brush piston skirts.

2. Examine each ring groove for burrs, dented edges and wide wear. Pay particular attention to the top compression ring groove, as it usually wears more than the others.
3. Measure piston-to-cylinder clearance as described in this chapter. If damage or wear indicates piston replacement, select a new piston as described under *Piston Clearance Measurement* in this chapter.
4. Oil the piston pin and install it in the connecting rod bearing. Slowly rotate the piston pin and check for radial and axial play (**Figure 75**). If there is play, the piston pin should be replaced, providing the rod bore is in good condition.
5. Measure the piston pin bore (**Figure 76**) with a snap gauge and measure the outside diameter of the

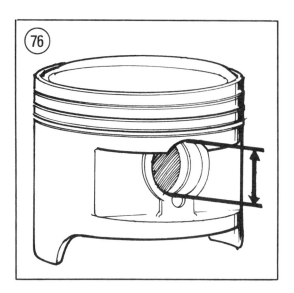

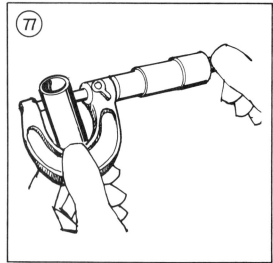

piston pin with a micrometer (**Figure 77**). Compare against dimensions given in **Table 1**. A machinist can do this for you if you do not have the measuring tools. Replace the piston and piston pin as a set if either are worn.

6. Check the piston skirt for galling and abrasion which may have been caused by piston seizure. If light galling is present, smooth the affected area with No. 400 emery cloth and oil or a fine oilstone. However, if galling is severe or if the piston is deeply scored, replace it.

Piston Clearance Measurement

1. Make sure the piston and cylinder walls are clean and dry.
2. Measure the inside diameter of the cylinder bore at a point 13 mm (1/2 in.) from the upper edge with a bore gauge.
3. Measure the outside diameter of the piston across the skirt (**Figure 78**) at right angles to the piston pin. Measure at a distance 10 mm (0.4 in.) up from the bottom of the piston skirt.
4. Piston clearance is the difference between the maximum piston diameter and the minimum cylinder diameter. Subtract the dimension of the piston from the cylinder dimension. If the clearance exceeds the dimension listed in **Table 1** the cylinder should be rebored to the next oversize and a new piston installed.

> *NOTE*
> *The new piston should be obtained before the cylinder is rebored so that the piston can be measured; slight manufacturing tolerances must be taken into account to determine the actual size and working clearance.*

5. To establish a final overbore dimension with a new piston, add the new piston skirt measurement to the specified piston-to-cylinder clearance. This will determine the dimension for the cylinder overbore size. Remember, do not exceed the cylinder maximum inside diameter listed in **Table 1**.
6. There are 2 oversize piston sizes available (0.25 mm and 0.50 mm oversize).

Piston Installation

1. Apply molybdenum disulfide grease to the inside surface of the connecting rod small end. Apply fresh engine oil to the piston pin and piston pin bore.
2. Insert the piston pin into the piston until its end extends slightly beyond the inside of the boss.
3. Place the piston over the connecting rod with the "IN" on the piston crown directed toward the "V" of the engine, toward the carburetors.
4. Line up the piston pin with the holes in the piston and connecting rod and push the pin into the

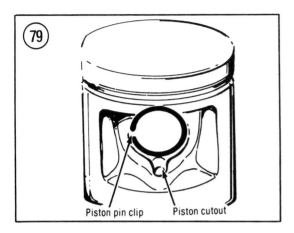

Piston pin clip   Piston cutout

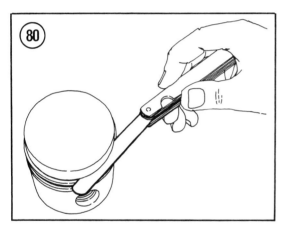

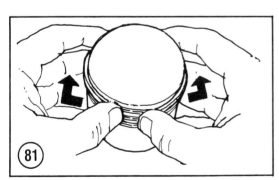

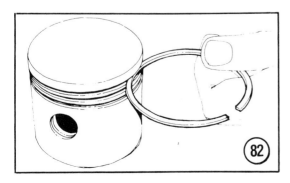

piston until its ends are even with the clip grooves. Be sure to install the piston to the correct rod as marked during removal.

NOTE
If the piston pin does not slide in easily, heat the piston until it is too warm to touch but not excessively hot (60° C/140° F). Continue to drive the piston pin while holding the piston so the rod does not have to take any shock. Drive the piston pin in until it is centered in the rod. If the pin is still difficult to install, use the special tool used during the removal sequence.

NOTE
In the next step, install the clips with the gap away from the cutout in the piston (Figure 79).

5. Install new piston pin clips in the ends of the pin boss (**Figure 73**). Make sure they are seated in the grooves.

6. Check installation by rocking the piston back and forth around the pin axis and from side to side parallel to the axis. It should rotate freely back and forth but not from side to side.

7. Repeat for the piston in the other cylinder.

8. Install the rings as described in this chapter.

9. Install the cylinders and cylinder heads as described in this chapter.

Piston Ring Removal/ Inspection/Installation

WARNING
The edges of all piston rings are very sharp, especially the flat rings of the oil ring assembly. Be careful when handling them to avoid cut fingers.

1. Measure the side clearance of each ring in its groove with a flat feeler gauge (**Figure 80**) and compare with dimensions listed in **Table 1**. If the clearance is greater than specified, the rings must be replaced. If the clearance is still excessive with the new rings, the piston must be replaced.

2. Remove the top ring with a ring expander tool or by spreading the ring ends with your thumbs and lifting the ring up and over the piston (**Figure 81**). Repeat for the remaining rings.

3. Carefully remove all carbon from the ring grooves. Inspect grooves carefully for burrs, nicks or broken and cracked lands. Recondition or replace the piston if necessary.

4. Roll each ring around its piston groove as shown in **Figure 82** to check for binding. Minor binding may be cleaned up with a fine-cut file.

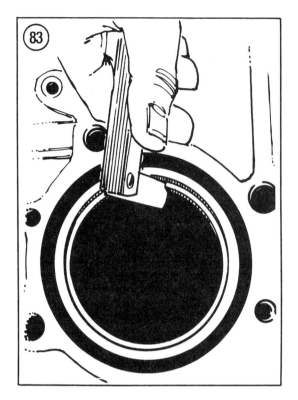

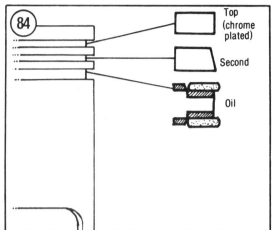

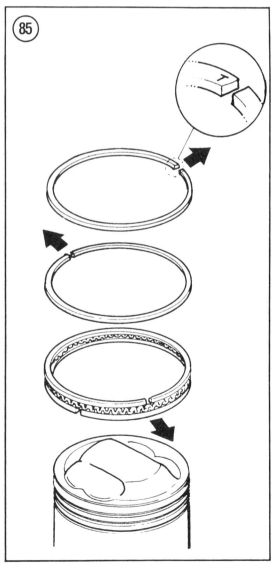

5. Measure the rings for wear as shown in **Figure 83**. Place each ring, one at a time, into its cylinder and push it in about 20 mm (3/4 in.) with the crown of the piston to ensure that the ring is square in the cylinder bore. Measure the gap with a flat feeler gauge and compare with dimensions listed in **Table 1**. If the gap is greater than specified, the ring(s) should be replaced. When installing new rings, measure their end gap in the same manner. If the gap is less than specified, carefully file the ends with a fine-cut file until the gap is correct.

6. Install the piston rings in the order shown in **Figure 84**.

NOTE
Install all rings with their markings facing up.

7. Install the piston rings—first the bottom, then the middle, then the top ring—by carefully spreading the ends with your thumbs and slipping the ring over the top of the piston. Remember that the piston rings must be installed with the marks on them facing up toward the top of the piston.

8. Make sure the rings are seated completely in their grooves all the way around the piston and that the end gaps are distributed around the piston as shown in **Figure 85**. The important thing is that the ring gaps are not aligned with each other when installed.

9. If new rings are installed, measure the side clearance of each ring in its groove with a flat feeler gauge (**Figure 80**) and compare to dimensions listed in **Table 1**.

OIL PUMP
DRIVE SPROCKETS
AND DRIVE CHAIN

Removal/Installation

1. Remove the clutch as described in Chapter Five.
2. Remove the bolt and washer (**Figure 86**) securing the oil pump driven sprocket.
3. As an assembly, slide off the oil pump driven sprocket (A, **Figure 87**), the drive chain (B, **Figure 87**), the oil pump drive sprocket and clutch outer housing bushing (C, **Figure 87**).
4. Inspect the drive chain and both sprockets (**Figure 88**) for wear or damage. Replace as a set if necessary.
5. Install by reversing these removal steps, noting the following.
6. Install the clutch outer housing bushing (**Figure 89**) onto the transmission main shaft prior to installing the sprockets and drive chain.
7. Position the oil pump driven sprocket with the "IN" mark facing in toward the crankcase and align the flats on the sprocket with the flats on the oil pump shaft.
8. Tighten the driven sprocket bolt to the torque specification listed in **Table 2**.

OIL PUMP

The oil pump is mounted within the crankcase. The engine must be removed from the frame and the crankcases disassembled to gain access to the oil pump.

Removal

1. Remove the engine as described in this chapter.
2. Separate the crankcase as described in this chapter.
3. Remove the bolts (**Figure 90**) securing the oil pump assembly to the left-hand crankcase half.

> *NOTE*
> ***Figure 90*** *is shown with the crankshaft and transmission assemblies removed for clarity. It is not necessary to remove any of these assemblies for this procedure.*

4. Remove the locating dowels and O-ring seals (**Figure 91**) from the left-hand crankcase half.
5. Remove the oil joint pipe and oil strainer from the oil pump assembly (**Figure 92**).

Installation

1. To prime the oil pump, add clean engine oil into one of the openings in the oil pump. Add oil until the oil drains out of the other opening.
2. Install a new O-ring seal (**Figure 93**) onto the oil pump body and then install the oil strainer (**Figure 94**) into the O-ring seal.
3. Install new O-ring seals (**Figure 95**) on the oil joint pipe. Install the 2 O-ring seals on the short

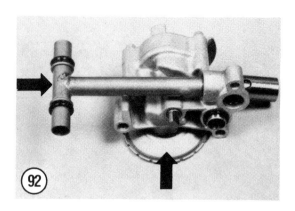

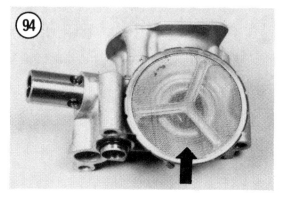

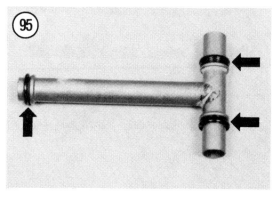

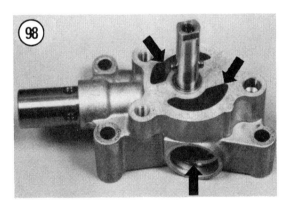

length of the oil joint pipe with the larger diameter portion toward the end of the pipe as shown in **Figure 96**.

4. Install the oil joint pipe onto the oil pump assembly.

5. Install the locating dowels and new O-ring seals (**Figure 91**) into the crankcase.

6. Install the mounting bolts and tighten to the torque specifications listed in **Table 2**.

7. Assemble the crankcase and install the engine as described in this chapter.

8. Refill the engine with the recommended type and quantity of engine oil as described in Chapter Three.

9. Start the engine and check for leaks.

Disassembly/Inspection/Assembly

> *NOTE*
> *Replacement parts are not available for the oil pump. If any of the external or internal components are worn or damaged, the entire oil pump assembly must be replaced.*

1. Inspect the outer cover and body for cracks.

2. Remove the bolts (**Figure 97**) securing the pump cover to the pump body. Remove the pump cover.

3. Withdraw the oil pump drive shaft, spacer and pin. Don't lose the pin; it will slide out of the shaft.

4. Remove the inner and outer rotors. Check all parts for scratches and abrasion.

5. Clean all parts in solvent and thoroughly dry with compressed air. Carefully scrub the strainer screen with a soft toothbrush; do not damage the screen.

6. Coat all parts with fresh oil prior to installation.

7. Inspect the interior passageways (**Figure 98**) of the oil pump body. Make sure that all oil sludge and foreign matter is removed.

8. Inspect the strainer screen for broken areas (**Figure 99**). This would allow small foreign particles to enter the oil pump and cause damage. If broken in any area, replace the strainer.

9. Install the outer rotor (**Figure 100**) and then the inner rotor (**Figure 101**) into the pump cover.

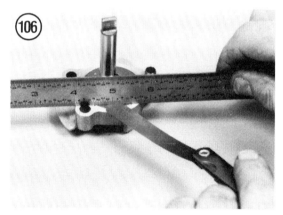

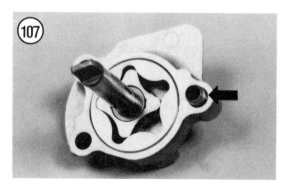

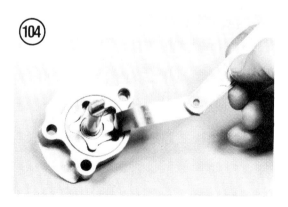

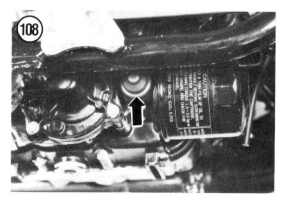

10. Install the oil pump drive shaft and pin (**Figure 102**). Mesh the pin into the groove in the inner rotor and install the spacer onto the shaft (**Figure 103**).

11. Check the clearance between the inner tip and outer rotor (**Figure 104**) with a flat feeler gauge. If the clearance is greater than the service limit in **Table 1** the oil pump must be replaced.

12. Check the clearance between the outer rotor and the body (**Figure 105**) with a flat feeler gauge. If the clearance is greater than the service limit in **Table 1** the oil pump must be replaced.

13. Check the rotor end clearance with a straightedge and flat feeler gauge (**Figure 106**). If the clearance is greater than the service limit in **Table 1** the oil pump must be replaced.

14. Install the locating dowel (**Figure 107**).

15. Install the body and tighten the screws (**Figure 99**) securely.

16. After the oil pump is assembled, turn the shaft and make sure the oil pump turns freely with no binding.

17. Install the oil pump as described in this chapter.

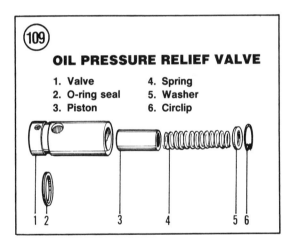

OIL PRESSURE RELIEF VALVE

1. Valve   4. Spring
2. O-ring seal   5. Washer
3. Piston   6. Circlip

1 2   3   4   5 6

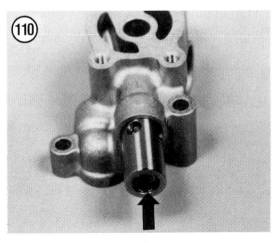

NOTE
*If the condition of the oil pump is doubtful, run the **Oil Pump Pressure Test** described in this chapter.*

Oil Pump Pressure Test

If the oil pump output is doubtful, the following test can be performed.

1. Warm the engine up to normal operating temperature (80° C/176° F). Shut off the engine.

2. Place the bike on the centerstand.

3. Check the engine oil level. It must be to the upper line; add oil if necessary. Do not run this test with the oil level low or the test readings will be false.

4. Pull the rubber boot back from the oil pressure switch (**Figure 108**).

5. Remove the electrical wire from the oil pressure switch.

6. Remove the oil pressure switch from the crankcase.

7. Screw a portable oil pressure gauge into the switch hole in the crankcase.

NOTE
These can be purchased in an automotive or motorcycle supply store or from a Honda dealer. The Honda parts are No. 07506-3000000 (Oil Pressure Gauge) and No. 07510-4220100 (Oil Pressure Gauge Attachment).

8. Start the engine and run it at 6,000 rpm. The standard pressure is 4.7-6.1 kg/cm^2 (52.7-72.5 psi) at 6,000 rpm and at 80° C (176° F). If the pressure is less than specified the oil pump must be replaced.

9. Remove the portable oil pressure gauge.

10. Apply a non-hardening liquid sealant to the switch threads prior to installation. Tighten the switch to the torque specifications listed in **Table 2**.

11. Install the electrical wire to the top of the switch. This connection must be free of oil to make good electrical contact.

12. Slide the rubber boot back into place on the switch.

OIL PRESSURE RELIEF VALVE

Refer to **Figure 109** for this procedure.

Disassembly/Inspection/Assembly

1. Remove the oil pump as described in this chapter.

2. Remove the circlip (**Figure 110**) securing the pressure relief valve.

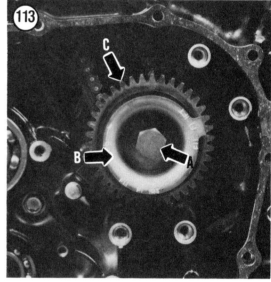

3. Remove the washer, spring and check valve.

4. Wash all parts in solvent and thoroughly dry with compressed air.

5. Inspect the check valve and the cylinder that it rides in for scratches or wear. Replace if defective.

6. Make sure the spring is not broken or distorted; replace if necessary.

7. Make sure the holes in the valve are not clogged.

8. Install the check valve, spring, washer and circlip.

9. Install the oil pump as decribed in this chapter.

PRIMARY DRIVE GEAR

Removal/Installation

1. Perform Steps 1-7 of *Clutch Removal* in Chapter Five.

2. Remove the bolts (A, **Figure 111**) securing the pulse generator units to the crankcase.

3. Remove the pulse generator units and rubber grommet (B, **Figure 111**) from the right-hand crankcase half.

4. To keep the primary drive gear from turning, insert a copper washer (or penny) into mesh with the primary drive gear and the clutch outer housing gear (**Figure 112**).

5. Remove the bolt (A, **Figure 113**) securing the pulse generator plate and the primary drive gear.

6. Remove the pulse generator plate (B, **Figure 113**) and the primary drive gear (C, **Figure 113**).

7. Inspect the gear teeth and internal splines of the primary drive gear (**Figure 114**). Replace if necessary.

8. While the pulse generator plate is removed, fill in the timing marks with white grease pencil or

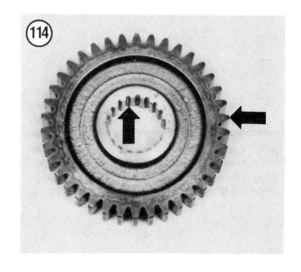

4

The procedure which follows is presented as a complete, step-by-step major lower-end rebuild that should be followed if an engine is to be completely reconditioned. However, if you're replacing a known failed part, the disassembly should be carried out only until the failed part is accessible; there's no need to disassemble the engine beyond that point so long as you know the remaining components are in good condition and that they were not affected by the failed part.

typewriter white correction fluid (**Figure 115**). This will make it easier to see the marks when checking ignition timing.

9. Install by reversing these removal steps, noting the following.

10. Align the flat on the crankshaft splines with the flat section on the primary drive gear and the pulse generator plate and install both parts.

11. Use the same tool set-up used in Step 4 to keep the primary drive gear from turning and tighten the bolt to the torque specifications listed in **Table 2**.

CRANKCASE AND CRANKSHAFT

Disassembly of the crankcase (splitting the case) and removal of the crankshaft assembly requires that the engine be removed from the frame.

The crankcase is made in 2 halves of precision diecast aluminum alloy and is of the "thin-walled" type. To avoid damage, do not hammer or pry on any of the interior or exterior projected walls. These areas are easily damaged. The cases are assembled with a coat of gasket sealer between the 2 halves and dowel pins align the halves when they are bolted together.

Disassembly

1. Prior to removing the clutch, loosen the bolt and washer (A, **Figure 116**) securing the primary drive gear to the end of the crankshaft.

NOTE
Wedge a soft copper washer (or penny) between the primary drive gear and the gear on the clutch outer housing to keep the primary drive gear from rotating during removal and installation of the bolt (B, Figure 116).

2. Remove the clutch as described in Chapter Five.

3. Remove the Allen bolt and washer (**Figure 117**) securing the output gear shaft.

NOTE
If the clutch has already been removed, install the drive shaft universal joint onto the splined end of the output gear shaft. Place a large screwdriver or drift between the 2 sections of the universal joint. Hold onto the screwdriver or large drift to prevent the gears from moving and remove the Allen bolt and washer on the output gear shaft.

4. Remove the engine from the frame as described in this chapter.

5. Remove all exterior engine assemblies as described in this chapter and other related chapters:
   a. Cylinder head (this chapter).
   b. Cylinder (this chapter).
   c. Piston and piston pin (this chapter).
   d. Alternator (this chapter).
   e. External shift mechanism (Chapter Five).
   f. Water pump (Chapter Eight).
   g. Starter gears (this chapter).
   h. Starter motor (Chapter Seven).
   i. Neutral indicator switch (Chapter Seven).

6. Loosen the bolt (**Figure 118**) securing the locking tab holding the rear cylinder cam chain in place. Move the tab up and out of the way.

7. Remove the cam chain from the timing sprocket.

8. Slide the timing sprocket (**Figure 119**) off of the crankshaft.

9. Loosen the bolt (**Figure 120**) securing the locking tab holding the front cylinder cam chain in place. Move the tab up and out of the way.

10. Remove the cam chain from the timing gear on the crankshaft.

11. Loosen the right-hand crankcase 6 mm and 8 mm bolts (**Figure 121**) in a crisscross pattern in 2-3 steps. Remove the bolts.

NOTE
Note the location of the copper washer (W, Figure 121) on the bolt and the ground strap (GS, Figure 121).

12. Loosen the left-hand crankcase 6 mm and 8 mm bolts (**Figure 122**) in a crisscross pattern in 2-3 steps. Remove the bolts.

13. Lay the crankcase assembly on 2 blocks of wood with the right-hand crankcase side up.

14. Using a soft-faced mallet, tap around the perimeter of the crankcase half and on the end of the crankshaft while pulling up on the right-hand crankcase half. Continue to tap until the crankcase halves separate.

15. Remove the right-hand crankcase half.

16. Remove the gearshift drum, shift forks and transmission shaft assemblies as described in Chapter Five.

17. Pull the crankshaft assembly straight up and out of the left-hand crankcase half.

18. Remove the oil pump assembly as described in this chapter.

19. Remove the oil jet (**Figure 123**) from each crankcase half.

20. Remove the oil pressure warning switch (**Figure 124**) from the left-hand crankcase half.

21. Remove the output gear case as described in this chapter.

Crankcase Inspection

1. Clean both crankcase halves inside and out with cleaning solvent. Thoroughly dry with compressed air and wipe off with a clean shop cloth. Be sure to remove all traces of the old gasket material from the mating surfaces.

2. Check the transmission, shift drum and output gear ball bearings for roughness and play by rotating them slowly by hand. Refer to **Figure 125** and **Figure 126**. If any roughness or play can be felt in a bearing, it must be replaced. Refer to *Crankcase Ball Bearing Replacement* in this chapter for the correct procedure.

NOTE
*Inspection of the crankshaft main bearing is covered under **Crankshaft Inspection** in this chapter.*

3. Carefully examine the cases for cracks and fractures. Also check the areas around the stiffening ribs, bearing bosses and threaded holes. If any damage is found, have it repaired by a shop specializing in the repair of precision aluminum castings or replace the crankcase halves as a set.

4. Make sure the crankcase studs are tight. If any are loose, tighten them to the torque specification listed in **Table 2**.

5. Inspect the camshaft drive chain and sprockets (**Figure 127**) for each cylinder. Check the sprockets for chipped or missing teeth; replace if necessary. If either of the sprockets is damaged, chances are the drive chain will also be damaged. If any one of the 3 parts is worn or damaged, replace all 3 parts as a set.

Crankcase Ball Bearing Replacement

The following special Honda tools may be required for bearing removal from the left-hand crankcase half:

    a. Bearing remover (20 mm): Honda part No. 07936-3710600.
    b. Remover handle: Honda part No. 07936-3710100.
    c. Remover weight: Honda part No. 07936-3710200.

1. On the right-hand crankcase half, remove the bolts and screw securing the bearing retainer and remove the bearing retainer.

2. The bearings are installed with a slight interference fit. The crankcase must be heated in an oven to about 100° C (212° F). An easy way to check the proper temperature is to drop tiny drops of water on the case; if they sizzle and evaporate immediately, the temperature is correct. Heat only one case at a time.

CAUTION
Do not heat the cases with a torch (propane or acetylene); never bring a flame into contact with the bearing or case. The direct heat will destroy the case hardening of the bearing and will likely cause warpage of the case.

3. Remove the case from the oven and hold onto the crankcase with a kitchen potholder, heavy gloves or heavy shop cloths—*it is hot*.

4. Hold the case with the bearing side down and tap it squarely on a piece of soft wood. Continue to tap until the bearing(s) fall out. Repeat for the other half.

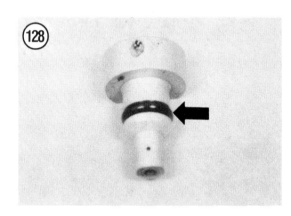

CAUTION
Be sure to tap the crankcase squarely on the piece of wood. Avoid damaging the sealing surfaces of the crankcase.

5A. On the right-hand crankcase half, if the bearings are difficult to remove, they can be gently tapped out with a socket or piece of pipe the same size as the bearing outer race.

5B. On the left-hand crankcase half, if the bearings are difficult to remove, special tools are required as the bearings are not accessible from the other side of the crankcase. Use the special Honda tools described in the introduction to this procedure:

    a. Attach the bearing remover to the bearing.
    b. Attach the remover handle and remover weight to the bearing remover.
    c. Move the weight up and down on the remover handle (similar to a body shop slide hammer) until the bearing is removed from the crankcase.
    d. If necessary, repeat this step for the other bearing.

NOTE
If the bearings or seals are difficult to remove or install, don't take a chance on

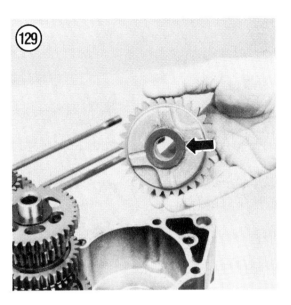

4

expensive damage. Have the work performed by a dealer or competent machine shop.

6. While heating the crankcase halves, place the new bearings in a freezer if possible. Chilling them will slightly reduce their overall diameter while the hot crankcase is slightly larger due to heat expansion. This will make installation easier.

7. Install the new bearing(s) in the heated cases. Press each bearing in by hand until it is completely seated. Do not hammer it in. If a bearing will not seat, remove it and cool it. Reheat the case and install the bearing again.

8. On bearings so equipped, install the bearing retainer and tighten the bolts and screw securely.

Assembly

Assemble all components into the right-hand crankcase half.

1. Install the output gear case as described in this chapter.

2. Apply Loctite Lock N' Seal to the the threads of the oil pressure switch. Install the switch and tighten to the torque specifications listed in **Table 2**.

3. Install a new O-ring seal (**Figure 128**) on each oil jet and install an oil jet into each crankcase half (**Figure 123**).

4. Refer to Chapter Five and reinstall the transmission shaft assemblies and the internal shift mechanism.

5. Apply a coat of cold grease to the thrust washer and place it on the output gear case final drive (**Figure 129**).

6. Place the output gear case final drive and thrust washer into place in the right-hand crankcase.

7. Insert the bushing into the output gear case final drive gear (**Figure 130**). Align the holes in the thrust washer and bushing with the inside diameter of the bearing in the crankcase.

8. Lightly oil the right-hand main bearing and the right-hand end of the crankshaft (primary drive gear splines).

9. Position the crankshaft so the connecting rods are toward the top of the crankcase. Position the front cylinder connecting rod so it fits into the cylinder relief in the crankcase and lower the crankshaft straight into the right-hand crankcase half (**Figure 131**).

10. Hold onto the connecting rods and turn the crankshaft slowly to make sure it spins freely. If not, repeat Step 9.

11. Install the oil pump assembly into the left-hand crankcase as described in this chapter.

12. Install the alignment dowels (**Figure 132**) into one of the crankcase halves.

13. Spray the sealing surface of both crankcase halves with contact cleaner. This will remove any traces of oil from the surfaces to achieve a better seal.

14. Apply a light even coat of liquid gasket sealer to the sealing surface of one crankcase half.

NOTE
Since the external finish of the engine is black, use a black colored sealer such as Permatex RTV Black Silicone Adhesive Sealer (part No. 16B) or equivalent.

15. Set the left-hand crankcase in place over the right-hand crankcase assembly as follows:

   a. Align the thrust washer and bushing on the output gear final drive gear with the output gear shaft.

   b. Slightly rotate the splines of the output gear case to align the raised cams (**Figure 133**) on the output gear shaft with the depressions (**Figure 134**) in the final drive gear.

   c. Push it down squarely into place until it reaches the crankshaft bearing. There is usually about 0.13 mm (1/2 in.) to go.

16. Lightly tap the case halves together with a plastic or rubber mallet until they seat.

CAUTION
Crankcase halves should fit together without force. If the crankcase halves do not fit together completely, do not attempt to pull them together with the crankcase screws. Separate the crankcase halves and investigate the cause of the interference. If the transmission shafts were disassembled, recheck to make sure that a gear is not installed backwards. Do not risk damage by trying to force the cases together.

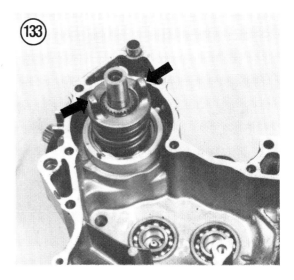

17. Rotate the crankshaft and transmission shafts by hand to make sure they rotate freely.

18. Install and tighten the left-hand crankcase 6 mm and 8 mm bolts (**Figure 122**) in a crisscross pattern in 2-3 steps. Tighten the bolts to the torque specifications listed in **Table 2**.

NOTE
*Note the location of the copper washer (W, **Figure 121**) on the bolt and the ground strap (GS, **Figure 121**).*

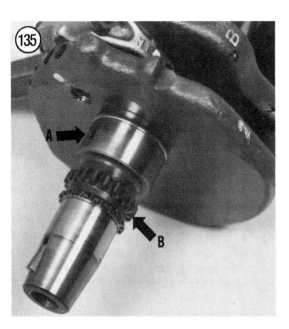

19. Install and tighten the right-hand crankcase 6 mm and 8 mm bolts (**Figure 121**) in a crisscross pattern in 2-3 steps. Tighten the bolts to the torque specifications listed in **Table 2**.

NOTE
The crankshaft has so much end float and it is so heavy that it may not want to rotate with the crankcase assembly on its side. Therefore it is necessary for the crankcase to be upright.

20. After the crankcase halves are completely assembled, turn the crankcase assembly upright. Once again rotate the crankshaft and transmission shafts by hand to make sure they rotate freely and that there is no binding. If any is present,

disassemble the crankcase halves and correct the problem.
21. Install all exterior engine assemblies as described in this chapter and other related chapters:
   a. Cylinder head (this chapter).
   b. Cylinder (this chapter).
   c. Piston and piston pin (this chapter).
   d. Alternator (this chapter).
   e. External shift mechanism (Chapter Five).
   f. Water pump (Chapter Eight).
   g. Starter gears (this chapter).
   h. Starter motor (Chapter Seven).
   i. Neutral indicator switch (Chapter Seven).
22. Install the Allen bolt and washer (**Figure 117**) securing the output gear shaft. Tighten to the torque specification listed in **Table 2**.
23. Install the primary drive gear as described in this chapter.
24. Install the clutch as described in Chapter Five.
25. Install the engine as described in this chapter.
26. Fill the engine with the recommended viscosity and quantity of engine oil. Refer to Chapter Three.

Crankshaft Inspection

1. Remove the connecting rods from the crankshaft as described in this chapter.
2. Clean crankshaft thoroughly with solvent. Clean oil holes with rifle cleaning brushes; flush thoroughly with new solvent and dry with compressed air. Lightly oil all bearing journal surfaces immediately to prevent rust.
3. Carefully inspect each journal (A, **Figure 135** and A, **Figure 136**) for scratches, ridges, scoring, nicks, etc. Very small nicks and scratches may be removed with fine emery cloth. More serious damage must be removed by grinding—a job for a machine shop or dealer.
4. If the surface on all journals is satisfactory, take the crankshaft to a dealer or machine shop to be checked for out-of-roundness, taper and wear on the bearing journals. Also check crankshaft runout. The service limit is listed in **Table 1**.
5. Inspect the sprocket teeth (front cylinder) for the cam chain (B, **Figure 135**). If damaged, the crankshaft must be replaced.
6. Inspect the splines (B, **Figure 136**) for the timing sprocket. If damaged, the crankshaft must be replaced.

Crankshaft Main Bearing Selection

1. Check the inside surface of the bearing inserts for wear, bluish tint (burned), flaking, abrasion and scoring. If the bearings are good, they may be reused. If the insert is questionable, replace it.

2. Clean the bearing surfaces of the crankshaft and the main bearing inserts. Measure the main bearing clearance by performing the following steps:

   a. Measure the inside diameter of the bearing insert with an inside micrometer (**Figure 137**).

   b. Measure the outside diameter of the crankshaft main bearing journal with a micrometer (**Figure 138**).

   c. Subtract the main bearing journal OD from the bearing insert ID. This will give you the clearance between the 2 parts. The service limit dimension is listed in **Table 1**.

3. If the bearing clearance is greater than specified, use the following steps for new bearing selection:

   a. The crankshaft main journals are marked with numbers "1" or "2" (**Figure 139**).

NOTE
The number on the left-hand end (end with the cam chain sprocket) relates to the bearing insert in the left-hand side and the number on the right-hand end (primary drive gear splines) relates to the bearing insert in the right-hand crankcase. Refer to **Figure 139**. *Remember the left-hand side relates to the engine as it sits in the bike's frame, not as it sits on your workbench.*

   b. If the main journal dimension is within the tolerances stated in **Table 3** the bearing can be simply selected by color-code. Select new main bearings by cross-referencing the main journal number (**Figure 139**) in the vertical column of **Table 3** to bearing insert ID (**Figure 137**) in the horizontal column. Where the 2 columns intersect, the new bearing color is indicated. **Table 4** gives the bearing insert color and thickness.

   c. If any main bearing journal measurements taken during inspection do not fall within the tolerance range listed in **Table 3**, the serviceability of the crankshaft must be carefully examined. If the main bearing journal in question is not tapered, out-of-round or scored the crankshaft may be still used, however, the bearing selection will have to be made based on the measured diameter of the bearing journal and not by the number code. Honda recommends the crankshaft be replaced whenever a main bearing journal dimension is beyond the specified range of the letter code.

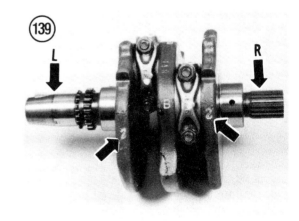

4. If the bearings require replacement, refer to *Crankshaft Main Bearing Replacement* in this chapter.

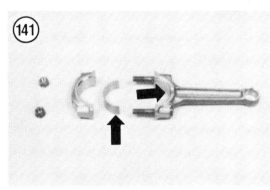

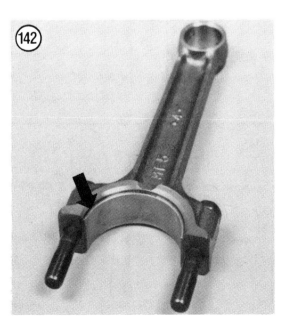

5. After new bearings have been installed, recheck clearance by repeating this procedure.

Crankshaft Main Bearing
Replacement

The crankshaft bearings must be removed and installed with a hydraulic press and special tools. This job is best left to an authorized dealer or machine shop.

> *CAUTION*
> *Do not try to drive out or drive in these bearings. The main bearings must be installed and aligned true to the centerline of the crankshaft.*

CONNECTING RODS

Removal/Installation

1. Remove the engine as described in this chapter.
2. Split the crankcases and remove the crankshaft assembly as described under *Crankcase Disassembly* in this chapter.

> *NOTE*
> *Prior to disassembly, mark the rods and caps. Mark them with an "L" for left-hand end (end with the cam chain sprocket) or "R" for the right-hand end (primary drive gear splines). Remember the left-hand side relates to the engine as it sits in the bike's frame, not as it sits on your workbench.*

3. Measure the connecting rod side clearance as described under *Connecting Rod Inspection* in this chapter.
4. Remove the nuts securing the connecting rod caps and remove the caps (**Figure 140**).
5. Carefully remove the connecting rods from the crankshaft.
6. Remove and mark the back of each bearing insert (**Figure 141**) with the cylinder "R" (right) or "L" (left) location and "U" (upper) or "L" (lower).
7. Install by reversing these removal steps, noting the following.
8. Install the bearing inserts into each connecting rod and cap. Make sure they are locked into place correctly (**Figure 142**).

> *NOTE*
> *If the old bearing inserts are reused, be sure they are installed into their original positions; refer to Step 6.*

9. Apply molybdenum disulfide grease to the bearing inserts, crankpins and connecting rod bolt threads. Install the connecting rods and rod caps. Tighten the cap nuts evenly in 2-3 steps to the torque specifications listed in **Table 2**.

10. After all rod caps have been installed, rotate the crankshaft several times and check that the bearings are not too tight. Make sure there is no binding.

Connecting Rod Inspection

1. Prior to removing the connecting rods from the crankshaft, measure the side clearance as follows:
   a. Insert a flat feeler gauge between the side of the connecting rod and the crankshaft as shown in **Figure 143**.
   b. Refer to the service limit dimension listed in **Table 1**.
   c. Replace the connecting rod(s) if it is worn to the service limit dimension or less.
2. Remove the connecting rods from the crankshaft as described in this chapter.
3. Clean the connecting rods and inserts in solvent and dry with compressed air.
4. Carefully inspect each rod journal on the crankshaft for scratches, ridges, scoring, nicks, etc. Very small nicks and scratches may be removed with fine emery cloth. More serious damage must be removed by grinding—a job for a machine shop or dealer.
5. If the surface on all journals is satisfactory, take the crankshaft to a dealer or machine shop to be checked for out-of-roundness, taper and wear on the rod bearing journals.

Connecting Rod Bearing Selection

1. Check the inside and outside surfaces of the bearing inserts for wear, bluish tint (burned), flaking, abrasion and scoring. If the bearings are good, they may be reused. If any insert is questionable, replace the entire set.
2. Measure the inside diameter of the small end of the connecting rod with an inside dial gauge (**Figure 144**). Check against the dimension listed in **Table 1**; replace the rod if necessary.
3. Clean the rod bearing surfaces of the crankshaft and the rod bearing inserts. Measure the rod bearing clearance by performing the following steps:
   a. Place a strip of Plastigage over each rod bearing journal parallel to the crankshaft (**Figure 145**). Do not place the Plastigage over an oil hole in the crankshaft.

> *NOTE*
> *Do not rotate connecting rod on the crankshaft while the Plastigage strips are in place.*

   b. Install the rod cap onto one rod and tighten the nuts to the torque specification listed in **Table 2**.

c. Remove the rod cap and measure the width of the flattened Plastigage material (**Figure 146**) following the manufacturer's instructions. Measure both ends of the Plastigage strip. A difference of 0.025 mm (0.001 in.) or more indicates a tapered journal. Confirm with a micrometer.
d. New bearing clearance and the service limit are listed in **Table 1**. Remove all of the Plastigage material from the crankshaft journals and the connecting rods.

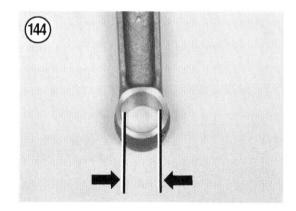

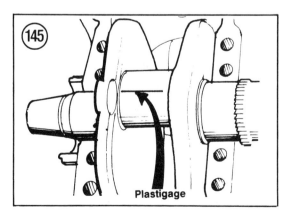

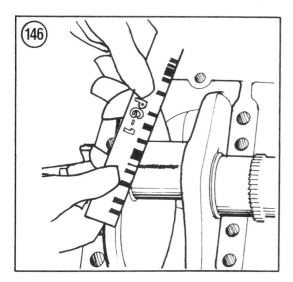

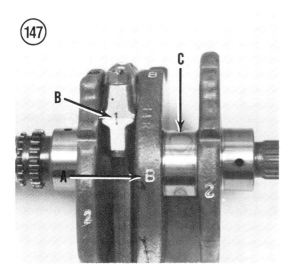

4. If the rod bearing clearance is greater than specified, use the following steps for new bearing selection:

    a. The crankshaft connecting rod journals are marked with letters "A" or "B" (A, **Figure 147**).

NOTE
The letter on the counterbalance weight refers to the rod journal to the left of the weight. The left-hand end is the end with the cam chain sprocket and the right-hand end is the end with the primary drive gear splines. Remember the left-hand side relates to the engine as it sits in the bike's frame, not as it sits on your workbench.

    b. The connecting rod and cap are marked with numbers "1" or "2" (B, **Figure 147**).

    c. Measure the rod journal (C, **Figure 147**) with a micrometer. If the rod journal dimension is within the tolerances stated for each letter code in **Table 5** the bearing can be simply selected by color-code.

    d. Select new bearings by cross-referencing the rod journal letters (A, **Figure 147**) in the horizontal column of **Table 5** to the rod bearing number (B, **Figure 147**) in the vertical column. Where the 2 columns intersect, the new bearing color is indicated. **Table 6** gives the bearing insert color and thickness.

5. If any rod bearing journal measurements taken during inspection do not fall within the tolerance range for the letter codes, the serviceability of the crankshaft must be carefully examined. If the rod bearing journal in question is not tapered, out-of-round or scored the crankshaft may be still used, however, the bearing selection will have to be made based on the measured diameter of the bearing journal and not by the letter code. Honda recommends the crankshaft be replaced whenever a rod bearing journal dimension is beyond the specified range of the stamped letter code.

6. After new bearings have been installed, recheck clearance by repeating this procedure.

7. Repeat Steps 1-6 for the other cylinder.

OUTPUT GEAR CASE

Removal/Installation

1. Disassemble the crankcase as described in this chapter.

2. Remove the bolts (**Figure 148**) securing the output gear case to the left-hand crankcase half.

3. Remove the output gear case. Don't lose the locating dowel.

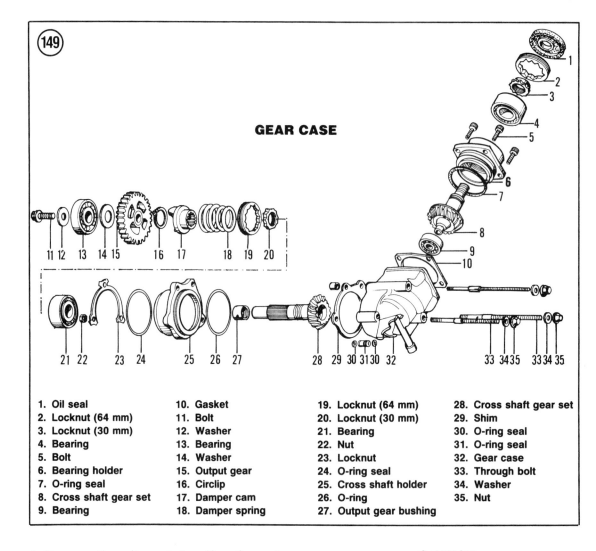

(149) GEAR CASE

1. Oil seal	10. Gasket	19. Locknut (64 mm)	28. Cross shaft gear set
2. Locknut (64 mm)	11. Bolt	20. Locknut (30 mm)	29. Shim
3. Locknut (30 mm)	12. Washer	21. Bearing	30. O-ring seal
4. Bearing	13. Bearing	22. Nut	31. O-ring seal
5. Bolt	14. Washer	23. Locknut	32. Gear case
6. Bearing holder	15. Output gear	24. O-ring seal	33. Through bolt
7. O-ring seal	16. Circlip	25. Cross shaft holder	34. Washer
8. Cross shaft gear set	17. Damper cam	26. O-ring	35. Nut
9. Bearing	18. Damper spring	27. Output gear bushing	

4. Remove the oil control orifice from the receptacle in the crankcase.

5. Clean the orifice in solvent and dry with compressed air. Make sure the orifice is clean to ensure maximum oil flow to the output gear assembly.

6. Install by reversing these removal steps, noting the following.

7. Install new O-ring seals on the oil control orifice. Install the oil control orifice in the crankcase.

Disassembly/Inspection/Assembly

Output gear case disassembly and assembly requires a considerable number of special Honda tools. The price of all of these tools could be more than the cost of most repairs done by a dealer.

Figure 149 shows the internal components of the output gear case.

CAUTION
Do not try to disassemble the gear case with makeshift tools. Approximately 13 special tools and a hydraulic press are required to disassemble and assemble the unit. If assembled incorrectly, the gear tooth contact pattern and set-up tolerance will be incorrect and the unit will be damaged.

ALTERNATOR ROTOR, STARTER CLUTCH ASSEMBLY AND GEARS

The alternator rotor, starter clutch assembly and gears can be removed with the engine in the frame. The starter motor can be left in place, if desired.

Refer to **Figure 150** for this procedure.

Removal/Installation

1. Place the bike on the centerstand.

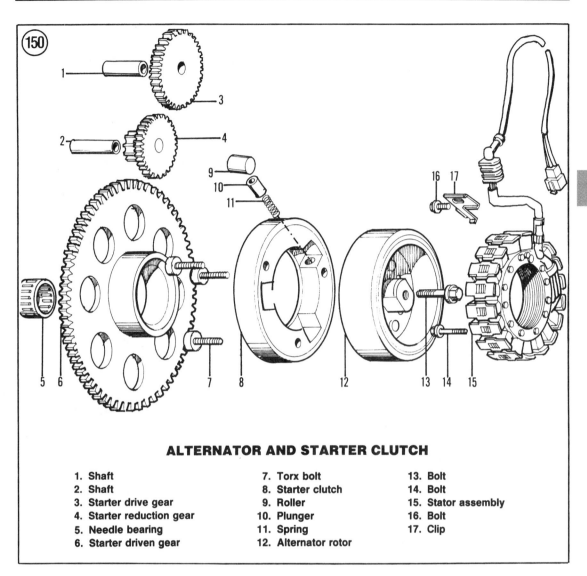

ALTERNATOR AND STARTER CLUTCH

1. Shaft	7. Torx bolt	13. Bolt
2. Shaft	8. Starter clutch	14. Bolt
3. Starter drive gear	9. Roller	15. Stator assembly
4. Starter reduction gear	10. Plunger	16. Bolt
5. Needle bearing	11. Spring	17. Clip
6. Starter driven gear	12. Alternator rotor	

2. Remove both side covers and the seat.

3. Disconnect the battery negative lead.

4. Disconnect the electrical connector (**Figure 151**) going to the alternator stator assembly.

5. Remove the screws (**Figure 152**) securing the left-hand rear crankcase cover and remove the cover.

6. Remove the bolt (A, **Figure 153**) securing the gearshift pedal to the gearshift spindle assembly.

7. Remove the bolts (B, **Figure 153**) securing the front left-hand footpeg and remove the footpeg/gearshift pedal assembly.

8. Remove the bolts securing the alternator cover (**Figure 154**) and remove the cover, gasket and the electrical harness from the frame. Note the path of the wire harness as it must be routed the same during installation.

9. Withdraw the starter drive gear and shaft (**Figure 155**).

10. Withdraw the starter reduction gear and shaft (**Figure 156**).

> *NOTE*
> *This shaft is longer than the shaft for the starter drive gear.*

> *CAUTION*
> *The bolt securing the alternator rotor has **left-hand threads**. The bolt must be turned **clockwise** for removal.*

11. Remove the bolt (**Figure 157**) securing the alternator rotor.

12. Turning a socket *clockwise*, remove the bolt securing the alternator rotor (A, **Figure 158**).

13. To keep the rotor from turning while removing the bolt, use one of the following:

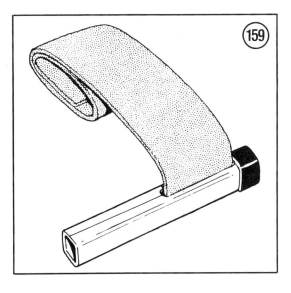

a. Use a strap wrench (**Figure 159**) on the outer perimeter of the rotor.

b. Use a large crescent wrench (B, **Figure 158**) on the flats on the inner boss of the rotor.

c. Shift the transmission into gear and hold the rear brake on.

14. Screw in the rotor puller (**Figure 160**) until it stops. Use the Honda rotor puller (part No. 07933-3290001), K & N rotor puller (part No. 81-0170) or equivalent.

> *CAUTION*
> *Don't try to remove the rotor without a puller; any attempt to do so will ultimately lead to some form of damage to the engine and/or rotor. Many aftermarket pullers are available from motorcycle dealers or mail order houses. The cost of one of these pullers is low and it makes an excellent addition to any mechanic's tool box. If you can't buy or borrow one, have the dealer remove the rotor.*

15. Turn the rotor puller with a wrench until the rotor is free.

> *NOTE*
> *If the rotor is difficult to remove, strike the puller with a hammer a few times. This will usually break it loose.*

> *CAUTION*
> *If normal rotor removal attempts fail, do not force the puller as the threads may be stripped out of the rotor causing expensive damage. Take the bike to a dealer and have the rotor removed.*

16. Remove the rotor and the starter driven gear from the crankshaft. The needle bearing may stay either on the crankshaft or in the starter driven gear.

Inspection

1. Place the alternator rotor and starter clutch assembly with the gear side facing up. Rotate the starter driven gear *clockwise* and pull up at the same time. Remove the starter driven gear from the starter clutch assembly.

2. Carefully inspect the inside of the rotor (**Figure 161**) for small bolts, washers or other metal "trash" that may have been picked up by the magnets. These small metal bits can cause severe damage to the alternator stator assembly.

3. Inspect the teeth on the starter driven gear (**Figure 162**). Check for chipped or missing teeth. Replace if necessary.

4. Inspect the teeth on the starter drive and reduction gears (**Figure 163**). Check for chipped or missing teeth. Look for uneven or excessive wear on the gear faces. Replace as a set if necessary.

5. Check the needle bearing (**Figure 164**) for wear or damage. It must rotate freely. Replace if necessary.

6. Check the rollers (A, **Figure 165**) in the starter clutch for uneven or excessive wear; replace as a set if any are bad.

7. To replace the rollers, perform the following:

    a. Remove the Torx bolts (B, **Figure 165**) securing the starter clutch to the back of the alternator.

    b. Remove the starter clutch assembly.

    c. Remove the roller, plunger and coil springs from each recess.

    d. Measure the inside diameter of the starter clutch (C, **Figure 165**) and compare to the dimension listed in **Table 1**. Replace if necessary.

    e. Install the spring, plunger and roller into each receptacle in the starter clutch.

    f. Apply Loctite Lock N' Seal to the threads of the Torx bolts prior to installing them and tighten to the torque specifications listed in **Table 2**.

8. Measure the OD of the starter driven gear contact surface where it rides against the rollers (**Figure 166**). Compare to dimensions listed in **Table 1**.

Installation

1. Install the roller bearing and starter driven gear onto the crankshaft (**Figure 154**).

2. Make sure the Woodruff key is in place on the crankshaft.

3. Align the Woodruff key with the slot in the rotor and push the alternator rotor/starter clutch assembly partially into place.

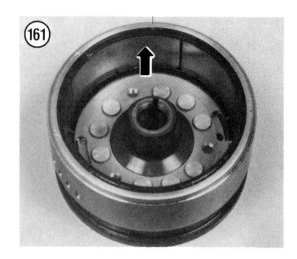

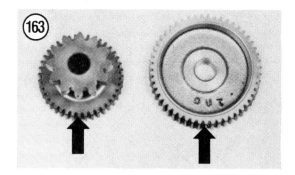

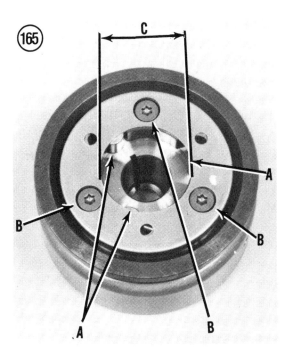

4. With your fingers, rotate the starter driven gear *clockwise* and push the rotor assembly all the way on until it seats.

> *CAUTION*
> *Remember, the bolt securing the alternator rotor has **left-hand threads**. The bolt must be turned **counterclockwise** for installation.*

5. Install the alternator rotor bolt.
6. Use the same tool set-up used for removal and tighten the bolt *counterclockwise* to the torque specification listed in **Table 2**.
7. Install the starter reduction gear and the long shaft.
8. Position the starter drive gear with the "OUT" mark facing toward the outside (**Figure 167**) and install the gear and shaft.
9. Install a new gasket and 2 locating dowels.
10. Install the alternator cover and tighten the bolts securely.
11. Route the alternator stator wire harness through the frame and connect the electrical connector.
12. Install the left-hand rear crankcase cover.
13. Install the gearshift pedal and tighten the bolts securely.
14. Install the left-hand front footpeg and tighten the bolts securely.
15. Connect the battery negative lead and install the seat and both side covers.

BREAK-IN PROCEDURE

If the rings were replaced, new pistons installed, the cylinders rebored or honed or major lower end work performed, the engine should be broken in just as though it were new. The performance and service life of the engine depends greatly on a careful and sensible break-in.

For the first 805 km (100 miles), no more than one-third throttle should be used and speed should be varied as much as possible within the one-third throttle limit. Prolonged steady running at one speed, no matter how moderate, is to be avoided as well as hard acceleration.

Following the *800 km (500 Mile) Service* described in this chapter more throttle should not be used until the motorcycle has covered at least 1,600 km (1,000 miles) and then it should be limited to short bursts of speed until 2,500 km (1,500 miles) have been logged.

The mono-grade oils recommended for break-in and normal use provide a better bedding pattern for rings and cylinders than do multi-grade oils. As a result, piston ring and cylinder bore life are greatly increased. During this period, oil consumption will be higher than normal. It is therefore important to frequently check and correct oil level. At no time during the break-in or later should the oil level be below the bottom line on the dipstick; if the oil level is low, the oil will become overheated resulting in insufficient lubrication and increased wear.

800 km (500 Mile) Service

It is essential that the oil and filter be changed after the first 800 km (500 mile). In addition, it is a good idea to change the oil and filter at the completion of the break-in (about 2,500 km/1,500 miles) to ensure that all of the particles produced during break-in are removed from the lubrication system. The small added expense may be considered a smart investment that will pay off in increased engine life.

Table 1 ENGINE SPECIFICATIONS

Item	Specification	Wear limit
General		
Engine type	Water-cooled, 4-stroke, SOHC, V-twin	
Bore and stroke	71.0 × 62.0 mm (2.80 × 2.44 in.)	
Displacement	490 cc (29.9 cid)	
Compression ratio	10.5 to 1	
Valve train	Hi-Vo multi-link drive chain, OHC and adjustable rocker arms	
Maximum horsepower		
VT500C	49.9 BHP @ 9,000 rpm	
VT500FT	48 BHP @ 9,000 rpm	
VT500E	50 BHP @ 9,000 rpm	
Maximum torque		
VT500C	4.3 kg/m (30.58 ft.-lb.) @ 7,000 rpm	
VT500FT	4.5 kg/m (32 ft.-lb.) @ 7,000 rpm	
VT500E	4.6 kg/m (33.27 ft.-lb.) @ 7,000 rpm	
Lubrication	Wet sump	
Air filtration		
1983-1984	Foam element type	
1985-1986	Paper element type	
Engine weight (dry)	64 kg (141 lb.)	
Cylinders		
Bore	71.000-71.015 mm (2.795-2.796 in.)	71.17 mm (2.802 in.)
Out-of-round	—	0.05 mm (0.002 in.)
Taper	—	0.05 mm (0.002 in.)
Piston/cylinder clearance	0.01-0.045 mm (0.0004-0.0018 in.)	0.32 mm (0.0126 in.)
Pistons		
Diameter	70.96-70.99 mm (2.7937-2.7949 in.)	70.84 mm (2.789 in.)
Clearance in bore	0.01-0.045 mm (0.0004-0.0018 in.)	0.32 mm (0.0126 in.)
Piston pin bore	18.002-18.008 mm (0.7087-0.7090 in.)	18.05 mm (0.71 in.)
Piston pin outer diameter	17.994-18.000 mm (0.7084-0.7087 in.)	17.80 mm (0.70 in.)

(continued)

Table 1 ENGINE SPECIFICATIONS (continued)

Item	Specification	Wear limit
Piston rings		
Number per piston		
Compression	2	
Oil control	1	
Ring end gap		
Top and second	0.20-0.30 mm (0.008-0.012 in.)	0.50 mm (0.002 in.)
Oil (side rail)	0.30-0.90 mm (0.012-0.035 in.)	1.10 mm (0.04 in.)
Ring side clearance		
Top and second	0.015-0.045 mm (0.006-0.0018 in.)	0.10 mm (0.004 in.)
Oil (side rail)	0.030-0.035 mm (0.0012-0.0014 in.)	0.1 mm (0.004 in.)
Connecting rod		
Small end inner diameter	18.016-18.034 mm (0.7093-0.7100 in.)	18.09 mm (0.712 in.)
Crankshaft		
Runout	—	0.05 mm (0.002 in.)
Main bearing oil clearance	0.025-0.041 mm (0.0010-0.0016 in.)	0.06 mm (0.002 in.)
Connecting rod oil clearance	0.028-0.052 mm (0.0011-0.0020 in.)	0.07 mm (0.003 in.)
Connecting rod big end side clearance	0.10-0.25 mm (0.004-0.010 in.)	0.4 mm (0.016 in.)
Camshaft		
Cam lobe height		
Intake	38.222 mm (1.5048 in.)	38.00 mm (1.496 in.)
Exhaust	38.126 mm (1.5010 in.)	37.90 mm (1.492 in.)
Runout	0.03 mm (0.001 in.)	0.05 mm (0.002 in.)
Oil clearance	0.141-0.220 mm (0.0055-0.0087 in.)	0.23 mm (0.009 in.)
Rocker arm bore	12.00-12.018 mm (0.4724-0.4731 in.)	12.05 mm (0.474 in.)
Rocker arm shaft	11.966-11.984 mm (0.4711-0.4718 in.)	11.83 mm (0.466 in.)
Valves		
Valve stem outer diameter		
Intake	5.475-5.490 mm (0.2156-0.2161 in.)	5.45 mm (0.215 in.)
Exhaust	6.565-6.570 mm (0.2585-0.2587 in.)	6.55 mm (0.258 in.)
Valve guide inner diameter		
VT500C and FT		
Intake and exhaust	5.500-5.515 mm (0.2165-0.2171 in.)	5.55 mm (0.219 in.)
VT500E		
Intake	5.500-5.520 mm (0.2165-0.2173 in.)	5.56 mm (0.219 in.)
Exhaust	6.600-6.620 mm (0.2598-0.2606 in.)	6.65 mm (0.262 in.)
Stem to guide clearance		
Intake	0.010-0.045 mm (0.0004-0.0018 in.)	0.10 mm (0.004 in.)
Exhaust	0.035-0.050 mm (0.0014-0.0020 in.)	0.11 mm (0.004 in.)
Valve seat width		
Intake and exhaust	0.9-1.1 mm (0.0354-0.0433 in.)	1.5 mm (0.059 in.)
Valve springs free length		
Intake		
Outer	46.0 mm (1.81 in.)	44.3 mm (1.74 in.)
Inner	37.18 mm (1.46 in.)	35.58 mm (1.401 in.)
Exhaust		
Outer	46.0 mm (1.81 in.)	44.3 mm (1.74 in.)
Inner	44.82 mm (1.76 in.)	43.32 mm (1.666 in.)
Cylinder head warpage		
VT500C and FT	—	0.25 mm (0.010 in.)
VT500E	—	0.10 mm (0.004 in.)
Oil pump		
Inner rotor tip to outer clearance	0.15 mm (0.006 in.)	0.20 mm (0.010 in.)
Outer rotor to body clearance	0.15-0.22 mm (0.006-0.009 in.)	0.35 mm (0.014 in.)
End clearance to body	0.02-0.07 mm (0.001-0.003 in.)	0.10 mm (0.004 in.)
Oil pump pressure (at switch)	5.4 ± 0.7 kg/cm^2 (62.6 ± 9.9 psi)	
Oil pump delivery	24 liters/min. @ 6,000 rpm (25.4 U.S. qt./min. @ 6,000 rpm)	

4

Table 2 ENGINE TORQUE SPECIFICATIONS

Item	N•m	ft.-lb.
Engine mounting bolts		
8 mm	20-30	14-22
10 mm	45-60	33-43
Sub-frame bolts		
Upper	30-45	22-25
Lower		
1985-1986 VT500C	20-30	14-22
All others	20-24	14-17
Cylinder head cover	8-12	6-9
Cam holder bolts and nuts	8-12	6-9
Cam sprocket bolts	20-25	14-18
Cylinder head bolts and nuts		
8 mm bolt	20-25	14-18
8 mm nut	20-25	14-18
10 mm nut	35-45	25-33
Crankcase bolts		
6 mm	8-12	6-9
8 mm	20-25	14-18
Connecting rod cap nuts	30-34	22-25
Output drive shaft bolt	35-45	25-33
Oil pipe bolts		
7 mm	8-12	6-9
10 mm	20-25	14-18
Alternator rotor bolt		
VT500C		
1983-1985	80-100	58-72
1986	100-120	72-87
VT500E	80-100	58-72
VT500FT	100-120	72-87
Oil pressure switch*	10-14	7-10
Starter clutch Torx bolts**	18-25	13-18

*Apply liquid sealant to the threads prior to installation.
**Apply Loctite 242 to the threads prior to installation.

Table 3 MAIN JOURNAL BEARING SELECTION

Main journal OD size code letter and dimension		
Crankcase inside dimension	Number 1 39.992-40.000 mm (1.5745-1.5748 in.)	Number 2 39-984-39-992 mm (1.5742-1.5745 in.)
44.010-44.020 mm (1.7326-1.7331 in.)	Brown (C)	Black (B)
44.000-44.010 mm (1.7322-1.7326 in.)	Black (B)	Blue (A)

Table 4 MAIN JOURNAL BEARING INSERT THICKNESS

Color	mm	in.
Brown (C)	1.989-1.999	0.0783-0.0787
Black (B)	1.994-2.004	0.0785-0.0789
Blue (A)	1.999-2.009	0.0787-0.0791

Table 5 CONNECTING ROD BEARING SELECTION

Crankpin journal OD side code letter and dimension		
Connecting rod ID code number and dimension	Letter A 39.982-39.990 mm (1.5740-1.5744 in.)	Letter B 39.974-39.982 mm (1.5737-1.5741 in.)
Number 1 43.000-43.008 mm (1.5354-1.5357 in.)	Brown	Black
Number 2 43.008-43.016 mm (1.6932-1.6935 in.)	Black	Blue

Table 6 CONNECTING ROD BEARING INSERT THICKNESS

Color	mm	in.
Blue	1.495-1.499	0.0589-0.0590
Black	1.491-1.495	0.0578-0.0589
Brown	1.487-1.491	0.0585-0.0587

CLUTCH AND TRANSMISSION

Refer to **Table 1** for all clutch specifications. **Tables 1-4** are at the end of this chapter.

CLUTCH OPERATION

The clutch is a wet multi-plate type which operates immersed in an oil supply shared with the transmission. It is mounted on the right-hand end of the transmission main shaft. The inner clutch hub is splined to the main shaft and the outer clutch housing can rotate freely on the main shaft. The outer clutch housing is geared to the crankshaft via the primary drive gear.

The clutch release mechanism is mounted within the right-hand crankcase and is operated by the clutch cable and hand lever mounted on the handlebar.

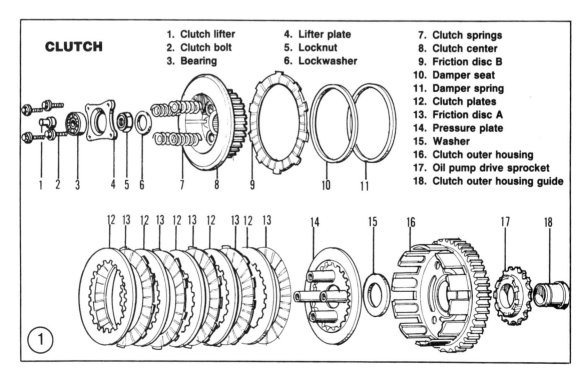

CLUTCH

1. Clutch lifter
2. Clutch bolt
3. Bearing
4. Lifter plate
5. Locknut
6. Lockwasher
7. Clutch springs
8. Clutch center
9. Friction disc B
10. Damper seat
11. Damper spring
12. Clutch plates
13. Friction disc A
14. Pressure plate
15. Washer
16. Clutch outer housing
17. Oil pump drive sprocket
18. Clutch outer housing guide

CLUTCH

Removal/Disassembly

Refer to **Figure 1** for this procedure.

The clutch assembly can be removed with the engine in the frame.

1. Drain the engine oil as described in Chapter Three.

2. Remove the exhaust system as described in Chapter Six.

3. Remove the rear brake pedal assembly as described in Chapter Eleven.

4. Place wood block(s) under the engine to support the bike securely.

5. Remove the bolts and nuts (**Figure 2**) securing the sub-frame and remove the sub-frame.

6. Disconnect the clutch cable from the clutch actuating lever (A, **Figure 3**).

7. Remove the bolts (B, **Figure 3**) securing the clutch cover. Remove the cover, gasket and locating dowels.

8. Using a crisscross pattern, remove the clutch bolts (**Figure 4**) securing the clutch lifter plate and remove the springs, lifter plate and bearing.

9. Place a copper washer (or penny) between the gears on the clutch outer housing and the primary drive gear (**Figure 5**). This will keep the clutch outer housing from turning during the following steps.

10. Remove the locknut and lockwasher.

11. Remove the clutch center, damper seat, damper spring, friction discs, clutch plates and pressure plate as an assembly.

12. Remove the washer and clutch outer housing.

13. Remove the bolt and washer (**Figure 6**) securing the oil pump driven gear.

14. As an assembly, slide off the oil pump driven gear (A, **Figure 7**), the chain (B, **Figure 7**) and the oil pump drive gear (C, **Figure 7**).

15. Slide off the clutch outer housing guide.

Inspection

1. Clean all parts in a petroleum based solvent such as kerosene and thoroughly dry with compressed air.

2. Measure the free length of each clutch spring as shown in **Figure 8**. If any of the springs are worn to the service limit shown in **Table 1**, they should be replaced. Replace all springs as a set.

> *NOTE*
> *In the following step, there are 2 different friction disc thicknesses, identified as A and B. Friction disc B is located next to the clutch center and is thicker than the remaining A friction discs.*

3. Measure the thickness of each friction disc at several places around the disc as shown in **Figure 9**. Replace any disc that is worn to the service limit listed in **Table 1**. For optimum performance, replace all discs as a set even if only a few need replacement.

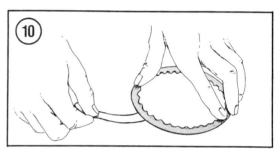

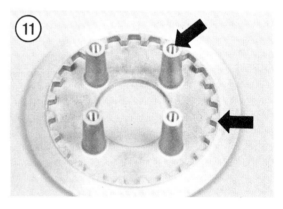

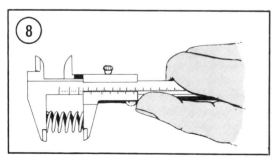

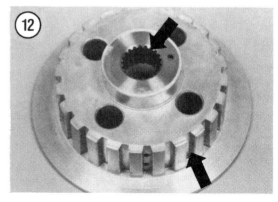

13

14

15

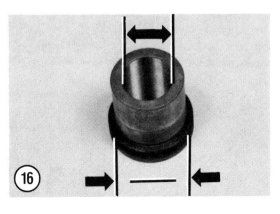

16

4. Check the clutch plates for warpage on a surface plate such as a piece of plate glass (**Figure 10**). Replace any that are warped to the service limit listed in **Table 1**. For optimum performance, replace all plates as a set even if only a few need replacement.

5. Inspect the grooves and studs in the pressure plate (**Figure 11**). If either show signs of wear or galling the pressure plate should be replaced.

6. Inspect the inner splines and outer grooves in the clutch center (**Figure 12**); if damaged, the clutch center should be replaced.

7. Inspect the teeth on the clutch outer housing (**Figure 13**). Remove any small nicks on the gear teeth with an oilstone. If damage is severe the clutch outer housing should be replaced.

8. Inspect the grooves in the clutch outer housing (**Figure 14**) for cracks, nicks or galling where it comes in contact with the friction disc tabs. If any severe damage is evident, the clutch housing must be replaced.

9. Measure the inside diameter of the clutch outer housing where the clutch outer housing guide rides (**Figure 15**). Replace if worn to the service limit listed in **Table 1**.

10. Measure the inside and outside diameter of the clutch outer housing guide (**Figure 16**). Replace if worn to the service limit listed in **Table 1**.

11. Check the bearing (**Figure 17**) in the lifter plate. It must rotate freely with no roughness or binding; replace if necessary.

12. Check the movement of the clutch lifter mechanism in the right-hand crankcase. If the arm binds or the return spring is weak or broken, it must be replaced. To remove the mechanism, perform the following:

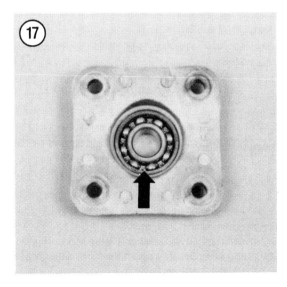

17

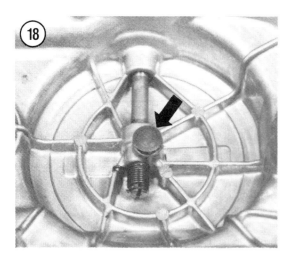

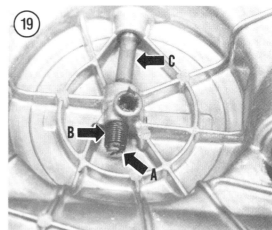

a. Remove the clutch lifter rod (**Figure 18**).
b. Remove the circlip (A, **Figure 19**) and return spring (B, **Figure 19**).
c. Withdraw the clutch actuating arm assembly (C, **Figure 19**) and O-ring from the right-hand crankcase cover.
d. Inspect the O-ring seal on the clutch actuating arm assembly; replace if necessary.
e. Check that the return spring is not bent or broken; replace if necessary.
f. Apply multipurpose grease to the clutch actuating arm and new O-ring seal.
g. Install the actuating arm into the crankcase cover.
h. Install the return spring and circlip.
i. Install the clutch lifter rod.
j. Move the clutch actuating arm back and forth to make sure is is operating smoothly with no binding.

Assembly/Installation

NOTE
If either or both friction discs and clutch plates have been replaced with new ones, apply new engine oil to all surfaces to avoid having the clutch lock up when used for the first time.

1. Install the clutch outer housing guide (**Figure 20**) onto the transmission main shaft.
2. Position the oil pump driven gear with the "IN" mark facing in toward the crankcase.
3. As an assembly, slide on the oil pump driven gear (A, **Figure 7**), the chain (B, **Figure 7**) and the oil pump drive gear (C, **Figure 7**).
4. Install the bolt and washer (**Figure 6**) securing the oil pump driven gear. Tighten the bolt to the torque specification listed in **Table 3**.

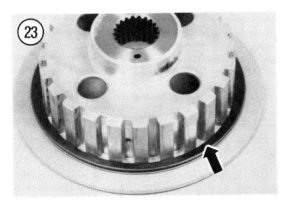

5. Install the clutch outer housing and washer.

CAUTION
The clutch outer housing and oil pump drive sprocket must be indexed correctly or the oil pump will not be driven; severe engine damage will result.

6. Align the bosses on the oil pump drive sprocket (A, **Figure 21**) with the depressions on the backside of the clutch outer housing (B, **Figure 21**). Gently move the oil pump drive chain and drive sprocket while pushing the clutch outer housing into place.

7. Push the clutch outer housing all the way in until it is completely seated and properly engaged with the oil pump drive sprocket. Once it is installed, rotate the clutch outer housing. The oil pump drive sprocket and drive chain must also move. If the oil pump drive chain does not move, repeat Step 6 until proper engagement is obtained between the clutch outer housing and oil pump drive sprocket.

8. Install the washer.

9. Onto the clutch center, perform the following:
   a. Install the damper seat (**Figure 22**) and the damper spring (**Figure 23**). Be sure to install the damper spring with the dished side facing up.
   b. Install the clutch disc B (thickest clutch disc) (**Figure 24**).
   c. Install a clutch plate (**Figure 25**), a friction disc (**Figure 26**) and then a clutch plate. Continue to install the friction discs and clutch plates, alternating them until all are installed. The last item installed is a friction disc (**Figure 27**).

d. Install the clutch pressure plate (A, **Figure 28**).

> *NOTE*
> *In the following step, do not tighten the bolts as some play is needed for final alignment of the friction tabs into the clutch outer housing.*

10. Install a couple of clutch springs, washers and clutch bolts (B, **Figure 28**) to hold this assembly together. Align the tabs (**Figure 29**) on the friction discs as this will make installation easier.

11. Slide this assembly onto the main shaft and into the clutch outer housing (**Figure 30**).

12. Install the lockwasher with the "OUTSIDE" facing toward the outside (**Figure 31**).

> *CAUTION*
> *Prior to installing the locknut, check to make sure the clutch outer housing is still properly meshed with the oil pump drive sprocket. Rotate the clutch outer housing; the oil pump drive sprocket and drive chain must also move. If the oil pump drive chain does not move, repeat Step 7 until proper engagement is obtained between the clutch outer housing and oil pump drive sprocket.*

13. Install a copper washer (or copper penny) into mesh with the primary drive gear and clutch outer housing (**Figure 5**). This will keep the clutch outer housing from turning in the next step.

14. Install the locknut (**Figure 32**) and tighten to the torque specification listed in **Table 3**.

15. Remove the bolts, washers and springs used in Step 10.

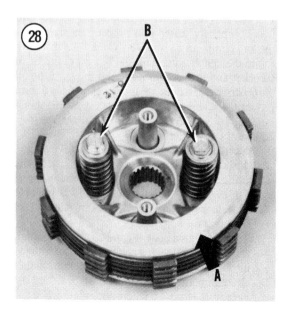

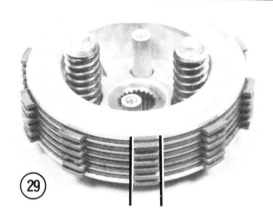

16. Install the clutch springs (**Figure 33**), lifter plate and clutch bolts (**Figure 4**). Tighten the bolts securely in a crisscross pattern in 2 or 3 stages.

17. Make sure the bearing is installed in the lifter plate.

18. Install the locating dowels and new gasket.

19. Make sure the lifter rod is in place in the clutch lifter mechanism. Install the right-hand crankcase cover and tighten the bolts to the torque specification listed in **Table 3**.

20. Install the sub-frame and tighten the bolts and nuts to the torque specifications listed in **Table 3**.

21. Install the clutch cable to the actuating lever.

22. Install the exhaust system as described in Chapter Six.

23. Install the rear brake pedal assembly as decribed in Chapter Eleven.

24. Fill the crankcase with the recommended viscosity and quantity of engine oil. Refer to Chapter Three.

25. Adjust the clutch as described in Chapter Three.

CLUTCH CABLE

Removal/Installation

In time the clutch cable will stretch to the point that it will have to be replaced.

1. Remove the seat and both side covers.

2. Remove the fuel tank as described in Chapter Six.

3. At the clutch lever, loosen the locknut and turn the adjuster barrel (**Figure 34**) all the way toward the cable sheath. Slip the cable end out of the hand lever.

4. At the right-hand crankcase cover, loosen the locknut (A, **Figure 35**) and the adjuster (B, **Figure 35**). Remove the cable end from the clutch lever.

5. Remove the retaining straps securing the clutch cable to the frame.

> *NOTE*
> *The piece of string attached in the next step will be used to pull the new clutch cable back through the frame so it will be routed in the exact same position.*

6. Tie a piece of heavy string or cord (approximately 2 m/7 ft. long) to the clutch mechanism end of the cable. Wrap this end with masking or duct tape. Do not use an excessive amount of tape. Tie the other end of the string to the right-hand footpeg.

7. At the handlebar end of the cable, carefully pull the cable (and attached string) out through the frame and from behind the steering head area.

Make sure the attached string follows the same path of the cable through the frame and behind the steering head area.

8. Remove the tape and untie the string from the old cable.

9. Lubricate the new cable as described in Chapter Three.

10. Tie the string to the clutch mechanism end of the new clutch cable and wrap it with tape.

11. Carefully pull the string back through the frame routing the new cable through the same path as the old cable.

12. Remove the tape and untie the string from the cable and the footpeg. Attach the new cable to the clutch lever and the clutch mechanism.

13. Install all clutch cable retaining straps onto the frame.

14. Install the fuel tank, side covers and seat.

15. Adjust the clutch cable as described in Chapter Three.

EXTERNAL SHIFT MECHANISM

The external shift mechanism is located on the same side of the engine as the clutch assembly and can be removed with the engine in the frame. To remove the shift drum and shift forks it is necessary to remove the engine and split the crankcase. That procedure is covered under *Internal Shift Mechanism* in this chapter.

Refer to **Figure 36** for this procedure.

Removal

1. Remove the clutch as described in this chapter.

2. Remove the bolts (**Figure 37**) securing the rear left-hand crankcase cover and remove the cover.

3. Remove the bolt (A, **Figure 38**) securing the gearshift pedal to the gearshift spindle assembly.

4. Remove the bolts (B, **Figure 38**) securing the front left-hand footpeg and remove the footpeg/gearshift pedal assembly.

5. Remove the bolt and washer (**Figure 6**) securing the oil pump driven gear.

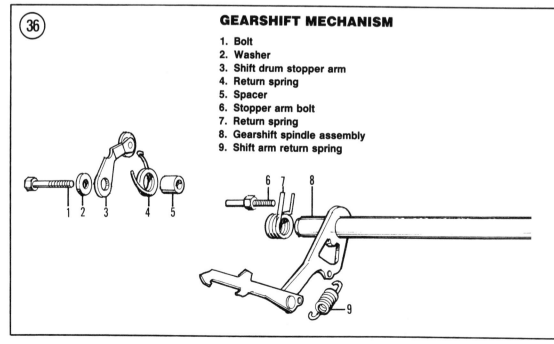

GEARSHIFT MECHANISM

1. Bolt
2. Washer
3. Shift drum stopper arm
4. Return spring
5. Spacer
6. Stopper arm bolt
7. Return spring
8. Gearshift spindle assembly
9. Shift arm return spring

6. Remove the oil pump driven gear (A, **Figure 7**), the drive chain (B, **Figure 7**) and the drive sprocket (C, **Figure 7**) at the same time. It is not necessary to remove the clutch outer housing guide from the transmission main shaft.

7. Disengage the gearshift arm from the shift drum and pull the gearshift spindle assembly out (**Figure 39**).

8. Remove the bolt, washer, return spring and shift drum stopper arm (**Figure 40**).

9. If the crankcase is going to be disassembled, remove the bolt (**Figure 41**) securing the shift drum cam plate. Remove the cam plate.

Inspection

1. Inspect the return spring on the gearshift arm assembly (A, **Figure 42**). If broken or weak it must be replaced.

2. Inspect the shift arm assembly spring (B, **Figure 42**). If broken or weak, remove and replace the spring.

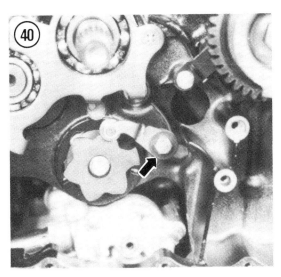

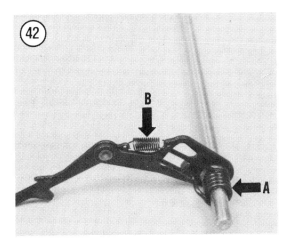

3. Inspect the gearshift spindle assembly shaft (**Figure 43**) for bending, wear or other damage; replace if necessary.

Installation

1. Align the hole in the backside of the shift drum cam plate with the pin on the shift drum (**Figure 44**) and install the cam plate. Install the bolt securing the cam plate and tighten to the torque specification listed in **Table 2**.
2. Install the shift drum stopper arm and index it into the shift drum cam plate. Install the return spring and the bolt and tighten to the torque specification listed in **Table 2**.
3. Install the gearshift spindle assembly. Make sure the return spring is correctly positioned onto the stopper plate bolt (**Figure 45**).
4. Make sure the clutch outer housing guide is installed on the transmission main shaft (**Figure 20**).
5. Assemble the oil pump driven gear, the drive chain and the drive sprocket as an assembly. The "IN" mark on the oil pump driven gear must face in toward the engine. The protruding bosses on the drive sprocket must face out away from the engine. Install this assembly onto the transmission main shaft and the oil pump drive shaft (**Figure 7**). Mesh the tab on the oil pump drive shaft with the slot in the oil pump driven gear.
6. Install the bolt and washer (**Figure 6**) securing the oil pump driven gear. Tighten the bolt to the torque specification listed in **Table 2**. Install the clutch as described in this chapter.
7. Install the front left-hand footpeg/gearshift pedal assembly. Tighten the bolts securely.
8. Align the punch marks on the gearshift arm and the gearshift spindle and install the gearshift arm onto the gearshift spindle assembly. Install and tighten the clamping bolt.

TRANSMISSION

The transmission is located within the engine crankcase. To gain access to the transmission and internal shift mechanism it is necessary to remove the engine and disassemble the crankcase. Once the crankcase is split, removal of the transmission main shaft is a simple task of pulling the assembly up and out of the crankcase.

Specifications for the transmission components are listed in **Table 3**.

Preliminary Inspection

After the transmission shaft assemblies have been removed from the crankcase halves, clean and inspect the assemblies prior to disassembling them.

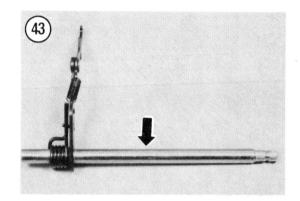

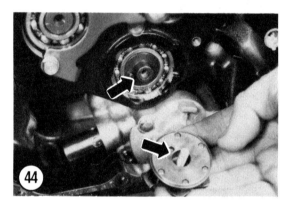

Place the assembled shaft into a large can or plastic bucket and thoroughly clean with a petroleum-based solvent such as kerosene and a stiff brush. Dry with compressed air or let it sit on rags to drip dry. Repeat for the other shaft assembly.

1. After they have been cleaned, visually inspect the components of the assemblies for excessive wear. Any burrs, pitting or roughness on the teeth of a gear will cause wear on the mating gear. Minor roughness can be cleaned up with an oilstone but there's little point in attempting to remove deep scars.

NOTE
Defective gears should be replaced. It's a good idea to replace the mating gear on the other shaft even though it may not show as much wear or damage.

2. Carefully check the engagement cogs. If any are chipped, worn, rounded or missing, the affected gear must be replaced.

3. Rotate the transmission bearings in the crankcases by hand. Refer to **Figure 46**. Check for roughness, noise and radial play. Any bearing that is suspect should be replaced.

4. If the transmission shafts are satisfactory and are not going to be disassembled, apply assembly oil or engine oil to all components and reinstall them in the crankcase as described in this chapter.

NOTE
If disassembling a used, well run-in transmission for the first time by yourself, pay particular attention to any additional shims that may have been added by a previous owner. These may have been added to take up the tolerance of worn components and must be reinstalled in the same position since the shims have developed a wear pattern. If new parts are going to be installed these shims may be eliminated. This is something you will have to determine upon reassembly.

Removal/Installation

1. Disassemble the crankcase as described in Chapter Four.

2. Remove the crankshaft as described in Chapter Four.

3. Remove the final drive damper gear, thrust washer (**Figure 47**) and the final drive damper gear bushing (**Figure 48**) from the output gear shaft.

4. Remove the main shaft assembly, countershaft assembly and shift forks as an assembly (**Figure 49**).

NOTE
Prior to installing any components, coat
all bearing surfaces with assembly oil.

5. Install the 2 transmission assemblies into the right-hand crankcase half as follows:

   a. Mesh the transmission assemblies together in their proper relationship to each other.

   b. Hold the thrust washer (**Figure 50**) on the countershaft assembly in place with your fingers.

   c. Install both assemblies into the right-hand crankcase.

   d. Make sure the thrust washer is still positioned correctly after the shaft assemblies are completely installed.

   e. After both shaft assemblies are installed, tap on the end of both shafts (**Figure 51**) with a plastic or rubber mallet to make sure they are completely seated.

NOTE
If the thrust washer on the end of the
shaft does not seat correctly it will hold
the transmission shaft up a little and
prevent the crankcase halves from
seating completely.

6. Install the shift forks with their marking facing down toward the right-hand crankcase. Install the "R," "C" and "L" shift forks into the grooves in their respective gears (**Figure 52**).

7. Make sure the shift drum bearing (**Figure 53**) is installed in the right-hand crankcase half.

8. Install the shift drum (**Figure 54**).

9. Mesh the pin followers of the shift forks into the grooves of the shift drum.

10. Install the shift fork shaft (**Figure 55**).

11. Make sure the pin followers are properly meshed with the grooves in the shift drum (**Figure 56**).

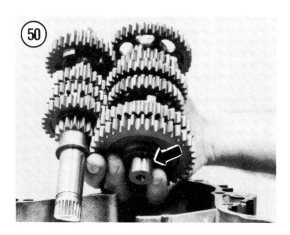

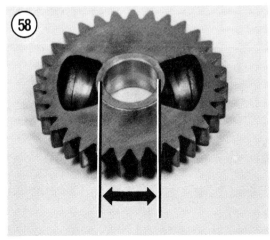

NOTE
The following procedure is best done with the aid of a helper as the assemblies are loose and won't spin very easily. Have the helper spin the transmission shafts while you turn the shift drum through all the gears.

12. Spin the transmission shafts and shift through the gears using the shift drum. Make sure you can shift into all gears. This is the time to find that something may be installed incorrectly—not after the crankcase is completely assembled.

13. Make sure the thrust washers (A, **Figure 57**) are in place on both shaft assemblies.

14. Install the crankshaft (B, **Figure 57**) as described in Chapter Four.

15. Assemble the crankcase as described in Chapter Four.

**Final Drive Damper
Gear Inspection**

Measure the inside diameter of the final drive damper gear (**Figure 58**). Refer to dimensions listed in **Table 4**. If the gear is worn to the service limit, the gear must be replaced.

Measure the inside and outside diameter of the final drive damper gear bushing (**Figure 59**). Refer to dimensions listed in **Table 3**. If the bushing is worn to the service limit, the bushing must be replaced.

**Main Shaft Disassembly/
Inspection/Assembly**

Refer to **Figure 60** for this procedure.

NOTE
*A helpful "tool" that should be used for transmission disassembly is a large egg flat (the type restaurants get their eggs in) (**Figure 61**). As you remove a part from the shaft, set it in one of the depressions in the same position from which it was removed. This is an easy way to remember the correct relationship of all parts.*

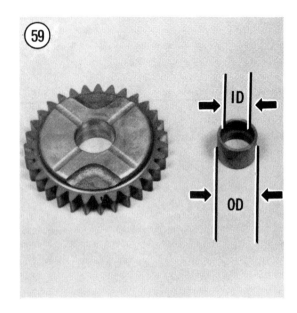

TRANSMISSION

1. Bearing
2. Thrust washer
3. Final drive gear
4. Countershaft 1st gear
5. Countershaft 1st gear bushing
6. Lockwasher
7. Splined washer
8. Countershaft 5th gear
9. Circlip
10. Countershaft 2nd gear
11. Splined bushing
12. Countershaft 3rd gear
13. Countershaft
14. Countershaft 6th gear
15. Countershaft 4th gear
16. Countershaft 4th gear bushing
17. Main shaft/1st gear

18. Main shaft 5th gear bushing
19. Main shaft 5th gear
20. Main shaft 2nd/3rd combination gear
21. Main shaft 6th gear bushing
22. Main shaft 6th gear
23. Main shaft 4th gear

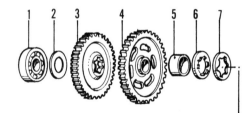

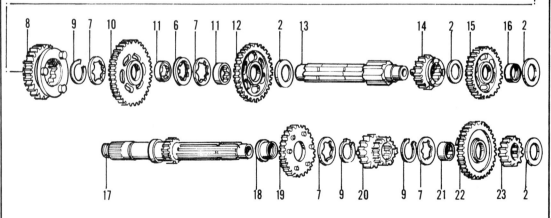

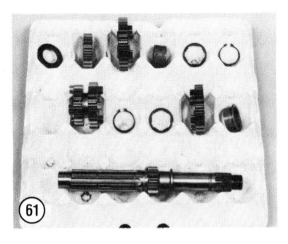

(61)

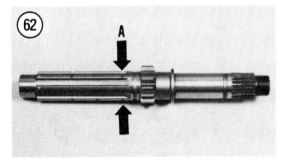

(62)

A

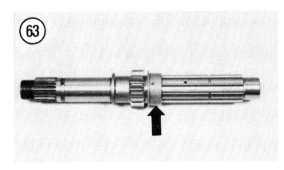

(63)

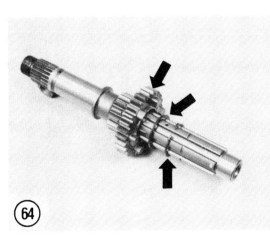

(64)

5

1. Clean the shaft as described under *Preliminary Inspection* in this chapter.
2. Slide off the thrust washer and the 4th gear.
3. Slide off the 6th gear, the 6th gear bushing and the splined washer.
4. Remove the circlip.
5. Slide off the 2nd/3rd combination gear.
6. Remove the circlip and slide off the splined washer.
7. Slide off the 5th gear and the 5th gear bushing.
8. Check each gear for excessive wear, burrs, pitting or chipped or missing teeth. Make sure the lugs of gears are in good condition.

NOTE
Defective gears should be replaced. It is a good idea to replace the mating gear on the countershaft even though it may not show as much wear or damage.

NOTE
The 1st gear is part of the main shaft. If the gear is defective, the shaft must be replaced.

9. Make sure that all gears and bushings slide smoothly on the main shaft splines.
10. Measure the outside diameter of the main shaft at location A as shown in **Figure 62**. Refer to the dimension listed in **Table 3**. If the shaft is worn to the service limit, the shaft must be replaced.
11. Measure the inside diameter of the main shaft 5th and 6th gears. Refer to dimensions listed in **Table 3**. If the gear(s) is worn to the service limit, the gear(s) must be replaced.
12. Measure the inside and outside diameter of the main shaft 5th gear bushing and the outside diameter of the 6th gear bushing. Refer to dimensions listed in **Table 3**. If the bushing(s) is worn to the service limit, the bushing(s) must be replaced.

NOTE
It is a good idea to replace all circlips every other time the transmission shaft is disassembled to ensure proper gear alignment.

13. Slide on the 5th gear bushing with the flange side on first (**Figure 63**).
14. Slide on the 5th gear (flush side on first), splined washer and circlip (**Figure 64**).
15. Position the 2nd/3rd combination gear with the larger diameter 2nd gear going on first. Slide on the 2nd/3rd combination gear and install the circlip and splined washer (**Figure 65**).
16. Align the oil hole in the 6th gear bushing with the oil hole in the main shaft (**Figure 66**) and slide

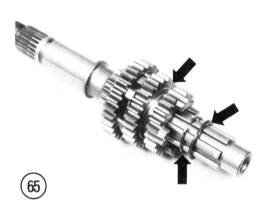

the bushing into place. This alignment is necessary for proper oil flow.

17. Install the 6th gear, the 4th gear and the thrust washer (**Figure 67**).

18. Before installation, double-check the placement of all gears (**Figure 68**). Make sure all circlips are seated in the main shaft grooves.

19. Make sure each gear engages properly with the adjoining gears where applicable.

**Countershaft Disassembly/
Inspection/Assembly**

Refer to **Figure 60** for this procedure.

> *NOTE*
> *Use the same large egg flat (used on the main shaft disassembly) during the countershaft disassembly. This is an easy way to remember the correct relationship of all parts.*

1. Slide off the thrust washer.

2. Slide off the 4th gear, the 4th gear bushing and the thrust washer.

3. Slide off the 6th gear.

4. From the other end of the shaft, slide off the thrust washer and the final drive gear.

5. Slide off the 1st gear and the 1st gear bushing.

6. Slide off the lockwasher, then rotate the splined washer in either direction so its tangs will clear the transmission spline grooves and slide it off of the shaft.

7. Slide off the 5th gear.

8. Remove the circlip and slide off the splined washer.

9. Slide off the 2nd gear and the 2nd gear splined bushing.

10. Slide off the lockwasher, then rotate the splined washer in either direction so its tangs will clear the transmission spline grooves and slide it off of the shaft.

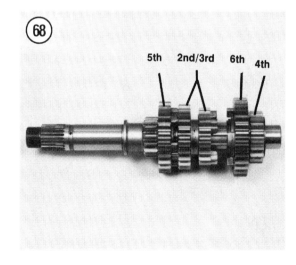

5th   2nd/3rd   6th   4th

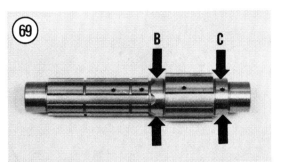

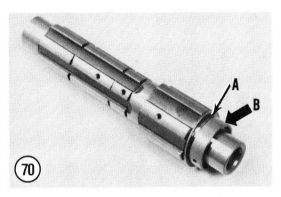

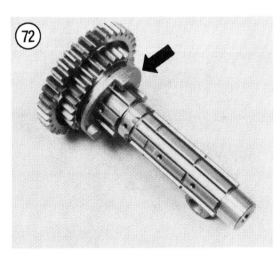

5

11. Slide off the 3rd gear, the 3rd gear splined bushing and the thrust washer.

12. Check each gear for excessive wear, burrs, pitting or chipped or missing teeth. Make sure the lugs on are in good condition.

NOTE
Defective gears should be replaced. It is a good idea to replace the mating gear on the main shaft even though it may not show signs of wear or damage.

13. Make sure all gears and gear bushings slide smoothly on the countershaft splines.

14. Measure the inside diameter of the 1st, 2nd, 3rd and 4th gears. Compare with the dimensions listed in **Table 3**.

15. Measure the outside diameter of the 1st, 2nd, 3rd and 4th gear bushings and the inside diameter of the 4th gear bushing. Compare with the dimensions listed in **Table 3**.

16. Measure the outside diameter of the shaft at locations B and C (**Figure 69**). Compare with dimensions listed in **Table 3**.

NOTE
It is a good idea to replace all circlips every other time the shaft is disassembled to ensure proper gear alignment.

17. Slide on the thrust washer (A, **Figure 70**).

18. Align the oil hole in the 4th gear bushing with the oil hole in the shaft (B, **Figure 70**) and slide on the bushing. This alignment is necessary for proper oil flow.

19. Slide the 4th gear (flush side on first) and the thrust washer (**Figure 71**).

20. Onto the other end of the shaft, slide on the 6th gear (**Figure 72**).

21. Slide on the thrust washer and the 3rd gear bushing (A, **Figure 73**).

22. Slide on the 3rd gear (B, **Figure 73**).

23. Slide on the splined washer (A, **Figure 74**). Rotate the splined washer in either direction so its tangs are engaged in the groove in the transmission shaft.

24. Slide on the splined lockwasher (B, **Figure 74**) so that the tangs go into the open areas of the splined washer and lock the washer in place.

25. Align the oil hole in the 2nd gear bushing with the oil hole in the shaft (**Figure 75**) and slide on the bushing. This alignment is necessary for proper oil flow.

26. Slide on the 2nd gear, splined washer (**Figure 76**) and install the circlip (**Figure 77**).

27. Align the oil hole in the 5th gear with the oil hole in the shaft (**Figure 78**) and slide on the gear (**Figure 79**). This alignment is necessary for proper oil flow.

28. Slide on the splined washer (**Figure 80**). Rotate the splined washer in either direction so its tangs are engaged in the groove in the transmission shaft.

29. Slide on the splined lockwasher (**Figure 81**) so that the tangs go into the open areas of the splined washer and lock the washer in place.

30. Align the oil hole in the 1st gear bushing with the oil hole in the shaft (**Figure 82**) and slide on the bushing. This alignment is necessary for proper oil flow.

31. Slide on the 1st gear (**Figure 83**) with the flush side on last.

32. Install the final drive gear with the shoulder side out (**Figure 84**) and the thrust washer (**Figure 85**).

33. Before installation, double-check the placement of all gears (**Figure 86**). Make sure all circlips are correctly seated in the countershaft grooves.

5

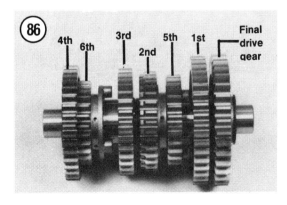

34. After both transmission shafts have been assembled, mesh the 2 assemblies together in the correct position (**Figure 87**). Check that all gears meet correctly. This is your last check prior to installing the assemblies into the crankcase; make sure they are correctly assembled.

INTERNAL SHIFT MECHANISM

Disassembly/Inspection/ Assembly

Refer to **Figure 88** for this procedure.

Refer to **Table 4** for shift fork, shift fork shaft and shift drum specifications.

The internal shift mechanism is removed during transmission removal as described in this chapter.

NOTE
Prior to removal or disassembly of any of the components, lay the assembly down on a piece of paper or cardboard and carefully trace around it. Write down the identifying numbers and letter next to the item. This will take a little extra time now but it may save some time and frustration later.

1. Slide the shift forks off the shift fork shaft.
2. Inspect each shift fork for signs of wear or cracking. Check for bending and make sure each fork slides smoothly on the shaft. Replace any worn or damaged forks.
3. Check for any arc-shaped wear or burned marks on the shift forks (**Figure 89**). This indicates that the shift fork has come in contact with the gear. The fork fingers have become excessively worn and the fork must be replaced.
4. Measure the inside diameter of each shift fork with an inside micrometer or snap gauge (**Figure 90**). Replace any that are worn to the service limit listed in **Table 4**.

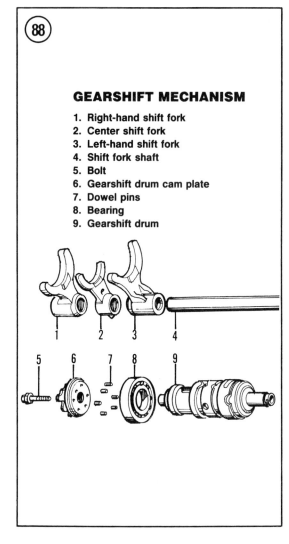

GEARSHIFT MECHANISM

1. Right-hand shift fork
2. Center shift fork
3. Left-hand shift fork
4. Shift fork shaft
5. Bolt
6. Gearshift drum cam plate
7. Dowel pins
8. Bearing
9. Gearshift drum

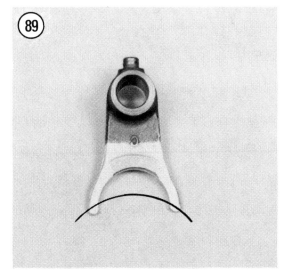

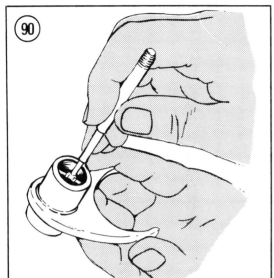

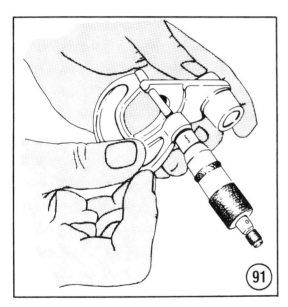

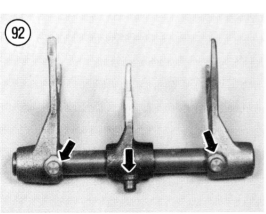

5. Measure the width of the gearshift fork fingers with a micrometer (**Figure 91**). Replace any that are worn to the service limit listed in **Table 6**.

6. Check the shift drum dowel pin (**Figure 92**) on each shift fork for wear or damage; replace the shift fork as necessary.

7. Roll the shift fork shaft on a flat surface such as a piece of plate glass and check for any bends. If the shaft is bent, it must be replaced.

8. Measure the outside diameter of the shift fork shaft with a micrometer. Replace if worn to the service limit listed in **Table 4**.

9. Check the grooves in the shift drum for wear or roughness (**Figure 93**). If any of the groove profiles have excessive wear or damage, replace the shift drum.

10. Measure the outside diameter of the shift drum at the location shown in **Figure 94**. Replace the shift drum if worn to less than the service limit dimension listed in **Table 4**.

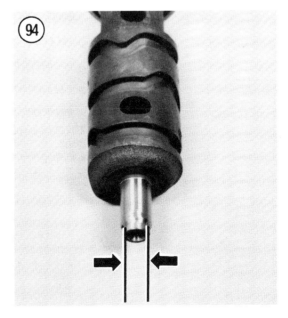

11. Inspect the shift drum bearing (**Figure 95**). It must rotate smoothly with no roughness or noise. If damaged the bearing must be replaced.

12. Inspect the ramps on the gearshift drum cam plate (**Figure 96**). The ramps must be smooth and free from burrs or nicks.

13. Inspect the pins in the gearshift drum cam plate (**Figure 97**). If worn or damaged the cam plate must be replaced.

14. Apply a light coat of oil to the shift fork shafts and the inside bores of the shift forks prior to installation.

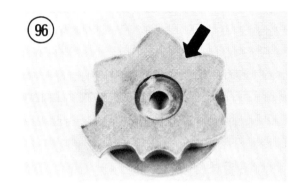

Table 1 CLUTCH SPECIFICATIONS

Item	Standard	Wear limit
Friction disc thickness		
Disc A	2.62-2.78 mm	2.3 mm (0.090 in.)
	(0.102-0.109 in.)	
Disc B	2.92-3.08 mm	2.6 mm (0.102 in.)
	(0.115-0.121 in.)	
Clutch plate warpage	—	0.30 mm (0.012 in.)
Clutch spring free length	39.0 mm (1.53 in.)	37.4 mm (1.47 in.)
Outer guide		
ID	21.991-22.016 mm	22.09 mm (0.869 in.)
	(0.866-0.867 in.)	
OD	31.959-31.975 mm	31.98 mm (1.259 in.)
	(1.258-1.259 in.)	
Clutch outer housing ID	32.000-32.025 mm	32.10 mm (1.263 in.)
	(1.2598-1.2608 in.)	

Table 2 CLUTCH AND GEARSHIFT MECHANISM TORQUE SPECIFICATIONS

Item	N·m	ft.-lb.
Clutch locknut	65-75	47-54
Right-hand crankcase cover bolts	8-12	6-9
Sub-frame bolts		
Upper	30-35	22-25
Lower		
1985-1986 VT500C	20-30	14-22
All others	20-24	14-17
Engine front mounting bolt and nut	45-60	33-43
Shift drum stopper arm bolt	8-12	6-9
Shift drum cam plate bolt	10-14	7-10
Primary drive gear	80-100	58-72
Oil pump driven sprocket bolt	8-12	6-9

Table 3 TRANSMISSION SPECIFICATIONS

Item	Specification	Wear limit
Gear backlash		
1st	0.089-0.170 mm (0.0035-0.0066 in.)	0.24 mm (0.009 in.)
2nd, 3rd, 4th and 5th	0.068-0.136 mm (0.0027-0.0054 in.)	0.18 mm (0.007 in.)
Gear ID main shaft		
5th	29.020-29.041 mm (1.1425-1.1433 in.)	29.06 mm (1.144 in.)
6th	28.020-28.041 mm (1.1031-1.1040 in.)	28.06 mm (1.105 in.)
Gear ID countershaft		
1st, 2nd, 3rd and 4th	28.000-28.021 mm (1.1023-1.1032 in.)	28.04 mm (1.1039 in.)
Gear bushing OD		
Main shaft		
5th	28.979-29.000 mm (1.1409-1.1417 in.)	28.94 mm (1.139 in.)
6th	27.979-28.000 mm (1.1015-1.1024 in.)	27.94 mm (1.100 in.)
Countershaft		
1st, 2nd, 3rd and 4th	27.959-27.980 mm (1.1007-1.1015 in.)	27.94 mm (1.100 in.)
Gear bushing ID		
Main shaft 5th	25.020-25.041 mm (0.9850-0.9859 in.)	25.06 mm (0.987 in.)
Countershaft 4th	25.000-25.021 mm (0.9843-0.9851 in.)	25.01 mm (0.9858 in.)
Main shaft OD		
At 5th gear bushing location A	24.959-24.980 mm (0.9826-0.9835 in.)	24.90 mm (0.980 in.)
Countershaft OD		
At 3rd and 4th gear bushing locations B and C	24.959-24.980 mm (0.9826-0.9835 in.)	24.90 mm (0.980 in.)
Damper shaft gear		
Gear ID	24.000-24.021 mm (0.944-0.9457 in.)	24.10 mm (0.949 in.)
Bushing OD	23.959-23.980 mm (0.9433-0.9441 in.)	23.70 mm (0.933 in.)
Bushing ID	20.020-20.041 mm (0.7882-0.7890 in.)	20.10 mm (0.791 in.)

(continued)

5

Table 3 TRANSMISSION SPECIFICATIONS (continued)

Item	Specification	Wear limit
Bushing clearance wear limits		
Main shaft		
5th gear to 5th gear bushing		0.10 mm (0.004 in.)
6th gear to 6th gear bushing		0.10 mm (0.004 in.)
5th gear bushing to shaft		0.060 mm (0.0024 in.)
Countershaft		
1st gear to 1st gear bushing		0.10 mm (0.004 in.)
2nd gear to 2nd gear bushing		0.10 mm (0.004 in.)
3rd gear to 3rd gear bushing		0.10 mm (0.004 in.)
4th gear to 4th gear bushing		0.060 mm (0.0024 in.)

Table 4 SHIFT FORK, SHIFT SHAFT AND SHIFT DRUM SPECIFICATIONS

Item	Specification	Wear limit
Shift fork ID	13.000-13.018 mm (0.5118-0.5125 in.)	13.037 mm (0.5133 in.)
Shift fork fingers	4.93-5.00 mm (0.194-0.197 in.)	4.63 mm (0.182 in.)
Shift fork shaft OD	12.996-12.984 mm (0.5105-0.5111 in.)	12.90 mm (0.5078 in.)
Shift drum end OD	13.996-13.984 mm (0.549-0.5506 in.)	13.90 mm (0.547 in.)

NOTE: If you own a VT500E, first check the Supplement at the back of the book for any additional service information.

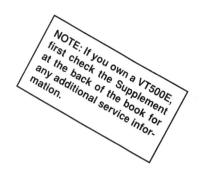

CHAPTER SIX

FUEL AND EXHAUST SYSTEMS

6

The fuel system consists of the fuel tank, shutoff valve, 2 Keihin constant velocity carburetors and the air filter.

The exhaust system consists of 2 exhaust pipes, a common collector and 1 or 2 mufflers.

The air filter must be cleaned frequently; the specific procedures and service intervals are covered in Chapter Three.

This chapter includes service procedures for all parts of the fuel and exhaust systems. Carburetor specifications are listed in **Table 1**. **Table 1** and **Table 2** are at the end of this chapter.

The carburetors on all U.S. models are engineered to meet stringent EPA (Environmental Protection Agency) regulations. The carburetors are flow tested and preset at the factory for maximum performance and efficiency within EPA regulations. Altering preset carburetor jet needle and pilot screw adjustments is forbidden by law. Failure to comply with EPA regulations may result in heavy fines.

CARBURETOR OPERATION

An understanding of the function of each of the carburetor components and their relation to one another is a valuable aid for pinpointing a source of carburetor trouble.

The carburetor's purpose is to supply and atomize fuel and mix it in correct proportions with air that is drawn in through the air intake. At the primary throttle opening (idle), a small amount of fuel is siphoned through the pilot jet by the incoming air. As the throttle is opened further, the air stream begins to siphon fuel through the main jet and needle jet. The tapered needle increases the effective flow capacity of the needle jet as it is lifted, in that it occupies decreasingly less of the area of the jet.

At full throttle the carburetor venturi is fully open and the needle is lifted far enough to permit the main jet to flow at full capacity.

The choke circuit is a "bystarter" system in which the choke lever opens a valve rather than closing a butterfly in the venturi area as on many carburetors. In the open position, the slow jet discharges a stream of fuel into the carburetor venturi, enriching the mixture when the engine is cold.

CARBURETOR SERVICE

Carburetor service (removal and cleaning) should be performed when poor engine performance or hesitation is observed. If, after servicing the carburetors and making the adjustments described in this chapter, the motorcycle does not perform correctly (and assuming that other factors affecting performance are correct, such as ignition timing and condition, valve adjustment, etc.), the motorcycle should be checked by a dealer or a qualified performance tuning specialist.

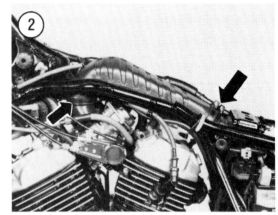

Removal/Installation

1. Place the bike on the centerstand and remove the right- and left-hand side covers (A, **Figure 1**).
2. Remove the seat (B, **Figure 1**) and disconnect the battery negative lead.
3. Remove the fuel tank as described in this chapter.
4. Loosen the clamping screws on the air filter connecting tube at the air filter box and at the carburetors (**Figure 2**). Remove the connecting tube from the frame.
5. Remove the screws (**Figure 3**) securing the throttle linkage cover and remove the cover.
6. At the hand throttle, loosen the throttle cable locknut and turn the adjusting barrel (**Figure 4**) all the way in. This provides the necessary slack for ease of cable removal at the carburetor assembly.
7. Pull back the rubber boots at the end of each choke cable.
8. Loosen the choke valve nut on each cable and remove the cable end (choke valve) from each carburetor (A, **Figure 5**).
9. On models so equipped, disconnect the lines (B, **Figure 5**) from the carburetors that go to the PCV valve. Move the lines out of the way.
10. Loosen the locknuts (A, **Figure 6**) securing the throttle cables to the cable bracket.
11. Disconnect the throttle cables (B, **Figure 6**) from the throttle wheel. Tie the loose ends of the cables onto the frame, out of the way.
12. Loosen the clamping screws on all of the carburetor bands (**Figure 7**).
13. Pull the carburetors and the rubber intake tubes from the inlet ports on the cylinder heads.
14. Slowly and carefully pull the carburetor assembly out toward the left-hand side. Be careful not to damage any of the carburetor components. This is a lot easier if you have one person on each side of the bike.

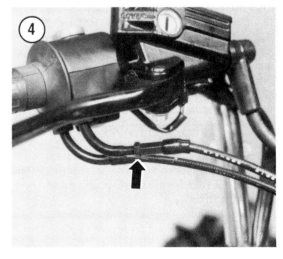

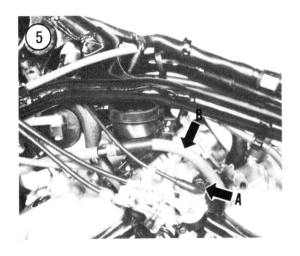

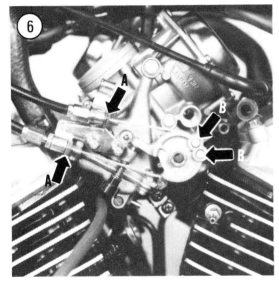

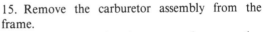

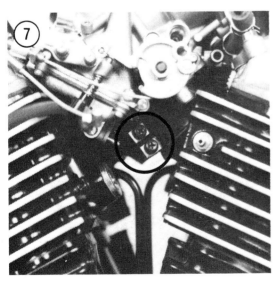

15. Remove the carburetor assembly from the frame.

16. Install by reversing these removal steps, noting the following.

17. Prior to installing the carburetor assembly, coat the inside surface of both rubber intake tubes with Armor All or rubber lube. This will make it easier to install the carburetor throats into the intake tubes.

18. Inspect the choke valve and spring for nicks, scratches or grooves; replace if necessary.

19. Be sure the throttle cables and choke cables are correctly positioned in the frame—not twisted or kinked and without any sharp bends. Tighten the locknuts securely.

20. Attach the "pull" throttle cable into the lower portion of the bracket and into the lower slot (**Figure 8**) in the throttle wheel.

21. Attach the "push" throttle cable into the upper portion of the bracket and into the upper slot (**Figure 9**) in the throttle wheel.

22. Adjust the throttle cable as described in Chapter Three.

23. Adjust the choke as described in this chapter.

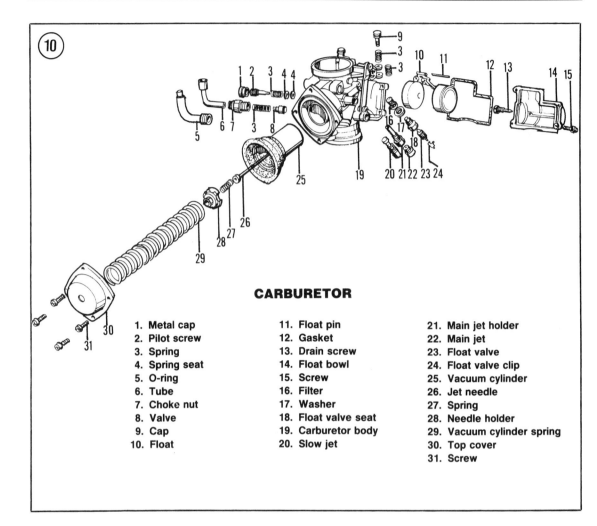

CARBURETOR

1. Metal cap	11. Float pin	21. Main jet holder
2. Pilot screw	12. Gasket	22. Main jet
3. Spring	13. Drain screw	23. Float valve
4. Spring seat	14. Float bowl	24. Float valve clip
5. O-ring	15. Screw	25. Vacuum cylinder
6. Tube	16. Filter	26. Jet needle
7. Choke nut	17. Washer	27. Spring
8. Valve	18. Float valve seat	28. Needle holder
9. Cap	19. Carburetor body	29. Vacuum cylinder spring
10. Float	20. Slow jet	30. Top cover
		31. Screw

**Disassembly/Cleaning/
Inspection**

Refer to **Figure 10** for this procedure.

It is recommended that only one carburetor be disassembled and cleaned at a time. This will prevent an accidental interchange of parts.

1. Remove the screws securing the carburetor top cover to the main body and remove the cover (A, **Figure 11**).

2. Remove the vacuum cylinder spring and vacuum cylinder assembly (**Figure 12**).

3. Put an 8 mm socket or screwdriver down into the vacuum cylinder cavity (**Figure 13**). Place the socket or screwdriver on the needle holder and turn the holder 60° in either direction to unlock it from the tangs within the vacuum cylinder. Remove the needle holder, jet needle spring and the jet needle (**Figure 14**).

4. Remove the screws (**Figure 15**) securing the float bowl to the main body and remove the float bowl.

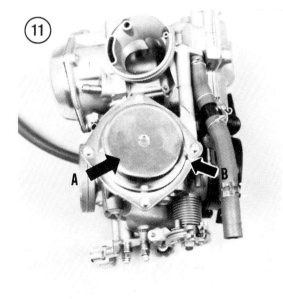

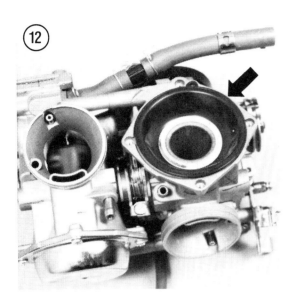

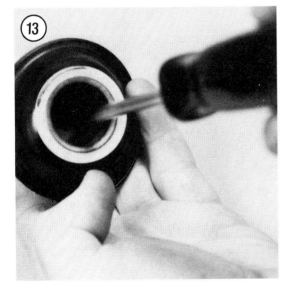

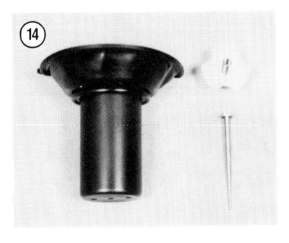

5. Remove the gasket from the float bowl (**Figure 16**).

6. Carefully push out the float pin (**Figure 17**).

7. Lift the float and needle valve (**Figure 18**) out of the main body.

8. Inspect the float valve seat (**Figure 19**) for grooves and nicks. If damaged it must be replaced.

9. Remove the float valve seat and filter (**Figure 20**).

10. Remove the main jet (**Figure 21**).

11. Remove the main jet holder (**Figure 22**).

12. Remove the slow jet (A, **Figure 23**).

13. The starter jet (B, **Figure 23**) is pressed into place and cannot be removed.

14. The needle jet (**Figure 24**) is not removable.

> *NOTE*
> *The pilot jets are covered by a metal plug (**Figure 25**) that has to be drilled out in order to remove the pilot jet. If removal is necessary, refer to the procedure in this chapter.*

15. Remove the drain screw (**Figure 26**) on float bowl. If necessary, clean out the drain tube outlet and reinstall the drain screw.

> *NOTE*
> *Further disassembly is neither necessary nor recommended. If throttle shafts or butterflies are damaged, take the carburetor body to a dealer for replacement.*

16. Clean all parts, except rubber or plastic parts, in a good grade of carburetor cleaner. This solution is available at most automotive or motorcycle supply stores in a small, resealable tank with a dip basket. If it is tightly sealed when not in use, the solution will last for several cleanings. Follow the manufacturer's instructions for correct soak time (usually about 1/2 hour).

> *NOTE*
> *It is recommended that one carburetor be cleaned at a time to avoid interchanging of parts.*

17. Remove the parts from the cleaner and blow dry with compressed air. Blow out the jets with compressed air. Do *not* use a piece of wire to clean them as minor gouges in a jet can alter flow rate and upset the fuel-air mixture.

18. Inspect the end of the float valve needle (**Figure 27**) and seat for wear or damage; replace either or both parts if necessary.

6

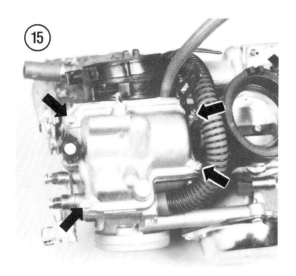

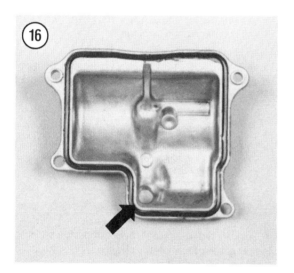

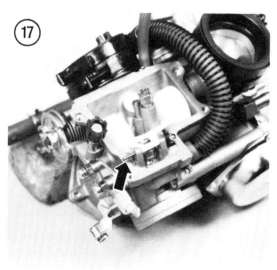

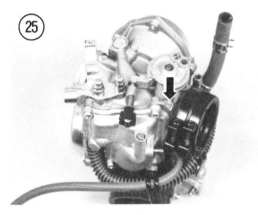

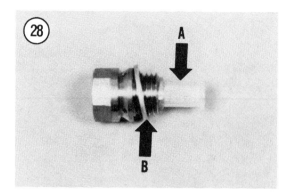

19. Inspect the filter (A, **Figure 28**) on the float valve seat. If damaged the float valve must be replaced.

20. If removed, inspect the pilot screw for wear or damage that may have occured during removal. Replace both pilot screws even if only 1 requires replacement. This is necessary for correct pilot screw adjustment as described in this chapter.

21. Repeat Steps 1-20 for the other carburetor.

22. Replace all O-rings and gaskets upon assembly. O-ring seals tend to become hardened after prolonged use and exposure to heat and therefore lose their ability to seal properly. Replace as necessary.

Assembly

1. If removed, screw the pilot screw into the exact same position (same number of turns) as recorded during disassembly.

> *NOTE*
> *If new pilot screws were installed, turn them out the number turns indicated in* **Table 1**, *from the* **lightly seated** *position.*

2. To assemble the vacuum cylinder, insert the jet needle (**Figure 29**) into the vacuum cylinder. Insert the needle holder and spring (**Figure 30**). Using an 8 mm socket or screwdriver (**Figure 13**), turn the needle holder 60° in either direction to lock the holder in place within the vacuum cylinder.

3. Install the vacuum cylinder into the carburetor body. Align the tab on the diaphragm with the hole (**Figure 31**) in the carburetor body.

4. Install the vacuum cylinder compression spring into the vacuum cylinder and index it onto the boss on the top cover (**Figure 32**).

5. Align the hole in the vacuum cylinder with the raised boss (B, **Figure 11**) on the top cover. Install the top cover and tighten the screws securely.

6. Install the slow jet (**Figure 33**).

7. Install the main jet holder (**Figure 34**) and the main jet (**Figure 35**).

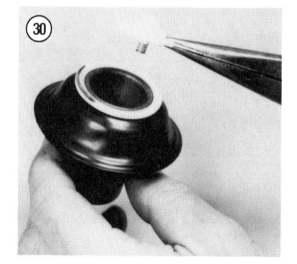

6

8. Make sure the gasket (B, **Figure 28**) is in place on the float valve and install the float valve seat and filter (**Figure 20**).

9. Install the needle valve onto the float.

10. Install the float and needle valve and install the float pin (**Figure 11**).

11. Inspect the float height and adjust if necessary as described in this chapter.

12. Install the gasket in the float bowl (**Figure 16**).

13. Install the float bowl (**Figure 15**) and tighten the screws securely.

14. After assembly and installation are completed, adjust the carburetors as described in this chapter and Chapter Three.

Separation/Assembly

1. Remove the carburetor assembly as described in this chapter.

2. Loosen the synchronizing screw (A, **Figure 36**) and remove the spring (B, **Figure 36**).

3. Remove the screw on each side securing the carburetors together. Refer to **Figure 37** and **Figure 38**.

4. Don't lose the throttle link thrust spring (**Figure 39**).

5. Carefully pull the carburetors apart.

6. Disconnect the fuel lines and T-fitting.

7. Loosen the throttle adjust screw (A, **Figure 40**).

8. Remove the nut (B, **Figure 40**) securing the throttle drum and remove the throttle drum and return spring.

9. Assemble by reversing these disassembly steps, noting the following.

10. Install new O-ring seals onto the air joint pipe and coat them with oil.

11. Tighten the throttle adjust screw until the throttle valve on the left-hand carburetor aligns with the small bypass hole in the venturi (A, **Figure 41**).

12. Turn the synchronizing screw until the throttle valve on the right-hand carburetor aligns with the small bypass hole in the venturi (B, **Figure 41**).

13. Using the throttle linkage (**Figure 42**), open the throttle a little then release it. The throttle should return smoothly with no drag.

14. If there is drag or the throttle does not move smoothly, recheck all previous steps until the problem is solved.

> *NOTE*
> *If the carburetors have been reassembled correctly and the throttle still does not operate correctly there may be internal damage to the throttle shafts or butterfly valves. Take the assembly to a dealer for inspection or replacement.*

Refilling Dry Float Bowls

After the carburetors are reassembled and installed on the engine the float bowls are all empty.

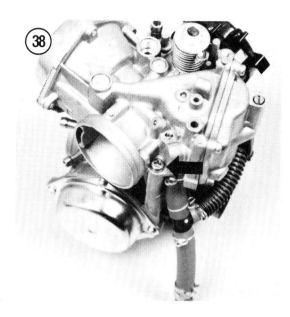

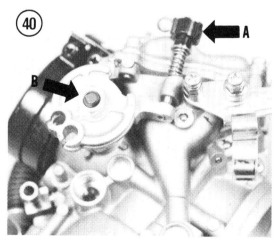

The engine must be running in order for fuel to flow from the fuel tank, through the vacuum controlled fuel shutoff valve and into the carburetors. To avoid prolonged cranking, use the following method to refill the carburetor float bowls before trying to start the engine.

> *WARNING*
> *Do not try to use a small funnel and a piece of fuel line because of the risk of fuel spillage.*

Purchase a small fuel tank like those used on a lawn mower. Attach the shutoff valve fuel line going to the carburetors (A, **Figure 43**) to the fitting on the small tank.

Secure the fuel tank to the frame with a bungee cord or hold it above the carburetor assembly (**Figure 44**) and pour some gasoline into the small fuel tank. Pour a small amount at a time as it will take very little to refill the bowls. The float bowls should fill up within 15-30 seconds. To check if there is fuel in the carburetors, slightly open one of the drain screws (B, **Figure 43**); if fuel flows out, the bowl has fuel in it.

Remove the temporary fuel tank.

Pilot Screw and Plug Removal

The pilot jets are covered by a metal plug (**Figure 25**) that has to be drilled out in order to remove the pilot jet. The pilot jets can be removed with the carburetor assembly either installed on the bike or removed. It is easier to perform this operation with

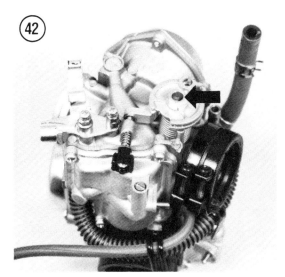

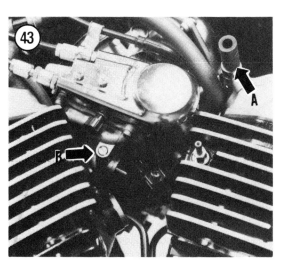

the carburetor assembly installed on the bike. Do not remove these plugs and jets unless you suspect they are not functioning properly.

> *CAUTION*
> *If the carburetor assembly is removed from the engine, put tape over all openings in the carburetor bodies to keep out metal shavings during the drilling operation.*

1. Use a small center punch and hammer to centerpunch the middle of the plug (**Figure 25**) for a drill guide.

> *CAUTION*
> *Be careful not to drill too far into the plug; you could damage the pilot screw.*

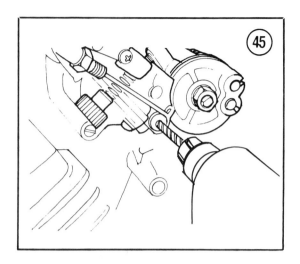

2. Drill through the plug (**Figure 45**) with a 4 mm (5/32 in.) drill bit. If available, attach a drill stop to the drill bit 3 mm (1/8 in.) from the end of the drill bit to prevent the accidental drilling of the pilot screw.

> *NOTE*
> *If you do not have a drill stop, wrap 8-10 layers of masking tape on the drill bit at the prescribed distance from the end. This can be used as a guide for the distance the drill bit has traveled. The tape will not stop the drill from traveling further in—it is only a visual guide.*

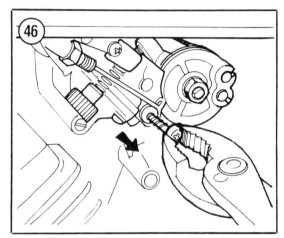

3. Force a 4 mm self-tapping screw into the drilled hole. Continue to turn the screw until the plug starts to rotate with the screw.
4. Withdraw the plug and screw with a pair of pliers (**Figure 46**) and blow away all metal shavings from the area.

> *NOTE*
> *Prior to removing the pilot screw, record the number of turns necessary until the screw lightly seats. Record the number of turns for each individual carburetor as the screws must be reinstalled into the exact same setting.*

5. Remove the pilot screw assembly.
6. Perform *Pilot Screw Adjustment and Plug Installation* in this chapter.

CARBURETOR ADJUSTMENTS

Float Adjustment

The carburetor assembly has to be removed and partially disassembled for this adjustment.
1. Remove the carburetors as described in this chapter.

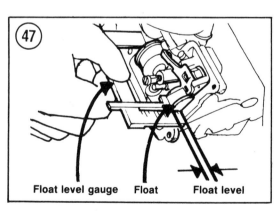

Float level gauge   Float   Float level

2. Remove the screws (**Figure 15**) securing the float bowls to the main bodies and remove them.
3. Hold the carburetor assembly with the carburetor inclined 15-45° from vertical so that the float arm is just touching the float needle. Use a float level gauge (Honda part No. 07401-0010001 or equivalant) and measure the distance from the

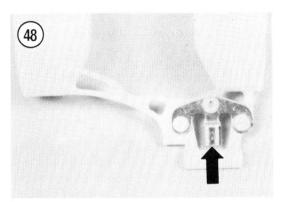

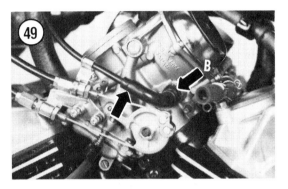

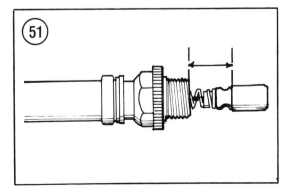

carburetor body to the float arm (**Figure 47**). The correct height is listed in **Table 1**.

4. Adjust by carefully bending the tang on the float arm (**Figure 48**).

5. If the float level is too high, the result will be a rich fuel-air mixture. If it is too low, the mixture will be too lean.

NOTE
The floats on both carburetors must be adjusted at the same height to maintain the same fuel-air mixture to both cylinders.

6. Reassemble and install the carburetors.

7. Refill the dry float bowls as described in this chapter.

Needle Jet Adjustment

The needle jet is *non-adjustable* on all models.

6

Choke Adjustment

First make sure the choke operates smoothly with no binding. The choke cable starts out as a single cable at the lever on the handlebar lever and about halfway down it branches out into 2 cables, one for each carburetor. If the cable binds, lubricate it as described in Chapter Three. If the cable still does not operate smoothly it must be replaced as described in this chapter.

NOTE
The choke circuit is a "bystarter" system in which the choke lever opens a valve rather than closing a butterfly in the venturi area as on other carburetors. In the open position, the slow jet discharges a stream of fuel into the carburetor venturi, enrichening the mixture when the engine is cold.

1. Remove both side covers and the seat.

2. Remove the fuel tank as described in this chapter.

3. Operate the choke lever and check for smooth operation of the cable and choke mechanism.

4. At the carburetor assembly, slide back the rubber boot on the choke cable (A, **Figure 49**).

5. Unscrew the choke valve nut (B, **Figure 49**) and remove the choke cable, valve and spring from the carburetor.

6. Move the lever all the way *down* to the fully closed position.

7. Using vernier calipers, measure the dimension shown in **Figure 50**. The correct dimension is between 10-11 mm (0.39-0.43 in.). Refer to **Figure 51**.

8. To adjust, perform the following:

   a. Loosen the locknut (A, **Figure 52**) on the choke cable at the lever.

   b. Turn the elbow (B, **Figure 52**) in either direction until the dimension at the cable end is correct.

   c. Tighten the locknut and recheck the dimension in Step 7.

9. Repeat Steps 4-8 for the other carburetor. The dimension in Step 7 must be the same for both carburetors. If you are unable to achieve the same dimension for both choke valves, the cable assembly must be replaced as described in this chapter.

10. Install the choke valve into the carburetor body.

11. Tighten the choke valve nut by hand then turn it an additonal 1/4 turn with a 14 mm wrench.

12. Reinstall the fuel tank, seat and side covers.

Pilot Screw Adjustment and Plug Installation

> *NOTE*
> *The pilot screws are pre-set at the factory. Adjustment is not necessary unless the carburetors have been overhauled or someone has misadjusted them.*

The air filter element must be cleaned before starting this procedure or the results will be inaccurate.

The plugs have to be removed from the carburetor bodies as described in this chapter.

1. For the preliminary adjustment, carefully turn the pilot screw on each carburetor in until it *lightly* seats and then back it out the number of turns listed in **Table 1**.

2. Start the engine and let it reach normal operating temperature. Stop-and-go riding for approximately 10-15 minutes is sufficient.

3. Shut the engine off and place the bike on the centerstand.

4. Connect a portable tachometer following the manufacturer's instructions. Use a tachometer that can register a change of 50 rpm. The bike's tachometer is not accurate enough at low rpm.

5. Start the engine and turn the large black plastic idle adjust screw (**Figure 53**) in or out to achieve the idle speed listed in **Table 1**.

6. Turn each pilot screw *out* 1/2 turn from the initial setting in Step 1. If the engine speed increases by 50 rpm or more, turn each pilot screw out by an additional 1/2 turn at a time until engine speed drops by 50 rpm or less.

7. Turn the idle adjust screw in or out again to achieve the idle speed listed in **Table 1**.

8. Turn the pilot screw on the left-hand carburetor *in* 1/2 turn at a time until engine speed drops by 50 rpm.

9. Turn the pilot screw on the left-hand carburetor *out* 1 turn from the position obtained in Step 8.

10. Turn the idle adjust screw in or out again to achieve the desired idle speed listed in **Table 1**.

11. Repeat Steps 8-10 on the right-hand carburetor pilot screw.

12. Turn the engine off and disconnect the portable tachometer.

13. After this adjustment is completed, test ride the bike. Throttle response from idle should be rapid and without any hesitation.

14. Use a suitable size drift and carefully drive a new plug (**Figure 54**) into each pilot screw bore in the carburetor body. The plug is fully seated when it is recessed into the hole by 1 mm.

High Elevation Adjustment

If the bike is going to be ridden for any sustained period of time at high elevation (2,000 m/6,500 ft.), the carburetors must be readjusted to improve performance and decrease exhaust emissions.

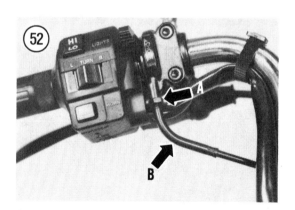

1. Remove each pilot screw plug as described in this chapter.

2. Start the engine and let it reach normal operating temperature. Stop-and-go riding for approximately 10 minutes is sufficient. Turn off the engine.

3. Connect a portable tachometer following the manufacturer's instructions. The bike's tach is not accurate enough at low rpm.

4. Turn each pilot screw *clockwise* 1/2 turn, as viewed from the side of the carburetor.

5. Restart the engine and turn the large idle screw (**Figure 53**) to achieve the idle speed listed in **Table 1**.

6. Turn the engine off and disconnect the portable tachometer.

7. Install new pilot screw plugs as described in this chapter.

8. When the bike is returned to lower elevation (near sea level), the pilot screws must be returned to their original position and the idle speed readjusted to the rpm listed in **Table 1**.

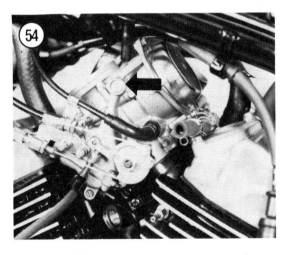

Rejetting The Carburetors

Do not try to solve a poor running engine problem by rejetting the carburetors if all of the following conditions hold true.

1. The engine has held a good tune in the past with the standard jetting.

2. The engine has not been modified.

3. The motorcycle is being operated in the same geographical region under the same general climatic conditions as in the past.

4. The motorcycle was and is being ridden at average highway speeds.

If those conditions all hold true, the chances are that the problem is due to a malfunction in the carburetor or in another component that needs to be adjusted or repaired. Changing carburetor jet size probably won't solve the problem. Rejetting the carburetors may be necessary if any of the following conditions hold true.

1. A non-standard type of air filter element is being used.

2. A non-standard exhaust system is installed on the motorcycle.

3. Any of the top end components in the engine (pistons, cams, valves, compression ratio, etc.) have been modified.

4. The motorcycle is in use at considerably higher or lower altitudes or in a considerably hotter or colder climate than in the past.

5. The motorcycle is being operated at considerably higher speeds than before and changing to colder spark plugs does not solve the problem.

6. Someone has previously changed the carburetor jetting.

7. The motorcycle has never held a satisfactory engine tune.

If it is necessary to rejet the carburetors, check with a dealer or motorcycle performance tuner for recommendations as to the size of jets to install for your specific situation.

If you do change the jets do so only one size at a time. After rejetting, test ride the bike and perform a spark plug test; refer to *Reading Spark Plugs* in Chapter Three.

THROTTLE CABLE REPLACEMENT

1. Place the bike on the centerstand and remove the right- and left-hand side covers.

2. Remove the fuel tank as described in this chapter.

3. Remove the screws securing the throttle linkage cover and remove the cover (**Figure 55**).

4. Disconnect the front brake light switch electrical connectors (A, **Figure 56**).

5. Remove the screws securing the right-hand switch/throttle housing halves together (B, **Figure 56**).

6. Remove the housing from the handlebar and disengage the throttle cables (C, **Figure 56**) from the throttle grip.

7. At the carburetor assembly, loosen the locknuts (A, **Figure 57**) securing the throttle cables to the cable bracket.

8. Disconnect the throttle cables (B, **Figure 57**) from the throttle wheel.

> *NOTE*
> *The piece of string attached in the next step will be used to pull the new throttle cables back through the frame so they will be routed in exactly the same position as the old ones.*

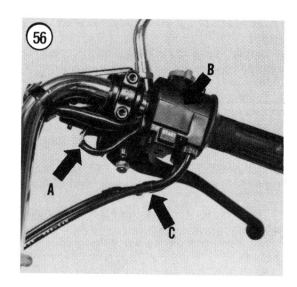

9. Tie a piece of heavy string or cord (approximately 7 ft./2 m long) to the carburetor end of the throttle cables. Wrap this end with masking or duct tape. Do not use an excessive amount of tape as it must be pulled through the frame loop during removal. Tie the other end of the string to the frame or air box.

10. At the throttle grip end of the cables, carefully pull the cables (and attached string) out through the frame, past the electrical harness and from behind the headlight housing. Make sure the attached string follows the same path as the cables through the frame.

11. Remove the tape and untie the string from the old cables.

12. Lubricate the new cables as described in Chapter Three.

13. Tie the string to the new throttle cables and wrap it with tape.

14. Carefully pull the string back through the frame routing the new cables through the same path as the old cables.

15. Remove the tape and untie the string from the cables and the frame.

> *CAUTION*
> *The throttle cables are the push/pull type and must be installed as described and shown in Step 16 and Step 17. Do **not** interchange the 2 cables.*

16. Attach the throttle "pull" cable to the bottom portion of the bracket and into the lower hole in the throttle wheel (**Figure 58**). The other end is attached to the front receptacle (A, **Figure 59**) of the throttle/switch housing.

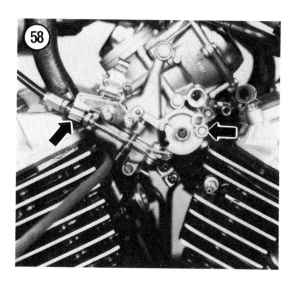

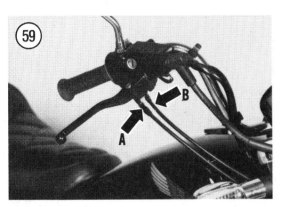

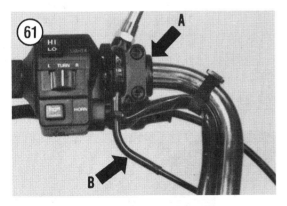

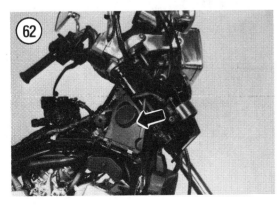

17. Attach the throttle "push" cable to the upper portion of the bracket and into the upper hole in the throttle wheel (**Figure 60**). The other end is attached to the rear receptacle (B, **Figure 59**) of the throttle/switch housing.

18. Install the throttle/switch housing and tighten the screws securely.

19. Attach the front brake light switch connectors.

20. Operate the throttle grip and make sure the carburetor throttle linkage is operating correctly, with no binding. If operation is incorrect or there is binding carefully check that the cables are attached correctly and there are no tight bends in the cables.

21. Install the carburetor assembly, fuel tank and seat.

22. Adjust the throttle cables as described in Chapter Three.

23. Test ride the bike slowly at first and make sure the throttle is operating correctly.

CHOKE CABLE REPLACEMENT

The choke cable starts out as a single cable at the lever on the handlebar lever and about halfway down it branches out into 2 cables, one for each carburetor.

1. Remove both side covers and the seat.

2. Remove the fuel tank as described in this chapter.

3. At the carburetor assembly, slide back the rubber boot on the choke cable (A, **Figure 49**).

4. Unscrew the choke valve nut (B, **Figure 49**) and remove the choke cable, valve and spring from the carburetor.

5. Repeat Step 3 and Step 4 for the other carburetor.

6. Remove the clutch switch wires at the clutch lever.

7. Remove the bolts and bracket (A, **Figure 61**) securing the clutch/choke bracket to the handlebar.

8. Remove the choke cable (B, **Figure 61**) from the choke lever assembly on the handlebar.

9. Remove the screw and remove the plastic trim panel (**Figure 62**) next to the right-hand side of the steering head.

NOTE
The piece of string attached in the next step will be used to pull the new choke cable back through the frame so it will be routed in the same position as the old cable.

10. Wrap the carburetor end of both choke cables together with masking tape.

11. Tie a piece of heavy string or cord (approximately 7 ft./2 m long) to the carburetor end

of the choke cables. Wrap this end with masking or duct tape. Do not use an excessive amount of tape as it must be pulled through the frame loop during removal. Tie the other end of the strings to the frame or air box.

12. Unhook the choke cables from any clips on the frame.

13. At the choke lever end of the cable, carefully pull the cable assembly (and attached strings) out through the frame and from behind the headlight housing. Make sure the attached strings follow the same path that the cable does through the frame.

14. Remove the tape and untie the strings from the old cable assembly.

15. Lubricate the new cable assembly as described in Chapter Three.

16. Tie the strings to the new choke cable assembly and wrap with tape.

17. Carefully pull the strings back through the frame routing the new cables through the same path as the old cables.

18. Remove the tape and untie the strings from the cable and the frame.

19. Attach the choke cable onto the choke lever assembly.

20. Install the choke valve into the carburetor body.

21. Tighten the choke valve nut by hand then turn it an additional 1/4 turn with a 14 mm wrench.

22. Repeat Step 20 and Step 21 for the other carburetor.

23. Install the switch/choke assembly on the handlebar and tighten the screws securely.

24. Attach the clutch switch wires to the clutch lever.

25. Operate the choke lever and make sure the carburetor choke linkage is operating correctly, with no binding. If operation is incorrect or there is binding carefully check that the cable is attached correctly and there are no tight bends in the cable.

26. Reinstall the fuel tank, seat and side covers.

27. Adjust the choke cable as described in this chapter.

FUEL SHUTOFF VALVE

Removal/Installation

Refer to **Figure 63** for this procedure.

1. Remove the fuel tank as described in this chapter.

2. Drain the fuel from the tank into a clean sealable metal container. If the fuel is kept clean it can be reused.

3. Place the fuel tank on its side on cloths to protect the finish.

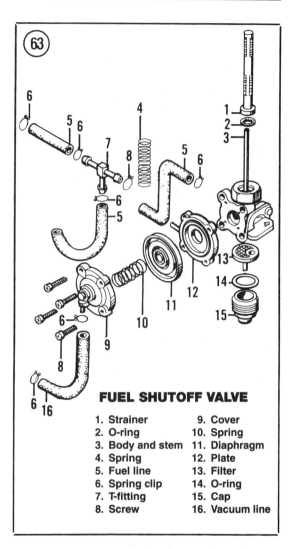

FUEL SHUTOFF VALVE

1. Strainer	9. Cover
2. O-ring	10. Spring
3. Body and stem	11. Diaphragm
4. Spring	12. Plate
5. Fuel line	13. Filter
6. Spring clip	14. O-ring
7. T-fitting	15. Cap
8. Screw	16. Vacuum line

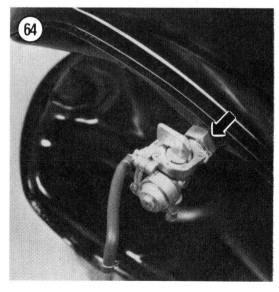

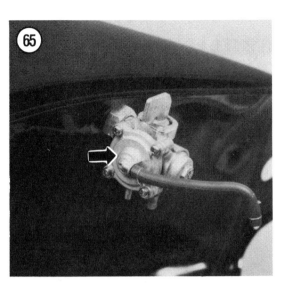

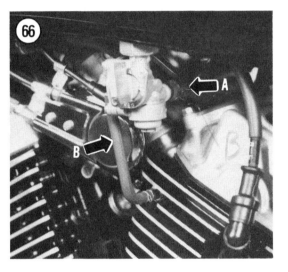

4. Unscrew the locknut securing the fuel shutoff valve to the fuel tank (**Figure 64**).

5. Remove the fuel filter from the shutoff valve. Clean it with a medium soft toothbrush and blow out with compressed air. Replace if defective.

6. To disassemble the vacuum controlled portion of the valve, perform the following:

     a. Remove the screws securing the cover and remove the cover and hose (**Figure 65**).

     b. Remove the spring, diaphragm and plate from the fuel shutoff valve.

     c. Inspect the diaphragm for deterioration or any holes.

     d. If any part of the vacuum controlled portion is defective the vacuum controlled portion must be replaced as an assembly (separate parts are not available). Honda does not provide test procedures for the vacuum controlled portion.

     e. Assemble by reversing these disassembly steps.

7. Install by reversing these removal steps, noting the following.

8. Be sure to install the gasket between the valve and the tank.

9. After installation is complete, thoroughly check for fuel leaks.

FUEL TANK

Removal/Installation

1. Place bike on the centerstand.

2. Remove the seat and both side panels.

3. Turn the fuel shutoff to the OFF position and disconnect the vacuum line (B, **Figure 66**) from the fitting on the cylinder head.

4. Disconnect the fuel line (A, **Figure 66**) from the carburetor assembly.

5. Remove the bolt and washer securing the rear of the fuel tank. Do not lose the metal spacer in the rubber cushion.

6A. On models equipped with the evaporative emission control system, perform the following:

     a. Lift up on the rear of the tank and pull the tank to the rear a short distance.

     b. Lift up the front of the tank and disconnect the vent line (**Figure 67**) going to the PCV valve.

     c. Remove the fuel tank.

6B. On all other models, lift up and pull the tank to the rear and remove it.

7. Install by reversing these removal steps.

CRANKCASE BREATHER SYSTEM (U.S. ONLY)

To comply with air pollution standards, the Honda V-twins are equipped with a crankcase breather system. The system draws blowby gases from crankcase and recirculates them into the fuel-air mixture and thus into the engine to be burned.

Inspection/Cleaning

Make sure all hose clamps are tight. Check all hoses for deterioration and replace as necessary.

Slide the drain tube out of the bracket on the battery holder. Remove the drain plug (**Figure 68**) from the drain hose and drain out all residue. This cleaning procedure should be done more frequently if a considerable amount of riding is done at full throttle or in the rain.

Install the drain plug and clamp.

EVAPORATIVE EMISSION CONTROL SYSTEM (1984-1986 CALIFORNIA MODELS ONLY)

Fuel vapor from the fuel tank is routed into a charcoal canister (**Figure 69**). This vapor is stored

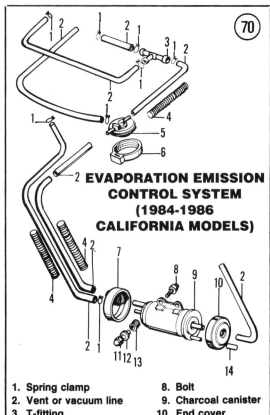

EVAPORATION EMISSION CONTROL SYSTEM (1984-1986 CALIFORNIA MODELS)

1. Spring clamp
2. Vent or vacuum line
3. T-fitting
4. Line protector
5. Purge control valve (PCV)
6. Valve holder
7. End cover
8. Bolt
9. Charcoal canister
10. End cover
11. Cap nut
12. Collar
13. Rubber grommet
14. Drain cap

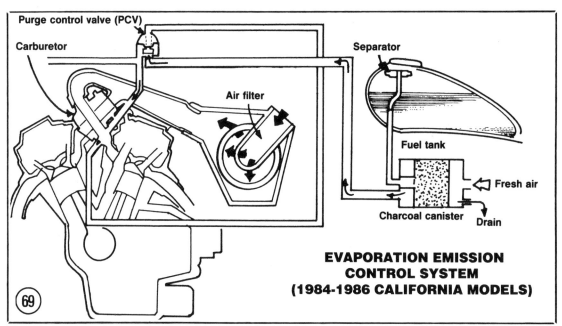

EVAPORATION EMISSION CONTROL SYSTEM (1984-1986 CALIFORNIA MODELS)

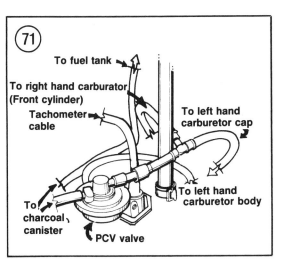

To fuel tank

To right hand carburator
(Front cylinder)

Tachometer
cable

To left hand
carbureter cap

To left hand
carburetor body

To
charcoal
canister

PCV valve

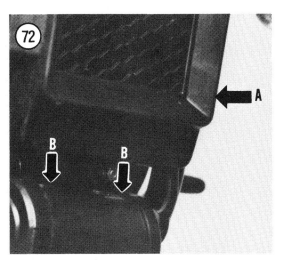

A

B   B

when the engine is not running. When the engine is running these vapors are drawn through a purge control valve and into the carburetor to be burned. Make sure all hose clamps are tight. Check all hoses for deterioration and replace as necessary (**Figure 70**).

Refer to **Figure 71** for correct hose routing to the PCV valve. When removing the hoses from the PCV valve, mark the hse and the fitting eith a piece of masking tape and identify ead as a set. These marks will be very helpful when re-attaching the hoses to the PCV valve.

Removal/Installation

1. Remove both side covers and the seat.
2. Remove the fuel tank as described in this chapter.
3. Remove the radiator trim panel (A, **Figure 72**).

NOTE
Prior to removing the hoses from the PCV valve, mark the hose and the fitting with a piece of masking tape to identify where the hose goes.

4. Disconnect the hoses from the PCV valve going to the charcoal canister.
5. Remove the hoses from the clip alongside the radiator.
6. Remove the bolts (B, **Figure 72**) securing the charcoal canister to the frame and remove the canister assembly.
7. Install by reversing these removal steps, noting the following.
8. Be sure to install the hoses to their correct place on the PCV valve.

EXHAUST SYSTEM (SHADOW)

1. Protector
2. Nut
3. Gasket
4. Exhaust pipe (rear cylinder)
5. Clamp
6. Bolt
7. Muffler gasket
8. Exhaust pipe (front cylinder)
9. Bolt
10. Protector
11. Nut
12. Power chamber
13. Protector
14. Bolt
15. Clamp
16. Muffler

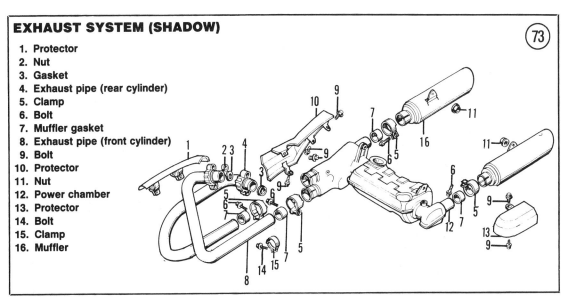

EXHAUST SYSTEM

The exhaust system consists of 2 exhaust pipes, a common collector and one or 2 mufflers depending on the model.

Removal/Installation

Refer to **Figure 73** (Shadow) or **Figure 74** (Ascot) for this procedure.
1. Place the bike on the centerstand.

2. Remove the nuts securing the exhaust pipe flanges to the front cylinder head (**Figure 75**) and the rear cylinder head (**Figure 76**).
3. Slide the flanges down.
4. Loosen the clamping bolts (**Figure 77**) securing each exhaust pipe to the power chamber.

NOTE
If difficult to remove, spray some WD-40 or equivalent on the clamping

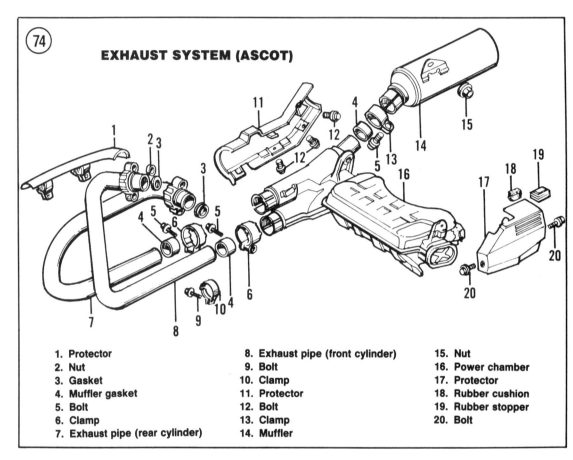

EXHAUST SYSTEM (ASCOT)

1. Protector	8. Exhaust pipe (front cylinder)	15. Nut
2. Nut	9. Bolt	16. Power chamber
3. Gasket	10. Clamp	17. Protector
4. Muffler gasket	11. Protector	18. Rubber cushion
5. Bolt	12. Bolt	19. Rubber stopper
6. Clamp	13. Clamp	20. Bolt
7. Exhaust pipe (rear cylinder)	14. Muffler	

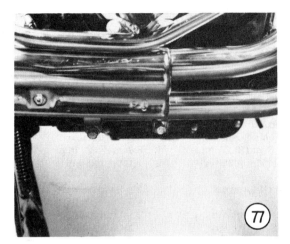

bolts to help loosen the exhaust pipes from the power chamber.

5. Remove the exhaust pipes from the power chamber.

6A. On VT500C models, remove the bolt, washer and nut (**Figure 78**) securing the mufflers to the rear footpeg bracket(s).

6B. On VT500FT models, remove the bolt, washer and nut (**Figure 79**) securing the muffler to the rear footpeg bracket.

NOTE
If difficult to remove, spray some WD-40 or equivalent on the clamping bolts to help loosen the mufflers from the power chamber.

7. Remove the muffler(s) from the power chamber.

8. On VT500FT models, remove the bolts securing the protective plate (**Figure 80**) and remove the protective plate.

9. Remove the bolt (**Figure 81**) on each side securing the power chamber to the frame and remove the power chamber.

10. Inspect the gaskets at all joints; replace as necessary.

11. Be sure to install a new gasket in each exhaust port in both cylinder heads.

12. Apply a light coat of multipurpose grease to the inside surface of the gaskets in the power chamber. This will make insertion of the exhaust pipes into the power chamber easier.

13. Install the assembly into position and install all bolts and nuts only finger-tight until the exhaust flange nuts and washers are installed and securely tightened. This will minimize an exhaust leak at the cylinder heads.

14. Tighten all bolts and nuts to the torque specifications listed in **Table 2**.

15. After installation is complete, make sure there are no exhaust leaks.

6

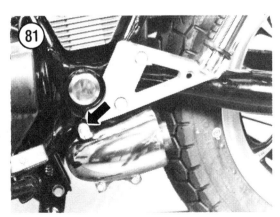

Table 1 CARBURETOR SPECIFICATIONS

	1983-1988 VT500E	1983 VT500C	1984 VT500C
Carburetor model No.	VD6UA	D64A	VD6HA VD6KA (Calif.)
Main jet number			
Front cylinder	No. 112	No. 112	No. 112
Rear cylinder	No. 122	No. 122	No. 122
Slow jet	No. 38	No. 38	No. 38
Jet needle clip setting	Non-adjustable	Non-adjustable	Non-adjustable
Float level	6.8 mm (0.27 in.)	6.8 mm (0.27 in.)	6.8 mm (0.27 in.)
Idle speed	1,100 ± 100 rpm	1,100 ± 100 rpm	1,100 ± 100 rpm
Pilot screw initial setting			
Front cylinder	2 1/4 turns out	2 1/4 turns out	2 1/4 turns out 1 3/4 turns out (Calif.)
Rear cylinder	2 1/4 turns out	2 1/4 turns out	2 1/4 turns out 1 3/4 turns out (Calif.)

	1985 VT500C	1986 VT500C
Carburetor model No.	VD6HC VD6LA (Calif.)	VD6HD VD6LB (Calif.)
Main jet number		
Front cylinder	No. 112	No. 112 (No. 108, Calif.)
Rear cylinder	No. 122	No. 120 (No. 115, Calif.)
Slow jet	No. 38	No. 38
Jet needle clip setting	Non-adjustable	Non-adjustable
Float level	6.8 mm (0.27 in.)	7.0 mm (0.28 in.)
Idle speed	1,100 ± 100 rpm	1,100 ± 100 rpm
Pilot screw initial setting		
Front cylinder	2 1/4 turns out 1 3/4 turns out (Calif.)	2 1/4 turns out 1 3/4 turns out (Calif.)
Rear cylinder	2 1/4 turns out 1 3/4 turns out (Calif.)	2 1/4 turns out 1 3/4 turns out (Calif.)

	1983 VT500FT	1984 VT500FT
Carburetor model No.	VD6HA	VD6JA VD6LA (Calif.)
Main jet number		
Front cylinder	No. 112	No. 112
Rear cylinder	No. 122	No. 120
Slow jet	No. 38	No. 38
Jet needle clip setting	Non-adjustable	Non-adjustable
Float level	6.8 mm (0.27 in.)	6.8 mm (0.27 in.)
Idle speed	1,100 ± 100 rpm	1,100 ± 100 rpm
Pilot screw initial setting		
Front cylinder	2 1/4 turns out	2 1/4 turns out 1 3/4 turns out (Calif.)
Rear cylinder	2 1/4 turns out	2 1/4 turns out 1 3/4 turns out (Calif.)

Table 2 EXHAUST SYSTEM TORQUE SPECIFICATIONS

Item	N·m	ft.-lb.
Exhaust pipe joint nut	8-14	6-10
Exhaust pipe clamping band bolts	20-28	14-20
Muffler clamp bolt	20-28	14-20

ELECTRICAL SYSTEM

The electrical system consists of the following:
a. Charging system.
b. Ignition system.
c. Lighting system.
d. Directional signal system.
e. Switches.
f. Electrical components.

Wiring diagrams are at the end of the book. **Tables 1-3** are located at the end of this chapter.

For complete spark plug and battery information, refer to Chapter Three.

CHARGING SYSTEM

The charging system consists of the battery, alternator and a voltage regulator/rectifier (**Figure 1**).

Alternating current generated by the alternator is rectified to direct current. The voltage regulator

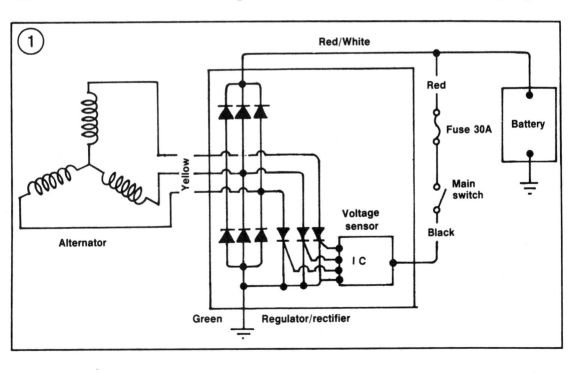

maintains the voltage to the battery and additional electrical loads (lights, ignition, etc.) at a constant voltage regardless of variations in engine speed and load.

Output Test

Whenever a charging system trouble is suspected, make sure the battery is fully charged and in good condition before going any further. Clean and test the battery as described in Chapter Three.

Prior to starting this test, start the bike and let it reach normal operating temperature; shut off the engine.

1. Remove the right-hand side cover and the seat.
2. Remove the headlight and disconnect the electrical wires going to the bulb.
3. Disconnect the regulator/rectifier 5-pin connector (**Figure 2**). Use a narrow blade screwdriver and carefully push the male end of the black wire out of the connector. Reconnect the connector with the black wire left out in the open, not connected.

> *NOTE*
> *Do not disconnect either the positive or negative battery cables; they are to remain in the circuit.*

4. Connect a 0-10 *DC* ammeter in line with the main fuse connectors (fusible link). Loosen the screws securing the fusible link (**Figure 3**) and remove the fusible link. Install an inline fuse/fuse holder (available at most auto supply or electronic supply stores) along with the ammeter as shown in **Figure 4**. Use alligator clips on the test leads for a good electrical connection.

> *CAUTION*
> *In order to protect the ammeter, always run the test with the inline fuse in the circuit. Do not try to test the charging system by connecting an ammeter between the positive battery terminal and the starter cable. The ammeter will burn out when the electric starter is operated.*

> *NOTE*
> *During the test, if the needle of the ammeter reads in the opposite direction on the scale, reverse the polarity of the test leads.*

5. Start the engine and gradually increase engine speed. Charging amperage should start at 1,000 rpm and should be a minimum of 11.8 amperes. At 5,000 rpm it should be a minimum of 25.6 amperes. If the charging amperage is not within specifications,

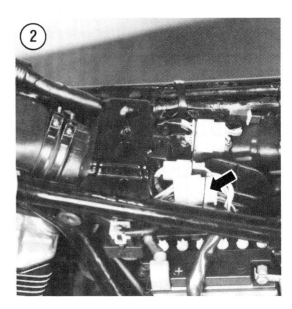

first check the alternator stator and then the voltage regulator/rectifier as described in this chapter.
6. Disconnect the ammeter and reinstall the fusible link.
7. Reinstall the headlight and reconnect the black wire to the voltage regulator/rectifier connector.

ALTERNATOR

An alternator is a form of electrical generator in which a magnetized field called a rotor revolves within a set of stationary coils called a stator. As the rotor revolves, alternating current is induced in the stator. The current is then rectified to direct current and used to operate the electrical accessories on the

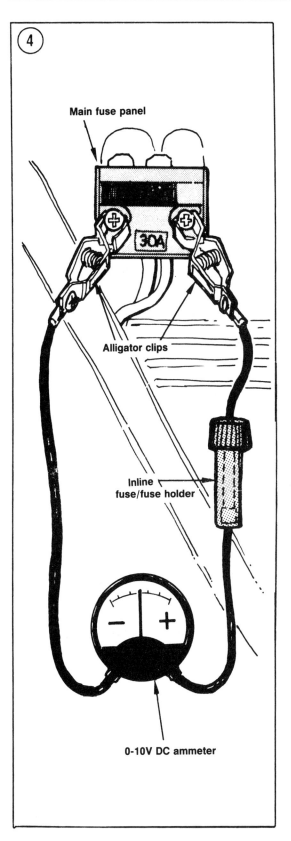

Main fuse panel

30A

Alligator clips

Inline fuse/fuse holder

0-10V DC ammeter

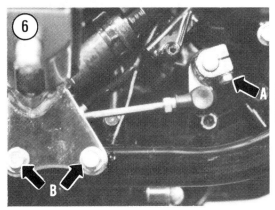

7

motorcycle and to charge the battery. The rotor is permanently magnetized.

Rotor removal/installation procedures are described in Chapter Four.

Rotor Testing

The rotor is permanently magnetized and cannot be tested except by replacement with a rotor known to be good. A rotor can lose magnetism from old age or a sharp blow. If defective, the rotor must be replaced; it cannot be remagnetized.

Stator Removal/Installation

1. Place the bike on the centerstand.
2. Remove both side covers and the seat.
3. Disconnect the battery negative lead.
4. Disconnect the electrical connector (**Figure 5**) going to the alternator stator assembly.
5. Remove the screws securing the left-hand rear crankcase cover and remove the cover.
6. Remove the bolt (A, **Figure 6**) securing the gearshift pedal to the gearshift spindle assembly.
7. Remove the bolts (B, **Figure 6**) securing the front left-hand front footpeg and remove the footpeg/gearshift assembly.

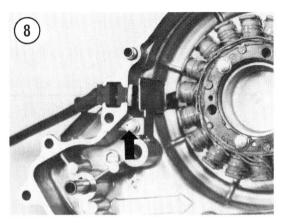

8. Remove the bolts securing the alternator cover (**Figure 7**) and remove the cover, gasket and the electrical harness from the frame. Note the path of the wire harness as it must be routed the same during installation.

9. Remove the electrical harness from the clips on the frame.

10. Remove the bolt and wire clamp (**Figure 8**) securing the wire to the housing.

11. Remove the bolts (**Figure 9**) securing the alternator stator to the alternator cover.

12. Carefully pull the rubber grommet and electrical wire harness from the alternator cover.

13. Install by reversing these removal steps, noting the following.

14. Be sure to install the wire clamp. If the clamp is left off the rotor may rub against the wires, wear off the insulation and cause a short in the circuit.

Stator Testing

1. Remove both side covers and the seat.

2. Disconnect the 3-pin alternator electrical connector (**Figure 5**).

3. Use an ohmmeter set at R×1 and check continuity between each yellow terminal. Replace the stator if any yellow terminal shows no continuity (infinite resistance) to any other. This would indicate an open in the winding.

4. Use an ohmmeter and check for continuity between each yellow terminal and ground. Replace the stator if any of the terminals show continuity (low resistance) to ground. This would indicate a short within a winding.

> *NOTE*
> *Prior to replacing the stator with a new one, check the electrical wires to and within the terminal connector for any opens or poor connections.*

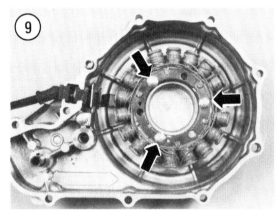

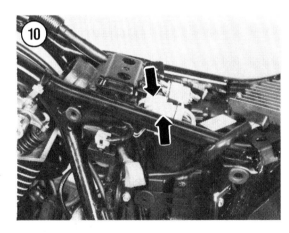

VOLTAGE REGULATOR/RECTIFIER

Removal/Installation

1. Remove both side covers and the seat.

2. Disconnect the battery negative lead.

3. Disconnect the 2 electrical connectors. One connector contains 5 wires and the other contains 3 wires (**Figure 10**).

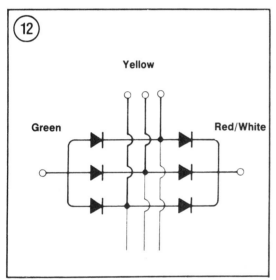

Yellow

Green   Red/White

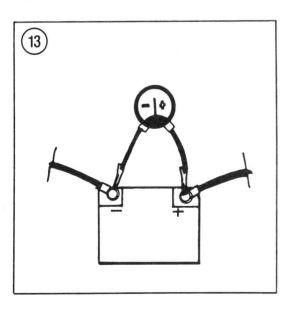

4. Remove the bolts securing the voltage regulator/rectifier to the battery holder and remove the voltage regulator/rectifier (**Figure 11**).

5. Carefully pull the voltage regulator/rectifier and the 2 electrical connectors and wires out from the frame.

6. Install by reversing these removal steps. Make sure all electrical connections are tight.

Testing

To test the voltage regulator/rectifier, disconnect the 2 electrical connectors from the harness. One connector contains 5 wires and the other contains 3 wires (**Figure 10**).

Make the following measurements using an ohmmeter and referring to **Figure 12**.

NOTE
The following tests are set up for a positive ground ohmmeter. If a negative ground ohmmeter is used the test results will be the opposite.

1. Connect the positive (+) ohmmeter lead to the yellow lead and the negative (–) ohmmeter lead to the green lead. There should be continuity (low resistance).

2. Reverse the ohmmeter leads and repeat Step 1. This time there should be no continuity (infinite resistance).

3. Connect the positive (+) ohmmeter lead to the red/white lead and the negative (–) ohmmeter lead to the yellow lead. There should be continuity (low resistance).

4. Reverse the ohmmeter leads and repeat Step 3. This time there should be no continuity (infinite resistance).

5. If the voltage regulator/rectifier fails to pass any of these tests the unit is defective and must be replaced.

Voltage Regulator
Performance Test

Connect a voltmeter to the battery negative and positive terminals (**Figure 13**). Leave the battery cables attached. Start the engine and let it idle; increase engine speed until the voltage going to the battery reaches 14.0-15.0 volts. At this point, the voltage regulator/rectifier should prevent any further increase in voltage. If this does not happen and voltage increases above specifications, the voltage regulator/rectifier is faulty and must be replaced.

IGNITION SYSTEM

The ignition system consists of 2 ignition coils, 2 spark units, 2 ignition pulse generators and 4 spark

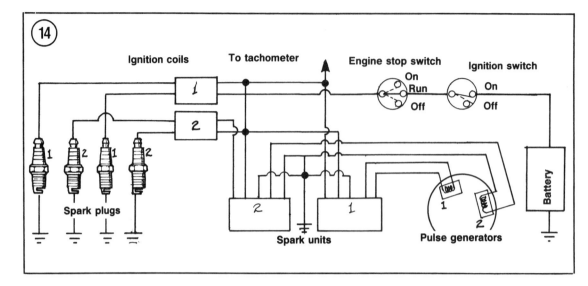

plugs (2 spark plugs per cylinder). Refer to **Figure 14** for a diagram of the ignition circuit.

The V-twins are equipped with a solid state capacitor discharge ignition (CDI) system that uses no breaker points. This system provides a longer life for components and delivers a more efficient spark throughout the entire speed range of the engine. Ignition timing is fixed with no means of adjustment. If ignition timing is incorrect it is due to a faulty unit within the ignition system.

Direct current charges the capacitor. As the piston approaches the firing position, a pulse from the pulse generator coil triggers the silicone controlled rectifier. The rectifier in turn allows the capacitor to discharge quickly into the primary circuit of the ignition coil, where the voltage is stepped up in the secondary circuit to a value sufficient to fire the spark plugs. Both spark plugs in the same cylinder will fire at the same time. The distribution of the pulses from the pulse generators is controlled by the rotation of the pulse generator plate that is attached to the primary drive gear.

CDI Precautions

Certain measures must be taken to protect the capacitor discharge system. Instantaneous damage to the semiconductors in the system will occur if the following precautions are not observed.
1. Never connect the battery backwards. If the connected battery polarity is wrong, damage will occur to the voltage regulator/rectifier, the alternator and the spark units.
2. Do not disconnect the battery when the engine is running. A voltage surge will occur which will damage the voltage regulator/rectifier and possibly burn out the lights.

3. Keep all connections between the various units clean and tight. Be sure that the wiring connections are pushed together firmly to help keep out moisture.
4. Do not substitute another type of ignition coil.
5. Each component is mounted within a rubber vibration isolator. Always be sure that the isolator is in place when installing any units in the system.

CDI Troubleshooting

Problems with the capacitor discharge system are usually the production of a weak spark or no spark at all.
1. Check all connections to make sure they are tight and free of corrosion.
2. Check the ignition coils as described in this chapter.

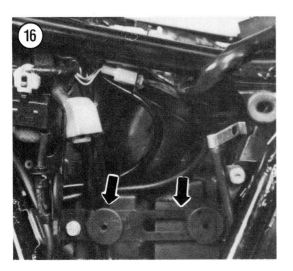

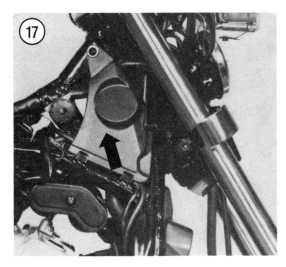

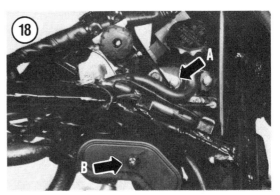

3. Check the ignition pulse generator coils with an ohmmeter:

   a. Remove the seat, both side covers and the fuel tank.

   b. Disconnect the 4-pin ignition pulse generator electrical connector (**Figure 15**).

   c. Connect the ohmmeter leads between the white and the yellow leads (rear cylinder) and then between the white and the blue leads (front cylinder).

   d. The resistance for each coil should be 480 ohms ±10% at 68° F (20° C). If the pulse generator coils do not meet these specifications the ignition pulse generator assembly must be replaced as described in this chapter. It cannot be serviced.

4. If the ignition coils and ignition pulse generator assembly check out okay, the spark units are at fault and must be replaced.

SPARK UNIT

Replacement

1. Remove the seat and both side covers.

2. Remove the battery as described in Chapter Three.

3. Disconnect the electrical connectors going to the spark units.

4. Remove the spark units (**Figure 16**) from the back of the battery compartment.

5. Install by reversing these removal steps. Make sure all electrical connections are tight and free of corrosion.

Testing

Honda does not provide test procedures or specifications for the spark units. If the ignition coils, the pulse generator assembly and the wiring harness are good and the ignition timing is not within specifications, replace the spark units with known good units.

IGNITION COIL

There are 2 ignition coils; one fires the plugs for the front cylinder and the other fires the plugs for the rear cylinder.

The ignition coil is a form of transformer which develops the high voltage required to jump the spark plugs gap. The only maintenance required is that of keeping the electrical connections clean and tight and occasionally checking to see that the coils are mounted securely.

Removal/Installation

1. Remove both side covers, seat and fuel tank.

2. Disconnect the battery negative lead.

3. Disconnect the spark plug leads.

4. Remove the screw and plastic trim panel on the right-hand side of the steering head (**Figure 17**).

5. Remove the trim panel on the right-hand side of the coil assembly (A, **Figure 18**).

7

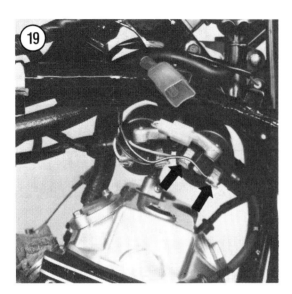

6. Disconnect the primary wire connectors (**Figure 19**) for both coils. The front cylinder's wires are yellow and black/white; the rear cylinder's wires are blue and black/white.

7. Remove the bolts (B, **Figure 18**) and brackets securing the ignition coils to the frame and remove both coils.

8. Install by reversing these removal steps; note the following.

9. Make sure all electrical connections are tight and free of corrosion.

10. Route the spark plug wires to the correct cylinder. Each spark plug wire is numbered next to the spark plug rubber boot.

Dynamic Test

Disconnect the high voltage lead from one of the spark plugs. Remove the spark plug from the cylinder head. Connect a new or known good spark plug to the high voltage lead and place the spark plug base on a good ground like the engine cylinder head (**Figure 20**). Position the spark plug so you can see the electrodes.

WARNING
If it is necessary to hold the high voltage lead, do so with an insulated pair of pliers. The high voltage generated could produce serious or fatal shocks.

Push the starter button to turn the engine over a couple of times. If a fat blue spark occurs the coil is in good condition; if not it must be replaced. Make sure that you are using a known good spark plug for this test. If the spark plug used is defective the test results will be incorrect.

Reinstall the spark plug in the cylinder head.

Continuity Test

1. Use an ohmmeter set at $R \times 10$ and measure between the 2 primary connector lugs on the coil. The specified resistance is 2.0 ohms.

2. Use an ohmmeter set at $R \times 1,000$ and measure between the 2 secondary leads (spark plug leads) with the spark plug caps in place. The specified resistance is 29,000-40,000 ohms.

3. Use an ohmmeter set at $R \times 10$ and measure between the 2 secondary leads (spark plug leads) with the spark plug caps removed. The specified resistance is 20.6-27.4 ohms.

4. If the coil(s) pass the test in Step 3 but fail Step 2, the spark plug caps may be faulty. Disconnect the spark plug leads from the ignition coil. Use an ohmmeter and check for continuity through the spark plug cap. (There should be high resistance). If there is no continuity at all the spark plug cap is faulty and must be replaced.

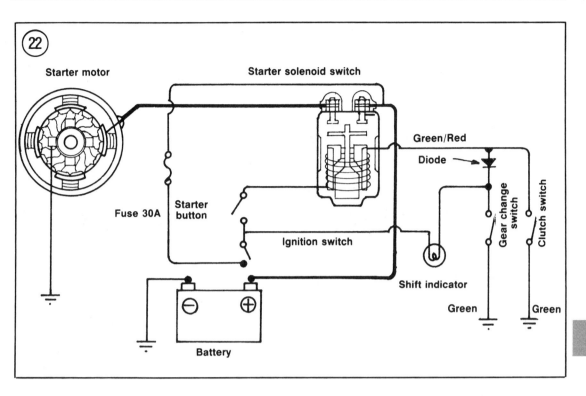

Starter motor

Starter solenoid switch

Green/Red

Diode

Gear change switch

Clutch switch

Fuse 30A

Starter button

Ignition switch

Shift indicator

Green

Green

Battery

5. If the coil(s) fail to pass any of these tests the coil should be replaced.

PULSE GENERATOR

Removal/Installation

1. Drain the engine oil as described in Chapter Three.
2. Remove the seat and both side covers.
3. Remove the fuel tank as described under in Chapter Six.
4. Perform Steps 1-7 of *Clutch Removal/Disassembly* in Chapter Five.
5. Disconnect the 4-pin ignition pulse generator electrical connector (**Figure 15**).
6. Remove the bolts securing each pulse generator (A, **Figure 21**) to the crankcase.
7. Carefully remove the rubber grommet (B, **Figure 21**) and electrical wires from the crankcase and remove the assembly from the frame.
8. Install by reversing these removal steps, noting the following.
9. Make sure the bolts securing the pulse generators are tight and that the wires are routed correctly in the frame.
10. Perform Steps 19-25 of *Clutch Assembly/Installation* in Chapter Five.
11. Refill the engine with the recommended viscosity and quantity of engine oil as described in Chapter Three.

STARTING SYSTEM

The starting system consists of the starter motor, starter gears, solenoid and the starter button.

The layout of the starting system is shown in **Figure 22**. When the starter button is pressed, it allows current flow through the solenoid coil. The solenoid coil contacts close, allowing electricity to flow from the battery to the starter motor.

> *CAUTION*
> *Do not operate the starter for more than 5 seconds at a time. Let it rest approximately 10 seconds, then use it again.*

The starter gears and starter clutch assembly are covered in Chapter Four.

Table 1, at the end of the chapter, lists possible starter problems, probable causes and most common remedies.

STARTER

Removal/Installation

1. Place the bike on the centerstand.
2. Remove the seat and both side covers.
3. Disconnect the battery negative lead.
4. Drain the coolant as described in Chapter Three.
5. Remove the exhaust pipe from the rear cylinder as described in Chapter Six.

6. Remove the right-hand coolant pipe as described in Chapter Eight.

7. Disconnect the electric starter cable from the starter (**Figure 23**).

8. Remove the bolts (**Figure 24**) securing the starter to the crankcase.

9. Pull the starter to the right and remove the starter from the crankcase.

10. Install by reversing these removal steps. Make sure the electrical wire connection is tight and free of corrosion.

11. Refill the cooling system as described in Chapter Three.

Disassembly/Inspection/ Assembly

The overhaul of a starter motor is best left to an expert. This procedure shows how to detect a defective starter.

1. Remove the case screws and separate the case and covers.

> *NOTE*
> *Write down the number of shims used on the shaft next to the commutator. Be sure to install the same number when assembling the starter.*

2. Clean all grease, dirt and carbon from the armature, case and end covers.

> *CAUTION*
> *Do not immerse brushes or the wire windings in solvent as the insulation may be damaged. Wipe the windings with a cloth lightly moistened with solvent and dry thoroughly.*

3. Measure the length of each brush (**Figure 25**) with a vernier caliper. If the length is 6.5 mm (0.26 in.) or less for any one of the brushs, the brush

holder assembly and cable terminal and brush assembly must be replaced. The brushes cannot be replaced individually.

4. To replace the brushes, perform the following:

> *NOTE*
> *Prior to removing the nuts and washers, write down their description and order. They must be reinstalled in the same order to insulate this set of brushes from the case.*

a. Remove the nuts, washers and O-ring (A, **Figure 26**) securing the cable terminal and brush assembly.

b. Slide the armature and brush holder assemblies partially out of the case.

c. Remove the old brush holders and install new brush holders.

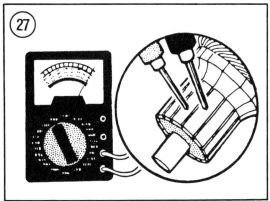

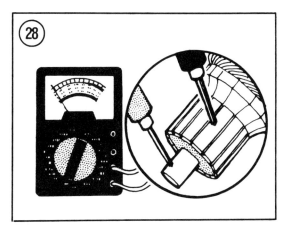

7

d. Slide the armature and brush holder assemblies back into the case.

e. Install the nuts and washers in the original order to secure the cable terminal and brush assembly.

5. Inspect the commutator. The mica in a good commutator is below the surface of the copper bars. On a worn commutator the mica and copper bars may be worn to the same level. If necessary, have the commutator serviced by a dealer or electrical repair shop.

6. Inspect the commutator copper bars for discoloration. If a pair of bars are discolored, grounded armature coils are indicated.

7. Use an ohmmeter and check for continuity between the commutator bars (**Figure 27**); there should be continuity (low resistance) between pairs of bars. Also check for continuity between the commutator bars and the shaft (**Figure 28**); there should be no continuity (infinite resistance). If the unit fails either of these tests the armature is faulty and must be replaced.

8. Use an ohmmeter and check for continuity between the starter cable terminal and the starter case; there should be no continuity (infinite resistance). Also check for continuity between the starter cable terminal and each brush wire terminal; there should be continuity (low resistance). If the unit fails either of these tests the case/field coil assembly must be replaced.

9. Assemble the case as follows:

a. Align the pin in the brush holder with the notch in the case (**Figure 29**).

b. Align the slot in the rear cover (B, **Figure 26**) with the pin on the brush holder (C, **Figure 26**).

c. Align the marks on the case and end covers (**Figure 30**).

10. Inspect the gear and O-ring seal (**Figure 31**). If the gear is chipped or worn the armature must be replaced. Replace the O-ring if it has hardened or is starting to deteriorate.

STARTER SOLENOID

Removal/Installation

1. Remove the seat and both side covers.
2. Disconnect the negative battery lead.
3. Disconnect the electrical connector (**Figure 32**) from the top of the main fuse holder.
4. Slide off the rubber protective boots and disconnect the electrical wires from the top terminals (**Figure 33**).
5. Remove the solenoid from the rubber mounting receptacle on the frame along with the main fuse holder that is attached to it.
6. Install by reversing these removal steps, noting the following.
7. If installing a new solenoid, transfer the fuse holder from the old solenoid to the new solenoid.

CLUTCH DIODE

Testing

1. Remove the seat and right-hand side cover.
2. Disconnect the clutch diode from the wire harness.
3. Use an ohmmeter and check for continuity between the 2 terminals on the clutch diode. There should be continuity (low resistance) in the normal direction and no continuity (infinite resistance) in the reverse direction. Replace the diode if it fails this test.

LIGHTING SYSTEM

The lighting system consists of a headlight, taillight/brake light combination, turn signals, indicator lights and speedometer and tachometer illumination lights. **Table 2** lists replacement bulbs for these components.

Always use the correct wattage bulb as indicated in this section. The use of a larger wattage bulb will give a dim light and a smaller wattage bulb will burn out prematurely.

Headlight Replacement

The headlight is equipped with a quartz halogen bulb. Special handling of the bulb is required as specified in this procedure.

Refer to **Figure 34** for this procedure.

NOTE
A round headlight assembly is used on 1985-1986 models. The lens and bulb are replaced as an assembly. Remove the headlight bezel screws to remove the bezel and headlight.

Refer to **Figure 34** for this procedure.

1. Remove the screw (**Figure 35**) on the bottom of the trim bezel securing the headlight assembly.
2. Pull out on the bottom of the headlight assembly and disengage it from the locating tab on top of the headlight housing.
3. Disconnect the electrical connector (A, **Figure 36**) from the headlight lens unit.

4. Remove the bulb cover (B, **Figure 36**).

CAUTION
Carefully read all instructions shipped with the replacement quartz halogen bulb. Do not touch the bulb glass with your fingers because of oil on your skin. Any traces of oil on the glass will drastically reduce the life of the bulb. Clean any traces of oil from the bulb with a cloth moistened in alcohol or lacquer thinner.

5. Remove the set spring (**Figure 37**) and bulb assembly (**Figure 38**). Replace with a new bulb assembly—do not touch the bulb with your fingers. Assemble by reversing this sequence.

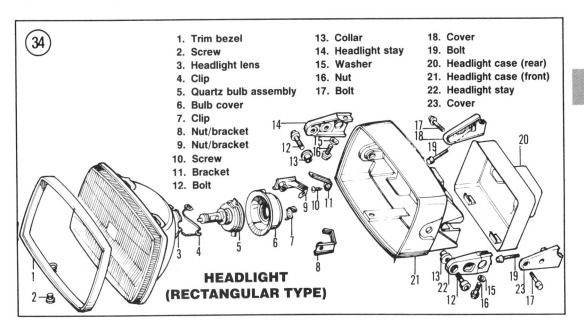

(34)

1. Trim bezel
2. Screw
3. Headlight lens
4. Clip
5. Quartz bulb assembly
6. Bulb cover
7. Clip
8. Nut/bracket
9. Nut/bracket
10. Screw
11. Bracket
12. Bolt

13. Collar
14. Headlight stay
15. Washer
16. Nut
17. Bolt

18. Cover
19. Bolt
20. Headlight case (rear)
21. Headlight case (front)
22. Headlight stay
23. Cover

7

HEADLIGHT (RECTANGULAR TYPE)

(35)

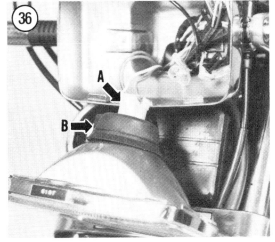

(36)

6. Install by reversing these removal steps.

7. Adjust the headlight as described in this chapter.

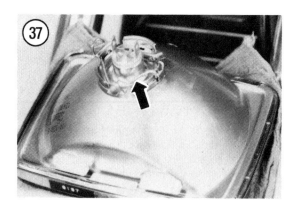

Headlight Housing
Removal/Installation

Refer to **Figure 34** for this procedure.

1. Remove the headlight (A, **Figure 39**) as described in this chapter.

2. Remove the Allen bolts (B, **Figure 39**) on each side securing the headlight case assembly to the case mounting bracket on the forks.

3. Disconnect all electrical connectors within the headlight housing (**Figure 40**).

4. Carefully withdraw the electrical connectors through the headlight housing and remove the housing.

5. To remove the assembly mounting bracket, remove the bolt securing each headlight bracket/turn signal assembly to the upper fork bridge. Remove both bracket assemblies.

6. Install by reversing these removal steps, noting the following.

7. Install the headlight bracket/turn signal bracket and align the index mark on the bracket with the index mark on the upper fork bridge.

8. Prior to installing the headlight lens assembly, check out the operation of the following items controlled by the electrical connections in the headlight housing:

   a. Headlight.

   b. Right and left turn signals.

9. Adjust the headlight as described in this chapter.

Headlight Adjustment

Adjust the headlight horizontally and vertically according to Department of Motor Vehicle regulations in your area.

To adjust the rectangular type headlight horizontally, loosen the bolt (B, **Figure 39**) on each side of the headlight mounting case. Move the headlight assembly either to the right or left until the headlight is positioned correctly. Tighten both bolts securely. To adjust the round type headlight horizontally, rotate the screw in the left-hand side of the trim bezel to redirect aim.

To adjust the headlight vertically, loosen the bolts (**Figure 41**) on each side of the headlight assembly. Position the headlight correctly. Tighten the bolts.

Taillight/Brake Light
Replacement (Ascot)

1. Remove the screws securing the lens and remove the lens.

2. Wash the inside and outside of the lens with a mild detergent and wipe dry. Wipe off the reflective base surrounding the bulbs with a soft cloth.

3. Inspect the lens gasket and replace if it is damaged or deteriorated.

4. Replace the bulb(s) and install the lens; do not overtighten the screws as the lens may crack.

Taillight/Brake Light Replacement (Shadow)

1. Remove the seat.

2. Push in on the bulb socket assembly (A, **Figure 42**) and turn clockwise until the socket assembly disengages from the assembly.

3. Remove the bulb from the socket assembly (**Figure 43**).

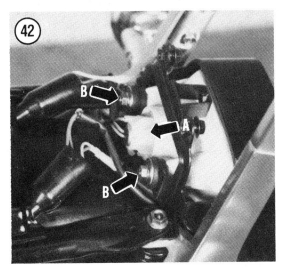

4. To remove the lens, remove the cap nuts and washers (B, **Figure 42**) securing the lens. Remove the lens assembly out toward the rear.

5. If the inside of the lens assembly is dirty, wash out the inside and outside of the lens with a mild detergent. Wipe dry with a cloth and then blow dry the inside with compressed air. If possible let the lens assembly dry in the sun or carefully blow dry with a portable hair drier. All moisture must be removed from within the lens assembly or the electrical connections within the socket assembly may rust or corrode.

6. Inspect the gasket on the bulb socket assembly and replace if it is damaged or deteriorated.

7. If removed, install the lens assembly; do not overtighten the cap nuts as the lens may crack.

8. Replace the bulb and bulb assembly.

9. Install the seat.

Turn Signal Light Replacement

1. Remove the screws (**Figure 44**) securing the lens and remove the lens.

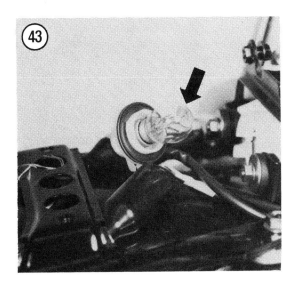

2. Wash the inside and outside of the lens with a mild detergent and wipe dry.

3. Inspect the lens gasket and replace if it is damaged or deteriorated.

4. Replace the bulb and install the lens; do not overtighten the screws as the lens may crack.

**Meter Illumination Light and
Indicator Light Replacement
(Ascot)**

1. Remove the instrument cluster (**Figure 45**) as described in this chapter.

2. Remove the nuts securing the metal mounting bracket to the rear of the instrument cluster. Remove the mounting bracket.

3. Remove the trip meter reset knob.

4. On the face of the instrument cluster, remove the Allen bolts in the 4 corners securing the meter cover and meter assemblies to the instrument cluster base. Remove the instrument cluster base.

5. Carefully pull the socket/bulb assembly out of the backside of the meter assembly.

6. Replace the defective bulb(s).

7. Assemble and install by reversing these disassembly steps.

**Meter Illumination Light and
Indicator Light Replacement
(Shadow)**

1. Remove the instrument cluster as described in this chapter.

2. Remove the Phillips screws securing the lower cover and remove the lower cover.

3. To replace the indicator lights, perform the following:
   a. Remove the Phillips screw securing the indicator panel to the mounting bracket and remove the indicator panel.
   b. Carefully remove the bulb(s) from the indicator panel.
   c. Replace the defective bulb(s).

4. To replace the meter illumination lights, perform the following:
   a. Remove the screws securing the meters to the instrument cluster.
   b. Withdraw the meters from the instrument cluster.
   c. Carefully pull the socket/bulb assembly out of the backside of the meter.
   d. Replace the defective bulb(s).

5. Assemble and install by reversing these disassembly steps.

SWITCHES

**Ignition Switch
Removal/Installation**

1. Remove the left-hand side cover and the seat.

2. Disconnect the battery negative lead.

3. Remove the headlight and case as described in this chapter.

CAUTION

The fork cover panel is plastic has one mounting post in the middle. This part can easily be broken if not removed carefully.

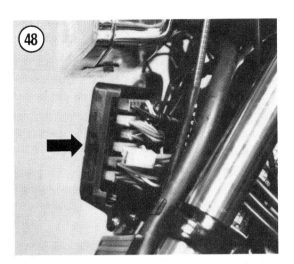

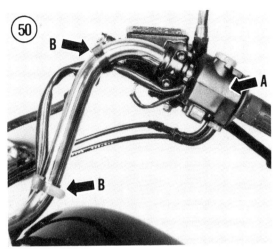

3. Push in on the lugs of the electrical switch portion, depressing them enough to clear the slots in the mechanical portion of the switch assembly.

4. Withdraw the electrical switch from the mechanical portion of the ignition switch.

5. Replace the defective component.

6. Assemble by reversing these disassembly steps.

**Engine Stop Switch and
Starter Button
Removal/Installation**

The engine stop switch and starter button are an integral part of the right-hand switch assembly. If either of these switches are faulty the entire switch assembly must be replaced.

1. Remove the headlight as described in this chapter.

CAUTION
The fork cover panel is plastic and has one mounting post in the middle. This part can easily be broken if not removed carefully.

2. Carefully pull on the *center* of the fork cover panel (**Figure 46**) and remove it from the rubber grommet on the lower fork bridge.

3. Remove the screws (**Figure 47**) securing the junction box to the lower fork bridge.

4. Carefully pull the junction box away from the lower fork bridge and remove the back cover from the junction box.

5. Disconnect the 11-pin electrical connector (going to the right-hand switch assembly) from the junction box panel (**Figure 48**).

6. Remove the screws clamping the right-hand switch assembly together (A, **Figure 50**).

7. Unhook any straps (B, **Figure 50**) securing the electrical wires to the handlebar.

4. Carefully pull on the *center* of the fork cover panel (**Figure 46**) and remove it from the rubber grommet on the lower fork bridge.

5. Remove the screws (**Figure 47**) securing the junction box to the lower fork bridge.

6. Carefully pull the junction box away from the lower fork bridge and remove the back cover from the junction box.

7. Disconnect the 2 white electrical connectors from the junction box panel (**Figure 48**).

8. Remove the bolts (**Figure 49**) securing the ignition switch to the upper fork bridge.

9. Install by reversing these removal steps.

**Ignition Switch
Disassembly/Assembly**

1. Open the wire clamp on the wire harness at the base of the switch.

2. Insert the ignition key and turn the tumbler in between the ON and OFF position. The key must be between the detents.

8. Remove the right-hand switch assembly and electrical wires from the frame.

9. Install a new switch by reversing these removal steps, noting the following.

10. Make sure all electrical connections are free of corrosion and are tight.

Headlight Dimmer Switch, Horn Button and Turn Signal Switch Removal/Installation

The headlight dimmer switch, horn button and turn signal switch are an integral part of the left-hand switch assembly. If any parts are faulty the entire switch assembly must be replaced.

1. Remove the headlight as described in this chapter.

> *CAUTION*
> *The fork cover panel is plastic and has one mounting post in the middle. This part can easily be broken if not removed carefully.*

2. Carefully pull on the *center* of the fork cover panel (**Figure 46**) and remove it from the rubber grommet on the lower fork bridge.

3. Remove the screws (**Figure 47**) securing the junction box to the lower fork bridge.

4. Carefully pull the junction box away from the lower fork bridge and remove the back cover from the junction box.

5. Disconnect the 11-pin electrical connector (going to the right-hand switch assembly) from the junction box panel (**Figure 48**).

6. Remove the screws clamping the left-hand switch assembly together (A, **Figure 51**).

7. Unhook any straps (B, **Figure 51**) securing the electrical wires to the handlebar.

8. Remove the left-hand switch assembly and electrical wires from the frame.

9. Install a new switch by reversing these removal steps, noting the following.

10. Make sure all electrical connections are free of corrosion and are tight.

Clutch Switch Testing/Replacement

1. Disconnect the electrical wires (**Figure 52**) from the clutch switch.

2. Use an ohmmeter and check for continuity between the 2 terminals on the clutch switch. There should be no continuity (infinite resistance) with the clutch lever released. With the clutch lever applied there should be continuity (low resistance). If the switch fails either of these tests the switch must be replaced.

3. Remove the screw securing the clutch switch and remove the clutch switch from the clutch lever assembly.

4. Install a new switch by reversing these removal steps, noting the following.

5. Make sure all electrical connections are free of corrosion and are tight.

Oil Pressure Switch Testing/Replacement

The oil pressure switch is located on the lower left-hand side of the crankcase just in front of the oil filter.

1. Drain the engine oil as described in Chapter Three.

2. Pull back the rubber boot and remove the screw securing the electrical connector (A, **Figure 53**) to the switch.

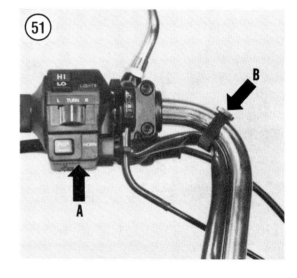

NOTE
Figure 53 is shown with the engine removed for clarity. The oil pressure switch can be removed with the engine in the frame.

3. Unscrew the switch (B, **Figure 53**) from the upper crankcase.

4. Use an ohmmeter and check for continuity between the electrical connector and the base of the switch. There should be no continuity (infinite resistance) with no pressure applied. With applied

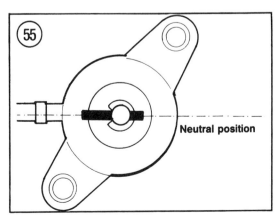

Neutral position

0.2-0.4 kg/cm² (2.8-5.6 psi) air pressure to the bottom of the switch there should be continuity (low resistance). If the switch fails either of these tests the switch must be replaced.

5. Apply a non-hardening sealer to the switch threads. Install the switch and screw it in until there are 2 threads exposed. Then tighten to 10-14 N•m (7-10 ft.-lb.).

6. Attach the electrical wire. Make sure the connection is tight and free from oil.

7. Slide the rubber boot back into position.

8. Refill the engine with the correct viscosity and quantity of engine oil; refer to Chapter Three.

Neutral Switch
Removal/Installation

1. Shift the transmission into NEUTRAL.

2. Remove the screws securing the left-hand rear crankcase cover and remove the cover.

3. Remove the bolt securing the gearshift pedal to the gearshift spindle assembly.

4. Remove the bolts securing the front left-hand footpeg and remove the footpeg/gearshift pedal assembly.

5. Remove the screw (**Figure 54**) securing the neutral indicator switch and remove the switch from the crankcase.

NOTE
Figure 54 is shown with the alternator cover removed for clarity.

6. Disconnect the electrical connector going to the neutral switch.

7. Remove the neutral switch and wiring harness from the frame.

8. Install by reversing these removal steps, noting the following.

9. Align the long end of the switch rotor pin with the electrical harness as shown in **Figure 55**. If the switch is installed with this pin 180° out, the neutral switch will not function properly.

Thermostatic Switch
Testing/Replacement

The thermostatic switch controls the radiator fan according to engine coolant temperature.

NOTE
If the cooling fan is not operating correctly, make sure that the inline fuse has not blown prior to starting this test.

NOTE
Use a kitchen type thermometer designed for deep fat frying or candy making. Do not use a medical type thermometer as it is rated for much lower temperatures.

7

1. Place the bike on the centerstand.

2. Remove the radiator filler cap and install a thermometer into the coolant.

3. Start the engine and let it idle. When the coolant temperature reaches 80-102° C (176-216° F) the cooling fan should start running. When the coolant temperature cools down to 83-97° C (200-207° F) the fan should stop running.

4. If the fan does not run at the specified temperature, shut the engine off.

5. Disconnect the electrical wires from the back of the thermostatic switch located on the lower left-hand side of the radiator.

6. Place a jumper wire between the black and green electrical wires.

7. Turn the ignition switch ON; the cooling fan should start running.

8. If the fan now runs, the thermostatic switch is defective and must be replaced.

9. If the fan does not run under any circumstances either the fan or the wiring to the fan is faulty. Replace the fan if the wiring checks out okay.

10. Turn the ignition switch OFF.

11. Drain the cooling system as described in Chapter Three.

12. Pull back the rubber boot (**Figure 56**) and carefully unscrew the switch from the radiator.

NOTE
***Figure 56** is shown with the radiator removed for clarity. It is easier but not necessary to remove the radiator in order to remove the thermostatic switch.*

13. Install a new O-ring seal on the switch and install the switch into the radiator.

14. Install all items removed.

15. Refill the cooling system with the recommended type and quantity of coolant. Refer to Chapter Three.

Temperature Sensor
Testing/Replacement

The engine must be cold for this test, preferably not operated for 12 hours.

1. Remove the seat and side covers.

2. Remove the fuel tank as described in Chapter Seven.

3. Remove the radiator filler cap cover from the frame.

4. Disconnect the green/blue electrical wire from the temperature sensor located on the thermostat housing (**Figure 57**).

NOTE
Use a kitchen type thermometer designed for deep fat frying or candy

making. Do not use a medical type thermometer as it is rated for much lower temperatures.

5. Remove the radiator filler cap and install a thermometer into the coolant.

6. Check the temperature of the coolant.

7. Start the engine and let it idle. Use an ohmmeter and check resistance between the terminal on the temperature sensor and ground. As the coolant temperature increases, compare to the temperature and resistance values listed in **Table 3**.

8. If the resistance values do not match those listed in **Table 3** the sensor must be replaced.

9. If faulty, remove the temperature sensor from the thermostat housing.

10. Apply a non-hardening sealer to the threads and install a new temperature sensor.

11. Connect the electrical wires to the temperature sensor.

12. Install all items removed.

Front Brake Light Switch
Testing/Replacement

1. Disconnect the electrical wires to the brake light switch (**Figure 58**).

2. Use an ohmmeter and check for continuity between the 2 terminals on the brake light switch. There should be no continuity (infinite resistance)

with the brake lever released. With the brake lever applied there should be continuity (low resistance). If the switch fails either of these tests the switch must be replaced.

3. Remove the screw securing the brake switch and remove the brake switch from the brake master cylinder.

4. Install a new switch by reversing these removal steps, noting the following.

5. Make sure all electrical connections are free of corrosion and are tight.

Rear Brake Light Switch
Testing/Replacement

On VT500C Shadow models, the rear brake light switch is located behind the right-hand rear footpeg bracket and is difficult to see.

1. Disconnect the electrical wires (A, **Figure 59**) to the rear brake light switch.

2. Use an ohmmeter and check for continuity between the 2 terminals on the brake light switch. There should be no continuity (infinite resistance) with the brake pedal released. With the brake pedal down or applied there should be continuity (low resistance). If the switch fails either of these tests the switch must be replaced.

3. Unhook the return spring and unscrew the locknut securing the rear brake light switch to the frame. Remove the switch from the frame.

4. Install a new switch by reversing these removal steps, noting the following.

5. Make sure all electrical connections are free of corrosion and are tight.

6. Adjust the switch as described in this chapter.

Rear Brake Light
Switch Adjustment

1. Turn the ignition switch to the ON position.

2. Depress the brake pedal. The light should come on just as the brake begins to work.

3. To make the light come on earlier, hold the switch body and turn the adjusting nut *clockwise* as viewed from the top (B, **Figure 59**). Turn *counterclockwise* to delay the light from coming on.

> *NOTE*
> *Some riders prefer the light to come on a little early. This way, they can tap the pedal without braking to warn drivers who are following too closely.*

ELECTRICAL COMPONENTS

This section contains information on electrical components other than switches.

Brake/Taillight Sensor Testing

The brake/taillight sensor is located on the left-hand side just behind the battery.

1. Turn the ignition switch to the ON position.

2. The indicator light should go on for a few seconds and then go off.

3. If the light does not go on, check for a burned-out indicator light or open in the electrical circuit from the sensor to the indicator light.

4. If the indicator light does not go out after a few seconds, check for a burned-out brake/taillight bulb or open in the electrical circuit from the brake/taillight to the sensor.

5. If necessary, replace the brake/taillight bulb.

6. If the brake/taillight bulb is okay, check for an open or short in the electrical circuit from brake/taillight to the sensor.

7. If the circuit is okay, replace the brake and taillight sensor.

Turn Signal Relay Replacement

1. Remove the seat and side covers.

2. Remove the fuel tank as described in Chapter Seven.

3. Remove the small side cover on the left-hand side of the steering head.

4. Remove the radiator filler cap cover on the right-hand side of the steering head.

7

5. Pull the turn signal relay (**Figure 60**) out of the rubber mount.

6. Install by reversing these steps.

Instrument Cluster
Removal/Installation

1. Remove the left-hand side cover and the seat.

2. Disconnect the battery negative lead.

3. Remove the headlight and case (A, **Figure 61**) as described in this chapter.

> *CAUTION*
> *The fork cover panel is plastic and has one mounting post in the middle. This part can easily be broken if not removed carefully.*

4. Carefully pull on the *center* of the fork cover panel (**Figure 46**) and remove it from the rubber grommet on the lower fork bridge.

5. Remove the screws (**Figure 47**) securing the junction box to the lower fork bridge.

6. Carefully pull the junction box away from the lower fork bridge and remove the back cover from the junction box.

7. Disconnect the brown electrical connector from the junction box panel (**Figure 48**).

8. Remove the speedometer and tachometer cables (B, **Figure 61**) from the meters.

9. Remove the nuts and lockwashers securing the instrument cluster to the upper fork bridge and remove the instrument cluster.

10. Install by reversing these removal steps.

Horn Removal/Installation

1. Carefully pull on the *center* of the fork cover panel (**Figure 46**) and remove it from the rubber grommets on the lower fork bridge.

2. Disconnect the electrical connections from the horn.

3. Remove the bolt (**Figure 62**) securing the horn to the mounting bracket and remove the horn.

4. Install by reversing these removal steps. Make sure the electrical connections are tight and free of corrosion.

Horn Testing

Remove the horn as described in this chapter. Connect a 12-volt battery to the horn. If the horn is good, it will sound. If not, replace it.

Temperature Gauge Testing

1. Remove the seat and both side covers.

2. Remove the fuel tank as described in Chapter Seven.

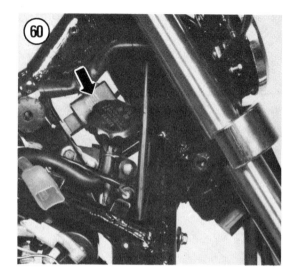

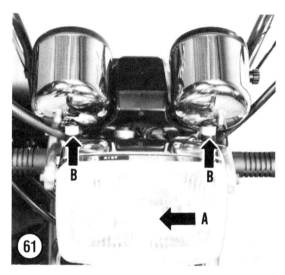

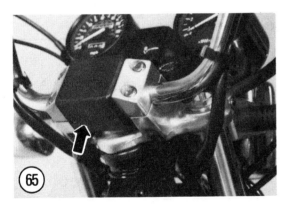

3. Remove the covers on both sides of the steering head.

4. Disconnect the electrical wire going to the temperature sensor on the thermostat housing (**Figure 57**).

5. Turn the ignition switch to the ON position.

> *CAUTION*
> *Do not short the temperature sensor wire to ground for longer than a few seconds or the temperature gauge will be damaged.*

6. Run a jumper wire from the electrical connector and short the other end to ground.

7. When the wire is grounded the gauge needle should move all the way to the right to the "H" position on the gauge face.

8. If the gauge fails the test the gauge must be replaced.

9. Remove the jumper wire and reconnect the temperature sensor wire to the sensor.

Fuses

There are 6 fuses used with the main fuse (fusible link) located next to the starter solenoid. The cooling fan has an inline fuse and the remaining 4 are located in the fuse panel at the base of the handlebar.

> *CAUTION*
> *When replacing a fuse, make sure the ignition switch is in the OFF position. This will lessen the chance of a short circuit.*

If the main fusible link blows, disconnect the electrical connector (**Figure 63**) and open the fuse door. Remove the Phillips screws securing the fusible link and replace it (**Figure 64**). There is a spare link inside the panel.

Four other fuses are located in the fuse panel at the base of the handlebar. Remove the screws securing the fuse holder cover and remove the cover (**Figure 65**).

Whenever a fuse blows, find out the reason for the failure before replacing the fuse (**Figure 66**). Usually the trouble is a short circuit in the wiring. This may be caused by worn-through insulation or a disconnected wire shorted to ground.

> *CAUTION*
> *Never substitute aluminum foil or wire for a fuse. Never use a higher amperage fuse than specified. An overload could cause a fire and complete loss of the motorcycle.*

7

Table 1 STARTER TROUBLESHOOTING

Symptom	Probable cause	Remedy
Starter does not work	Low battery	Recharge battery
	Worn brushes	Replace brushes
	Defective relay	Repair or replace
	Defective switch	Repair or replace
	Defective wiring connection	Repair wire or clean connection
	Internal short circuit	Repair or replace defective component
Starter action is weak	Low battery	Recharge battery
	Pitted relay contacts	Clean or replace
	Worn brushes	Replace brushes
	Defective connection	Clean and tighten
	Short circuit in commutator	Replace armature
Starter runs continuously	Stuck relay	Replace relay
Starter turns; does not turn engine	Defective starter clutch	Replace starter clutch

Table 2 REPLACEMENT BULBS

| Item | Wattage | | Number |
	VT500C and FT	VT500E	U.S.
Headlight (quartz bulb)	12 V 60/55W	12 V 60/55W	H4
Tail/brakelight	12 V 8/27W	12 V 21/5W	SAE No. 1157
Turn signals			
Front	12 V 23/8W	12 V 21W	SAE No. 1034
Rear	12 V 23W	12 V 21W	SAE No. 1073
Instrument lights	12 V 3W	12 V 3W	—
Indicator lights	12 V 3W	12 V 3W	—
High beam indicator	12 V 3W	12 V 3W	—
Oil pressure warning	12 V 3W	12 V 3W	—
Neutral indicator	12 V 3W	12 V 3W	—
Position light	12 V 8W	12 V 4W	SAE No. 1034

Table 3 TEMPERATURE SENSOR READINGS

Temperature	Resistance (ohms)
140° F (60° C)	104.0
185° F (85° C)	43.9
230° F (110° C)	20.3
248° F (120° C)	16.1

CHAPTER EIGHT

COOLING SYSTEM

The pressurized cooling system consists of the radiator, water pump, thermostat, electric cooling fan and a coolant reserve tank. The system uses a 0.75-1.05 kg/cm^2 (10.7-14.9 psi) radiator fill cap and is designed to operate with a 180° F (82° C) thermostat, which is located on the right-hand side of the engine.

The water pump requires no routine maintenance and is replaced as a complete unit if defective.

It is important to keep the coolant level between the 2 marks on the coolant reserve tank (**Figure 1**). Always add coolant to the reserve tank (**Figure 2**), not to the radiator. If the cooling system requires repeated refilling, there is probably a leak somewhere in the system. Perform the *Cooling System Inspection* in Chapter Three.

> *CAUTION*
> *Drain and flush the cooling system at least every 2 years. Refill with a mixture of ethylene glycol antifreeze (formulated for aluminum engines) and distilled water. Do not reuse the old coolant as it deteriorates with use. Do **not** operate the cooling system with only distilled water (even in climates where antifreeze protection is not required). This is important because the engine is all aluminum; it will not rust but it will oxidize internally and have to be replaced. Refer to **Coolant Change** in Chapter Three.*

This chapter describes repair and replacement of cooling system components. **Table 1** at the end of this chapter lists all of the cooling system specifications. For routine maintenance of the system, refer to Chapter Three.

Drain and flush the cooling system at least every 2 years. Refill with a mixture of ethylene glycol antifreeze, formulated for aluminum engines, and distilled water. Refer to *Coolant Change* in Chapter Three.

> *WARNING*
> *Do not remove the radiator filler cap (**Figure 3**) when the engine is hot. The coolant is very hot and is under pressure. Severe scalding could result if the coolant comes in contact with your skin.*

The cooling system must be cool prior to removing any component of the system.

There are 3 different types of hose clamps used on the coolant hoses. Always install the same type of clamp to its original position as in some cases the clearance is so minimal there is only room for one type of clamp. Throughout the text there is mention of loosening the clamping screws. In some cases a spring type clamp may be used on the same hose at the other end, therefore there is only one clamping screw to be loosened.

Major components of the cooling system are shown in **Figure 4**.

COOLING SYSTEM CHECK

Two checks should be made before disassembly if a cooling system fault is suspected.

1. Run the engine until it reaches operating temperature. While the engine is running a pressure surge should be felt when the upper radiator hose is squeezed.

2. If a substantial coolant loss is noted one of the head gaskets may be blown. In extreme cases sufficient coolant will leak into a cylinder(s) when the bike is left standing for several hours so the engine cannot be turned over with the starter. White smoke (steam) might also be observed at the muffler(s) when the engine is running. Coolant may also find its way into the oil. Unscrew the dipstick and look at the oil residue on it. If the oil looks like a "green chocolate malt" there is coolant in the oil system. If so, correct the cooling system problem immediately.

> *CAUTION*
> *After the cooling system problem is corrected, drain and thoroughly flush out the engine oil system to eliminate all coolant residue. Refill with fresh engine oil; refer to Chapter Three.*

RADIATOR

Removal/Installation

1. Remove the seat and both side covers.

2. Drain the cooling system as described in Chapter Three.

3. Remove the screw securing the plastic trim panel (**Figure 5**) and remove the trim panel from each side of the steering head.

4. Disconnect the overflow tube from the radiator filler neck.

5. On models so equipped, remove the gasoline evaporation canister assembly (A, **Figure 6**) and hoses from the area below the radiator.

6. Remove the screws securing the black radiator cover (B, **Figure 6**) and remove the radiator cover.

7. Disconnect the cooling fan 2-pin electrical connector.

8. Pull back the rubber boot and disconnect the electrical wires from the thermostatic switch coupler at the base of the radiator.

9. Loosen the clamping screws on the upper and lower radiator hose bands.

10. Remove the radiator upper mounting bolt.

11. Pull the radiator slightly forward while working both radiator hoses loose from the radiator. Pull the radiator forward and up and out of the lower receptacles on the frame.

12. Install by reversing these removal steps, noting the following.

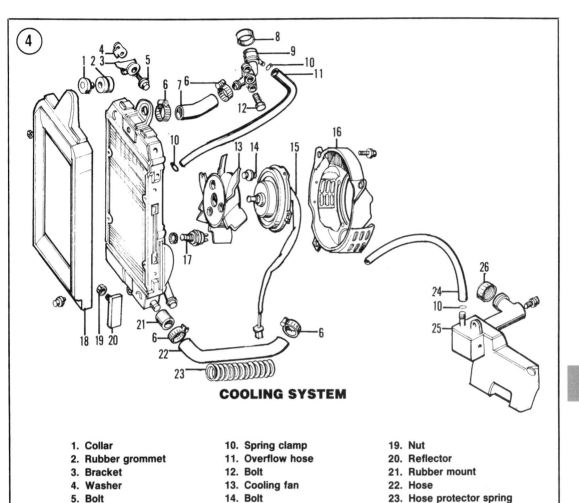

COOLING SYSTEM

1. Collar
2. Rubber grommet
3. Bracket
4. Washer
5. Bolt
6. Hose clamp
7. Hose
8. Hose clamp
9. Filler neck
10. Spring clamp
11. Overflow hose
12. Bolt
13. Cooling fan
14. Bolt
15. Fan motor
16. Fan shroud
17. Thermostat switch
18. Radiator cover
19. Nut
20. Reflector
21. Rubber mount
22. Hose
23. Hose protector spring
24. Reserve tank tube
25. Reserve tank
26. Reserve tank cap

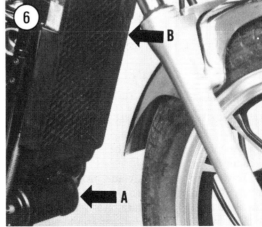

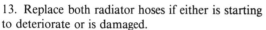

13. Replace both radiator hoses if either is starting to deteriorate or is damaged.

14. Refill the cooling system with the recommended type and quantity of coolant. Refer to Chapter Three.

Inspection

1. Flush off the exterior of the radiator with a garden hose on low pressure. Spray both the front and the back to remove all road dirt and bugs. Carefully use a whisk broom or stiff paint brush to remove any stubborn dirt.

> *CAUTION*
> *Do not press too hard or the cooling fins*
> *and tubes may be damaged.*

2. Carefully straighten out any bent cooling fins with a broad tipped screwdriver or putty knife.

3. Check for cracks or leakage (usually a moss-green colored residue) at the filler neck, the inlet and outlet hose fittings and the upper and lower tank seams (**Figure 7**).

4. If the condition of the radiator is doubtful, have it pressure checked as described in Chapter Three. The radiator can be pressure-checked while removed or installed on the bike.

COOLING FAN

Removal/Installation

1. Remove the radiator as described in this chapter.

2. Remove the bolts securing the fan shroud and fan assembly and remove the assembly from the radiator (**Figure 8**).

3. To remove the fan blade from the motor, remove the nut and washers (**Figure 9**) securing the fan blade to the motor and remove the fan blade.

4. To remove the fan motor, perform the following:

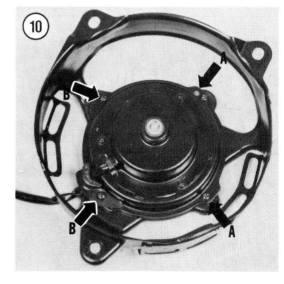

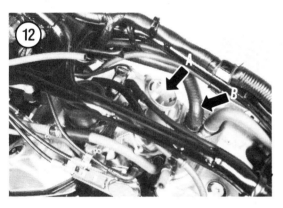

a. Remove the screws (A, **Figure 10**) securing the fan assembly to the fan shroud.

b. Remove the screw and plate (B, **Figure 10**) holding the electrical wires in place.

c. Remove the fan motor.

5. Install by reversing these removal steps, noting the following.

6. Apply Loctite Lock 'N Seal to the threads on the fan motor shaft prior to installing the fan blade nut. Install the washer, lockwasher and nut and tighten the nut securely.

7. Refill the cooling system with the recommended type and quantity of coolant. Refer to in Chapter Three.

THERMOSTAT

Removal/Installation

1. Remove the seat and both side covers.

2. Remove the fuel tank as described in Chapter Six.

3. Remove the screw securing the plastic trim panel and remove the trim panel from each side of the steering head.

4. Drain the cooling system as described in Chapter Three.

5. Loosen the clamping screws (**Figure 11**) on the air filter interconnecting tube. Pull the tube off of the carburetors then from the air filter air box and remove the interconnecting tube.

6. Place a clean shop cloth into each carburetor venturi (A, **Figure 12**) to prevent the entry of dirt and coolant.

7. Disconnect the thermostat hoses from the front and rear (B, **Figure 12**) cylinder heads.

8. Disconnect the electrical wires from the turn signal relay (A, **Figure 13**) and remove the relay from its rubber mount.

9. Disconnect the temperature sensor wire (B, **Figure 13**) from the thermostat housing.

10. Disconnect the overflow tube (C, **Figure 13**) from the filler neck.

11. Remove the bolts securing the ignition coil mounting bracket and lower the ignition coils (D, **Figure 13**). It is not necessary to remove the ignition coils.

12. Remove the bolts (E, **Figure 13**) securing the thermostat housing and filler neck.

13. Remove the bolts (**Figure 14**) securing the thermostat housing cover and remove the cover and the O-ring seal.

14. Remove the thermostat from the housing.

15. If necessary, test the thermostat as described in this chapter.

16. Install by reversing these removal steps, noting the following.

8

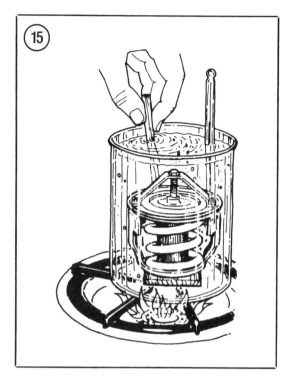

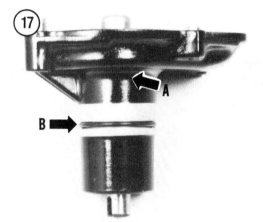

17. Make sure the O-ring seal in the thermostat housing cover is in good condition. If it has started to deteriorate or become brittle with age it should be replaced as it will no longer seal properly.
18. Refill the cooling system with the recommended type and quantity of coolant. Refer to Chapter Three.

Testing

Test the thermostat to ensure proper operation. The thermostat should be replaced if it remains open at normal room temperature or stays closed after the specified temperature has been reached during the test procedure.

Place the thermostat on a small piece of wood in a pan of water (**Figure 15**). Place a thermometer in the pan of water (use a cooking or candy thermometer that is rated higher than the test temperature). Gradually heat the water and continue to gently stir the water until it reaches 176-183° F (80-84° C). At this temperature the thermostat valve should open.

> *NOTE*
> *Valve operation is sometimes sluggish;*
> *it usually takes 3-5 minutes for the valve*
> *to operate properly.*

If the valve fails to open, the thermostat should be replaced (it cannot be serviced). Be sure to replace it with one of the same temperature rating.

WATER PUMP

Mechanical Seal Inspection

1. Remove the bolts securing the left-hand rear crankcase cover and remove the cover.
2. Check the lower area of the water pump (**Figure 16**) for signs of coolant leakage (usually a moss-green colored residue).
3. If the mechanical seal is leaking the coolant will drip out of the weep hole (A, **Figure 17**) in the bottom of the water pump.
4. If the mechanical seal is leaking, the water pump assembly must be replaced. It cannot be serviced.

Removal/Installation

Refer to **Figure 18** for this procedure.
1. Remove the engine as described in Chapter Four.
2. Remove the bolts securing the water pump cover and remove the cover and the hose (**Figure 19**). Don't lose the locating dowels.
3. Withdraw the water pump from the crankcase (**Figure 20**).

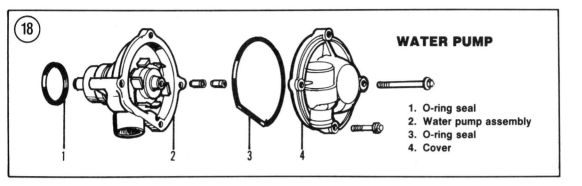

WATER PUMP

1. O-ring seal
2. Water pump assembly
3. O-ring seal
4. Cover

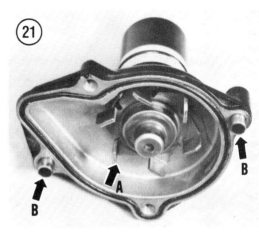

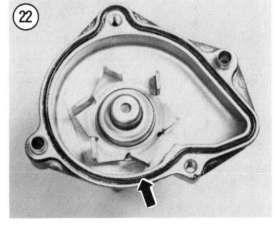

Inspection

1. Inspect the water pump assembly for wear or damage.

2. Rotate the impeller to make sure the bearings are not worn or damaged. If the bearings are damaged, the assembly must be replaced, as it cannot be serviced.

3. Check the impeller blades (A, **Figure 21**); straighten any that are bent.

4. Remove the O-ring seal (**Figure 22**) in the water pump assembly. Replace with a new one.

5. Inspect the cover and inlet and outlet pipes for cracks or damage (**Figure 23**). If damaged, the assembly must be replaced; it cannot be serviced.

6. If removed, install the locating dowels (B, **Figure 21**) into the water pump assembly.

Installation

1. Within the crankcase, rotate the oil pump shaft so the tab on the end of the shaft is vertical.
2. Apply a coat of clean engine oil to the O-ring seal (B, **Figure 17**) on the water pump housing.
3. Position the groove on the water pump shaft vertically so it will align with the tab on the oil pump shaft.
4. Install the water pump into the crankcase and slightly wiggle the water pump impeller to assure proper alignment of the tab and groove. Push the water pump assembly all the way on until it is properly seated against the crankcase. The assembly should fit snugly without using any force. If it will not fit properly, withdraw the assembly and realign the tab of the oil pump shaft and the groove on the water pump.

CAUTION
Do not install the cover nor any bolts until the assembly is completely seated against the crankcase. Do not try to force the assembly into place with the mounting screws.

5. Make sure the dowel pins are installed in the water pump assembly.
6. Make sure the O-ring seal is installed in the water pump assembly.
7. Install the water pump cover and the bolts and tighten the bolts securely.
8. Install the engine into the frame as described in Chapter Four.
9. Refill the cooling system with the recommended type and quantity of coolant. Refer to Chapter Three.
10. Start the bike and check for leaks.

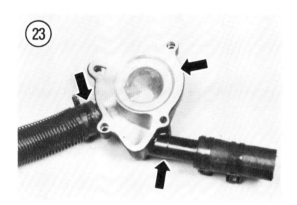

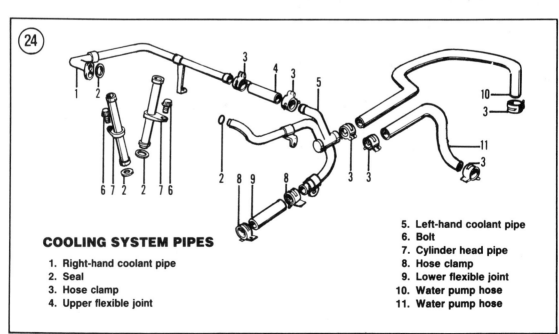

COOLING SYSTEM PIPES

1. Right-hand coolant pipe
2. Seal
3. Hose clamp
4. Upper flexible joint
5. Left-hand coolant pipe
6. Bolt
7. Cylinder head pipe
8. Hose clamp
9. Lower flexible joint
10. Water pump hose
11. Water pump hose

COOLANT PIPES

Removal/Installation

Refer to **Figure 24** for this procedure.
1. Drain the coolant as described in Chapter Three.
2. Remove the bolts securing the coolant pipe on the right-hand side (**Figure 25**).

3. Loosen the hose clamps on the upper flexible joint (A, **Figure 26**) between the right- and left-hand coolant pipes.
4. Loosen the hose clamp on the lower flexible joint (B, **Figure 26**) between the water pump and the left-hand coolant pipes.
5. Remove the bolts securing the coolant pipe on the left-hand side (C, **Figure 26**).
6. Install by reversing these removal steps, noting the following.
7. Install new O-ring seals on all metal pipes.
8. Refill the cooling system with the recommended type and quantity of coolant. Refer to Chapter Three.

HOSES

Hoses deteriorate with age and should be replaced periodically or whenever they show signs of cracking or leakage. To be safe, replace the hoses every 2 years. The spray of hot coolant from a cracked hose can injure the rider and passenger. Loss of coolant can also cause engine damage.

Whenever any component of the cooling system is removed, inspect the hose(s) and determine if replacement is necessary.

8

Table 1 COOLING SYSTEM SPECIFICATIONS

Coolant capacity	
Total system	
VT500C	
1983-1984	1.7 liters (1.8 U.S. qt.)
1985-1986	2.0 liters (2.1 U.S. qt.)
VT500FT	1.7 liters (1.8 U.S. qt.)
VT500E	2.0 liters (1.76 Imp. qt.)
Radiator and engine	
VT500C	
1983-1984	1.2 liters (1.3 U.S. qt.)
1985-1986	1.55 liters (1.64 U.S. qt.)
VT500FT	1.2 liters (1.3 U.S. qt.)
VT500E	1.55 liters (1.36 Imp. qt.)
Reserve tank	
VT500C	
1983-1984	0.5 liters (0.5 U.S. qt.)
1985-1986	0.45 liters (0.47 U.S. qt.)
VT500FT	0.5 liters (0.5 U.S. qt.)
VT500E	0.45 liters (0.4 Imp. qt.)
Radiator cap relief pressure	0.75-1.05 kg/cm^2 (10.7-14.9 psi)
Thermostat	
Begins to open	80-84° C (176-183° F)
Valve lift	Minimum of 8 mm @ 95° C (203° F)
Boiling point (50:50 mixture)	
Unpressurized	107.7° C (226° F)
Pressurized (cap on)	125.6° C (258° F)
Freezing point (hydrometer test)	
55:45 water:antifreeze	−32° C (−25° F)
50:50 water:antifreeze	−37° C (−34° F)
45:55 water:antifreeze	−44.5° C (−48° F)

NOTE: If you own a VT500E, first check the Supplement at the back of the book for any additional service information.

CHAPTER NINE

FRONT SUSPENSION AND STEERING

This chapter describes repair and maintenance procedures for the front wheel, forks and steering components.

Front suspension torque specifications are covered in **Table 1**. **Tables 1-4** are at the end of this chapter.

FRONT WHEEL

Removal

1. Place the bike on the centerstand or place wood blocks under the engine or frame to support it securely with the front wheel off the ground.
2. Remove the speedometer cable set screw. Pull the speedometer cable (A, **Figure 1**) free from the speedometer gear box.
3. Remove the bolts (B, **Figure 1**) securing the brake caliper assembly to the front fork and tie it up to the front fork.

> *NOTE*
> *Insert a piece of vinyl tubing or wood in the caliper in place of the brake disc. That way if the brake lever is inadvertently squeezed, the pistons will not be forced out of the cylinder. If this does happen, the caliper may have to be disassembled to reseat the pistons and the system will have to be bled. By using the wood, bleeding the brake is not necessary when installing the wheel.*

4. Remove the chrome cap (**Figure 2**) from the axle pinch bolt and remove the axle pinch bolt.

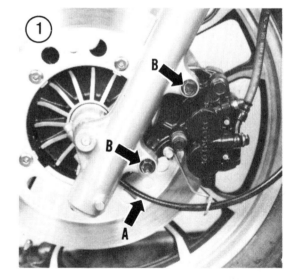

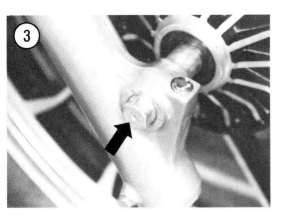

5. Unscrew and withdraw the front axle (**Figure 3**).

6. Pull the wheel down and forward and remove it.

CAUTION
*Do not set the wheel down on the disc surface as it may get scratched or warped. Set the wheel on 2 blocks of wood (**Figure 4**).*

Installation

1. Make sure the axle bearing surfaces of the fork slider and axle are free from burrs and nicks.

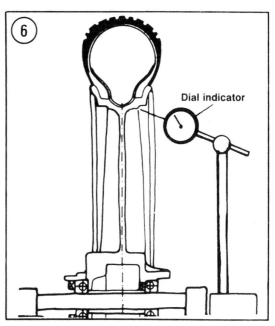

Dial indicator

2. Remove the vinyl tubing or piece of wood from the brake caliper.

3. Position the wheel into place.

4. Position the speedometer housing tang *behind* the raised boss on the left-hand fork (**Figure 5**).

5. Insert the front axle from the right-hand side and screw it into the left-hand fork leg.

6. Tighten the front axle to the torque specification listed in **Table 1**.

7. Install the pinch bolt and tighten it to the torque specification listed in **Table 1**. Install the chrome cap into the pinch bolt.

8. Install the caliper, being careful not to damage the brake pads.

9. Tighten the caliper mounting bolts to the torque specifications listed in **Table 1**.

10. Slowly rotate the wheel and install the speedometer cable into the speedometer housing. Install the cable set screw.

11. After the wheel is completely installed, rotate it several times and apply the brakes a couple of times to make sure that it rotates freely and that the brake pads are against the disc correctly.

Inspection

Measure the axial and radial runout of the wheel with a dial indicator as shown in **Figure 6**. The maximum axial and radial runout is 2.0 mm (0.08 in.). If the runout exceeds this dimension, check the wheel bearing condition.

If the wheel bearings are okay, the alloy wheel will have to be replaced as it cannot be serviced. Inspect the wheel for signs of cracks, fractures, dents or bends. If it is damaged in any way, it must be replaced.

> *WARNING*
> *Do not try to repair any damage to an alloy wheel as it will result in an unsafe riding condition.*

Check axle runout as described under *Front Hub Inspection* in this chapter.

FRONT HUB

Inspection

Inspect each wheel bearing prior to removing it from the wheel hub.

> *CAUTION*
> *Do not remove the wheel bearings for inspection purposes as they will be damaged during the removal process. Remove wheel bearings only if they are to be replaced.*

1. Perform Steps 1-3 of *Disassembly* in this chapter.
2. Turn each bearing by hand. Make sure bearings turn smoothly.
3. On non-sealed bearings, check the balls for evidence of wear, pitting or excessive heat (bluish tint). Replace the bearings if necessary; always replace as a complete set. When replacing the bearings, be sure to take your old bearings along to ensure a perfect matchup.

> *NOTE*
> *Fully sealed bearings are available from many bearing specialty shops. Fully sealed bearings provide better protection from dirt and moisture that may get into the hub.*

4. Check the axle for wear and straightness. Use V-blocks and a dial indicator as shown in **Figure 7**. If the runout is 0.2 mm (0.01 in.) or greater, the axle should be replaced.

Disassembly

Refer to **Figure 8** for this procedure.
1. Remove the front wheel as described in this chapter.
2. Remove the spacer (**Figure 9**) and grease seal (**Figure 10**) from the right-hand side.

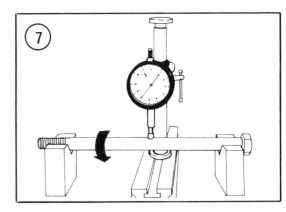

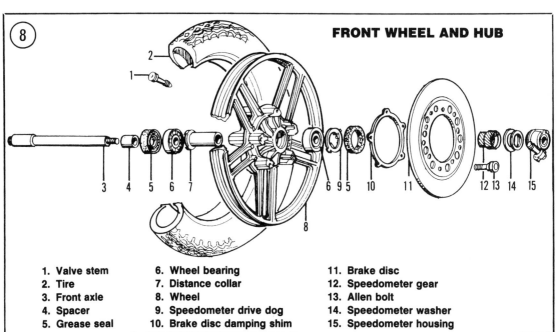

FRONT WHEEL AND HUB

1. Valve stem	6. Wheel bearing	11. Brake disc
2. Tire	7. Distance collar	12. Speedometer gear
3. Front axle	8. Wheel	13. Allen bolt
4. Spacer	9. Speedometer drive dog	14. Speedometer washer
5. Grease seal	10. Brake disc damping shim	15. Speedometer housing

3. Remove the speedometer housing (**Figure 11**), the grease seal and speedometer drive dog (**Figure 12**) from the left-hand side.

4. Before proceeding further, inspect the wheel bearings as described in this chapter. If they must be replaced, proceed as follows.

5. Remove the bolts (**Figure 13**) securing the brake disc. Remove the disc and the single damping shim located between the disc and the hub.

6A. A special Honda tool set-up can be used to remove the wheel bearings as follows:

  a. Install the 15 mm bearing remover (Honda part No. 07746-0050400) into the right-hand bearing.

  b. Turn the wheel over (left-hand side up) on the workbench so the bearing remover is touching the workbench surface.

  c. From the left-hand side of the hub, install the bearing remover expander (Honda part No. 07746-050100) into the bearing remover. Using a hammer, tap the expander into the bearing remover with a hammer.

  d. Stand the wheel up to a vertical position.

  e. Tap on the end of the expander (**Figure 14**) and drive the right-hand bearing out of the hub. Remove the bearing and the distance collar.

  f. Repeat for the left-hand bearing.

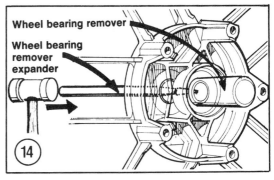

Wheel bearing remover

Wheel bearing remover expander

6B. If special tools are not available, perform the following:

    a. To remove the right- and left-hand bearings and distance collar, insert a soft aluminum or brass drift into one side of the hub.

    b. Push the distance collar over to one side and place the drift on the inner race of the lower bearing.

    c. Tap the bearing out of the hub with a hammer, working around the perimeter of the inner race.

    d. Repeat for the other bearing.

7. Clean the inside and the outside of the hub with solvent. Dry with compressed air.

Assembly

1. On non-sealed bearings, pack the bearings with a good quality bearing grease. Work the grease in between the balls thoroughly; turn the bearing by hand a couple of times to make sure the grease is distributed evenly inside the bearing.

2. Blow any dirt or foreign matter out of the hub prior to installing the bearings.

> *CAUTION*
> *Install non-sealed bearings with the single sealed side facing outward (**Figure 15**). Tap the bearings squarely into place and tap on the outer race only. Use a socket (**Figure 16**) that matches the outer race diameter. Do not tap on the inner race or the bearing might be damaged. Be sure that the bearings are completely seated.*

3. Install the right-hand bearing and press the distance collar into place.

4. Install the left-hand bearing.

5. Install the single damping shim onto the hub and then install the brake disc. Install the bolts and tighten to the torque specifications listed in **Table 1**.

6. Install the grease seal on the right-hand side.

7. Align the tangs of the speedometer drive gear (A, **Figure 17**) with the drive dog (B, **Figure 17**) in the hub and install the speedometer gear box.

8. Install the spacer on the right-hand side.

9. Instal the front wheel as described in this chapter.

WHEEL BALANCE

    An unbalanced wheel is unsafe. Depending on the degree of unbalance and the speed of the motorcycle, the rider may experience anything from a mild vibration to a violent shimmy which may even result in loss of control.

    On alloy wheels, weights are attached to the rim. A kit of Tape-A-Weight or equivalent may be

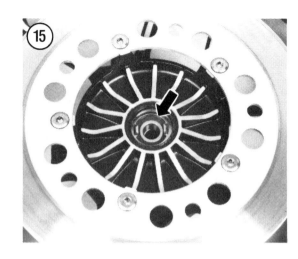

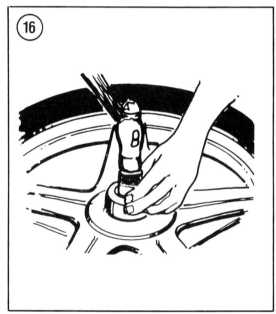

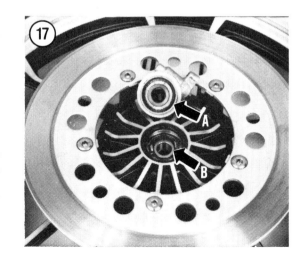

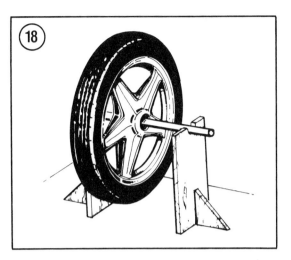

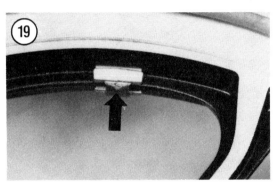

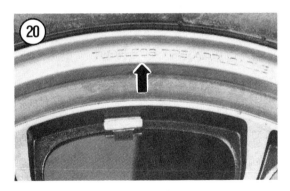

purchased from most motorcycle supply stores. This kit contains test weights and strips of adhesive-backed weights that can be cut to the desired weight and attached directly to the rim.

Before you attempt to balance the wheel, check to be sure that the wheel bearings are in good condition and properly lubricated and that the brakes do not drag. The wheel must rotate freely.

1. Remove the wheel as described in this chapter or Chapter Ten.

2. Mount the wheel on a fixture such as the one shown in **Figure 18** so it can rotate freely.

3. Give the wheel a spin and let it coast to a stop. Mark the tire at the lowest point.

4. Spin the wheel several more times. If the wheel keeps coming to rest at the same point, it is out of balance.

5. Tape a test weight to the upper (or light) side of the wheel.

6. Experiment with different weights until the wheel, when spun, comes to a rest at a different position each time.

7. Remove the test weight and install the correct size adhesive-backed or clamp-on weight (**Figure 19**).

TIRE CHANGING

The rim of the alloy wheel is aluminum and the exterior appearance can easily be damaged. Special care must be taken with tire irons when changing a tire to avoid scratches and gouges to the outer rim surface. Insert scraps of leather between the tire iron and the rim to protect the rim from gouges. Honda offers rim protectors (part No. 07772-0020200) for this purpose that are very handy to use. All models are factory-equipped with tubeless tires and wheels designed specifically for use with tubeless tires.

> *WARNING*
> *Do not install tubeless tires on wheels designed for use only with tube-type tires. Personal injury and tire failure may result from rapid tire deflation while riding. Wheels for use with tubeless tires are so marked (**Figure 20**).*

Removal

1. Remove the valve core to deflate the tire.

2. Press the entire bead on both sides of the tire into the center of the rim. Lubricate the beads with soapy water.

3. Insert the tire iron under the bead next to the valve (**Figure 21**). Force the bead on the opposite side of the tire into the center of the rim and pry the bead over the rim with the tire iron.

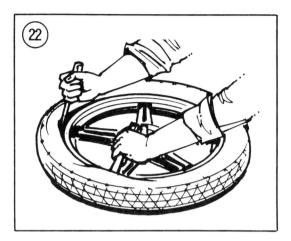

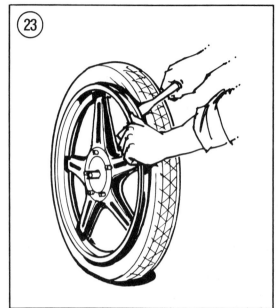

4. Insert a second tire iron next to the first to hold the bead over the rim. Then work around the tire with the first tire iron, prying the bead over the rim (**Figure 22**).

5. Stand the tire upright. Insert the tire iron between the second bead and the side of the rim that the first bead was pried over (**Figure 23**). Force the bead on the opposite side from the tire iron into the center of the rim. Pry the second bead off the rim, working around as with the first.

6. Honda recommends that the tire valve stem be replaced whenever the tire is removed from the wheel.

Installation

1. Carefully inspect the tire for any damage, especially inside.

2. A new tire may have balancing rubbers inside. These are not patches and should not be disturbed. A colored spot near the bead indicates a lighter point on the tire. This spot (**Figure 24**) should be placed next to the valve stem.

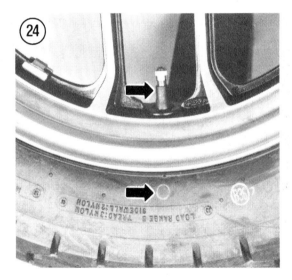

3. Lubricate both beads of the tire with soapy water.

4. Place the backside of the tire into the center of the rim. The lower bead should go into the center of the rim and the upper bead outside. Work around the tire in both directions (**Figure 25**). Use a tire iron for the last few inches of bead (**Figure 26**).

5. Press the upper bead into the rim opposite the valve (**Figure 27**). Pry the bead into the rim on both sides of the initial point with a tire iron, working around the rim to the valve (**Figure 28**).

6. Check the bead on both sides of the tire for even fit around the rim.

7. Bounce the wheel several times, rotating it each time. This will force the tire beads against the rim flanges. After the tire beads are in contact with the rim evenly, inflate the tire to seat the beads.

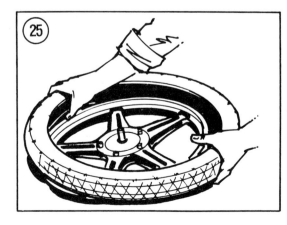

NOTE
If you are unable to get an airtight seal this way, install an inflatable band around the circumference of the tire. Slowly inflate the band until the beads are seated against the rim flanges, then inflate the tire. If you still encounter trouble, deflate the inflation band and the tire. Apply additional lubricant to the beads and repeat the inflation procedure. Also try rolling the tire back and forth while inflating it.

8. Inflate the tire to more than the recommended inflation pressure for the initial seating of the rim flanges. Once the beads are seated correctly, deflate the tire to the correct pressure. Refer to **Table 2**.

WARNING
Never exceed 4.0 kg/cm² (56 psi) inflation pressure as the tire could burst causing severe injury. Never stand directly over the tire while inflating it.

TIRE REPAIRS

Patching a tubeless tire on the road is very difficult. If both beads are still in place against the rim, a can of pressurized tire sealant may inflate the tire and seal the hole. The beads must be against the wheel for this method to work.

Another solution is to carry a spare inner tube that could be temporarily installed and inflated. This will enable you to get to a service station where the tire can be correctly repaired. Be sure that the tube is designed for use with a tubeless tire.

Honda (and the tire industry) recommends that the tubeless tire be patched from the inside. Therefore, do not patch the tire with an external type plug. If you find an external patch on a tire, it is recommended that it be patch-reinforced from the inside.

Due to the variations of material supplied with different tubeless tire repair kits, follow the instructions and recommendations supplied with the repair kit.

Honda recommends that the valve stem be replaced each time the tire is removed from the wheel.

HANDLEBAR

Removal

1. Remove the left-hand side cover.
2. Disconnect the battery negative lead.
3. Remove the fuel tank as described in Chapter Six.

4. Remove the right-hand rear view mirror (A, **Figure 29**).

5. Disconnect the brake light switch electrical connector (B, **Figure 29**).

6. Remove the screws securing the right-hand handlebar switch assembly (C, **Figure 29**) and remove the electrical wires from the clips (D, **Figure 29**) on the handlebar.

> *CAUTION*
> *Cover the frame with a heavy cloth or plastic tarp to protect it from accidental spilling of brake fluid. Wash any spilled brake fluid off any painted or plated surface immediately, as it will destroy the finish. Use soapy water and rinse thoroughly.*

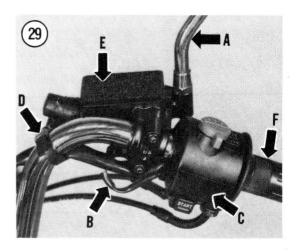

7. Remove the 2 bolts and clamp securing the brake master cylinder (E, **Figure 29**) and lay it over the frame. Keep the reservoir in the upright position to minimize loss of brake fluid and to keep air from entering into the brake system. It is not necessary to remove the hydraulic brake line.

8. Remove the throttle assembly (F, **Figure 29**) and carefully lay the throttle assembly and cables over the fender or back over the frame. Be careful that the cables do not get crimped or damaged.

9. Remove the left-hand rear view mirror (A, **Figure 30**).

10. Disconnect the clutch switch wires and remove the electrical wires from the clips (B, **Figure 30**) on the handlebar.

11. Remove the 2 bolts securing the clutch/choke lever assembly (C, **Figure 30**). Disconnect the choke cable from the choke lever. Remove the assembly and lay the assembly and cables over the fender or back over the frame. Be careful that the cables do not get crimped or damaged.

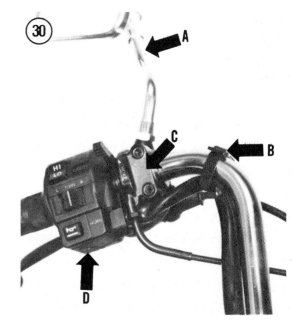

12. Remove the screws securing the left-hand handlebar switch assembly (D, **Figure 30**) and remove the electrical wires from the clips on the handlebar.

13. Remove the screws securing the fuse panel cover (**Figure 31**) and remove the cover.

14. Remove the screw securing the fuse panel (A, **Figure 32**) to the handlebar upper holder.

15. Remove the plastic plugs (B, **Figure 32**) and remove the Allen bolts securing the handlebar upper holder in place.

16. Move the handlebar upper holder and fuse panel up, then remove the handlebar.

17. To maintain a good grip on the handlebar and to prevent it from slipping down, clean the knurled section of the handlebar with a wire brush. It should be kept rough so it will be held securely by the

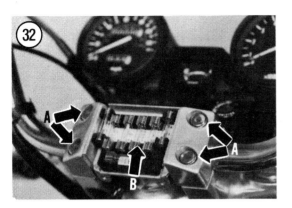

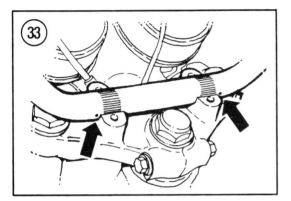

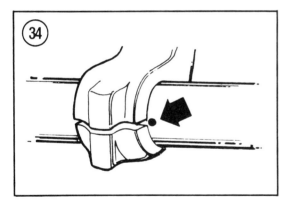

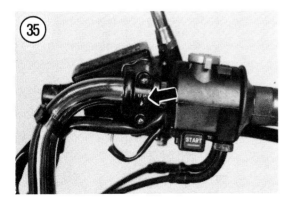

holders. The handlebar holder and the holders on the upper fork bridge should also be kept clean and free of any metal that may have been gouged loose by handlebar slippage.

Installation

1. Position the handlebar on the upper fork bridge so the punch mark on the handlebar is aligned with the top surface of the raised portion of the upper fork bridge (**Figure 33**).
2. Install the handlebar holder and install the Allen bolts. Tighten the forward bolts first and then the rear bolts. Tighten all bolts to the torque specification listed in **Table 3**. Install the plastic plugs.
3. Install the fuse panel onto the handlebar upper holder. Install the screws and tighten securely.
4. Install the fuse panel cover and install the screws.
5. After installation is complete, recheck the alignment of the handlebar punch mark.
6. Apply a light coat of multipurpose grease to the throttle grip area on the handlebar prior to installing the throttle grip assembly.

NOTE
*When installing all assemblies, align the punch mark on the handlebar with the slit on the mounting bracket (**Figure 34**).*

7. Install the throttle grip assembly and right-hand switch assembly.
8. Install the brake master cylinder onto the handlebar. Install the clamp with the punch mark facing down or with the "UP" arrow (**Figure 35**) facing up and align the clamp mating surface with the punch mark on the handlebar. Tighten the upper bolt first and then the lower bolt.

WARNING
After installation is completed, make sure the brake lever does not come in contact with the throttle grip assembly when it is pulled on fully. If it does the brake fluid may be low in the reservoir; refill as necessary. Refer to Chapter Twelve.

9. Attach the choke cable to the choke lever.
10. Install the clutch/choke lever assembly and tighten the bolts securely.
11. Install the left-hand handlebar switch assembly.
12. Install the clips onto the electrical wires on the handlebar.
13. Connect the battery negative lead to the battery.
14. Install the fuel tank, seat and rear view mirrors.
15. Adjust the throttle and clutch operation as described in Chapter Three.

STEERING HEAD AND STEM

Disassembly

Refer to **Figure 36** for this procedure.

1. Remove the front wheel as described in this chapter.

2. Remove the handlebar (A, **Figure 37**) as described in this chapter.

3. Remove the instrument cluster (B, **Figure 37**) as described in Chapter Seven.

4. Remove the headlight assembly as described in Chapter Seven.

5. Remove the ignition switch as described in Chapter Seven.

6. Loosen the upper fork bridge bolts.

7. Remove the steering stem nut and washer (C, **Figure 37**).

8. Remove the front forks (D, **Figure 37**) as described in this chapter.

9. Remove the upper fork bridge (E, **Figure 37**).

10. Disconnect the electrical connector from the horn and remove the horn.

11. Remove the screws securing the junction box to the lower fork bridge.

12. Move the junction box out and remove the rear cover.

13. Disconnect all electrical connectors from the junction box.

14. Remove the steering stem adjusting nut. To loosen the nut, use a large drift and hammer or use the easily improvised tool shown in **Figure 38**.

15. Have an assistant hold a large pan under the steering stem to catch the loose ball bearings and carefully lower the steering stem assembly down and out of the steering head (**Figure 39**).

NOTE
There are 37 balls total—18 on the top and 19 on the bottom. These balls are all the same size.

Inspection

1. Clean the bearing races in the steering head and the bearings with solvent.

2. Check the welds around the steering head for cracks and fractures. If any are found, have them repaired by a competent frame shop or welding service.

3. Check the bearings for pitting, scratches or discoloration indicating wear or corrosion.

4. Check the races for pitting, galling and corrosion. If any of these conditions exist, replace the races as described in this chapter.

5. Check the steering stem for cracks and check its race for damage or wear. Replace if necessary.

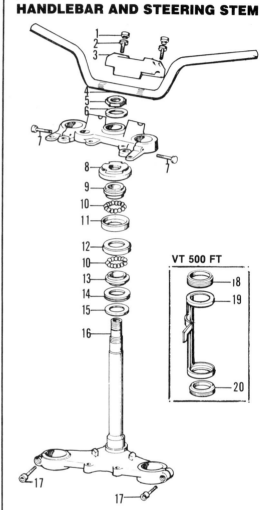

HANDLEBAR AND STEERING STEM

VT 500 FT

1. Cap
2. Allen bolt
3. Cover
4. Handlebar
5. Steering stem locknut
6. Washer
7. Upper fork bridge
8. Adjusting nut
9. Top bearing inner race
10. Steel balls #8 (1/4 in. dia.)
    Quantity—18 top, 19 lower
11. Top bearing outer race
12. Lower bearing outer race
13. Lower bearing inner race
14. Dust seal
15. Washer
16. Steering stem
17. Bolt
18. Rubber grommet
19. Front cover stay
20. Rubber grommet

36

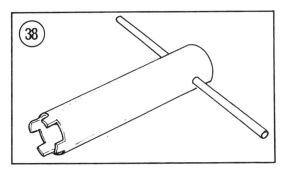

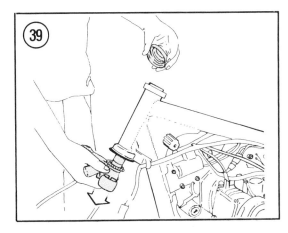

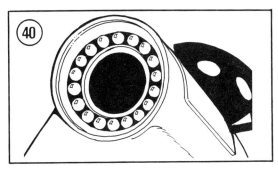

Assembly

Refer to **Figure 36** for this procedure.

1. Make sure both steering head bearing outer races are properly seated in the steering head tube.

2. Apply a coat of cold grease to the top bearing race cone and fit 18 balls into it (**Figure 40**).

3. Apply a coat of cold grease to the bottom bearing race cone and fit 19 balls into it (**Figure 41**). The grease will hold the balls in place.

4. Install the steering stem into the steering head tube and hold it firmly in place.

5. Install the top bearing inner race.

6. Install the steering stem adjusting nut and tighten it until it is snug against the top race, then back it off 1/8 turn.

> *NOTE*
> *The steering stem adjusting nut should be just tight enough to remove play, both vertical and horizontal, yet loose enough so that the assembly will turn to both lock positions under its own weight after a light push.*

7. Install the upper fork bridge, washer and the steering stem nut. Tighten the nut only finger-tight at this time.

> *NOTE*
> *Step 8 and Step 9 must be performed in this order to assure proper upper and lower fork bridge to fork alignment.*

8. Install the fork tubes in the lower fork bridge and continue to slide the fork tubes into position. Align the top of each fork tube so it is flush with the top surface of the upper fork bridge.

9. Tighten these items in the following order:
   a. Lower fork bridge bolts.
   b. Stem nut.
   c. Upper fork bridge bolts.

Tighten all items to the torque specifications listed in **Table 1**.

9

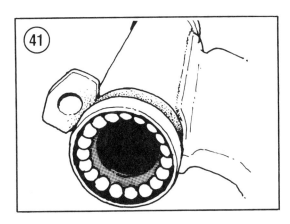

10. Install the horn and connect the electrical connector to the horn.

11. Connect all electrical connectors to the junction box.

12. Install the junction box cover and move the junction box into position.

13. Install the screws securing the junction box to the lower fork bridge.

14. Install the ignition switch, headlight assembly and the instrument cluster as described in Chapter Seven.

15. Install the handlebar as described in this chapter.

16. Complete the installation of the front forks as described in this chapter.

Steering Stem Adjustment

If play develops or there is binding in the steering system, it may only require adjustment. However, don't take a chance on it. Disassemble the steering stem assembly and look for possible damage as described in this chapter.

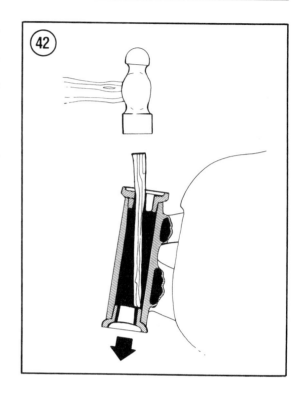

STEERING HEAD BEARING RACES

The headset and steering stem bearing races are pressed into place. Because they are easily bent, do not remove them unless they are worn and require replacement.

The top and bottom bearing races are not the same size. The bottom race is the slightly larger of the two. Be sure that you install them in the proper ends of the frame steering head tube.

**Steering Head Bearing
Outer Race Replacement**

To remove the headset race, insert a hardwood stick or soft punch into the head tube (**Figure 42**) and carefully tap the race out from the inside. After it is started, tap around the race so that neither the race nor the steering head tube are damaged.

To install the steering head bearing race, tap it in slowly with a block of wood, a suitable size socket or piece of pipe (**Figure 43**). Make sure that the race is squarely seated in the steering head race bore before tapping it into place. Tap the race in until it is flush with the steering head surface.

**Steering Stem Lower Bearing and
Race and Grease Seal
Removal/Installation**

*NOTE
Do not remove the steering stem lower bearing race unless it is going to be replaced with a new bearing race. Do*

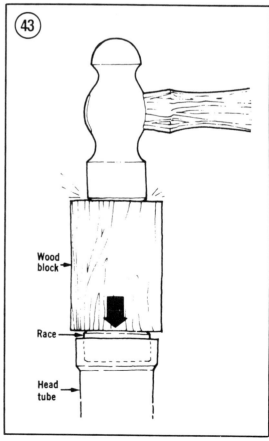

not reinstall a bearing race that has been removed as it is no longer true to alignment.

1. To remove the steering stem lower bearing inner race, try twisting and pulling it up by hand. If it will not come off, carefully pry it up from the base of the steering stem with a screwdriver; work around in a circle, prying a little at a time. Remove the bearing inner race, dust seal and dust seal washer.

2. Slide on a new dust seal washer and dust seal over the steering stem.

3. Slide the lower bearing inner race over the steering stem. Tap the race down with a long piece of metal pipe that fits the inner race diameter or use

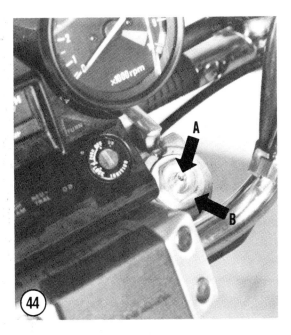

a piece of hardwood; work around in a circle so the bearing and inner race will not be bent. Make sure it is seated squarely and is all the way down.

FRONT FORKS

The front suspension uses a spring controlled, hydraulically damped, telescopic fork with air assist.

Before suspecting major trouble, drain the front fork oil and refill with the proper type and quantity; refer to in Chapter Three. If you still have trouble, such as poor damping, a tendency to bottom or top out or leakage around the rubber seals, follow the service procedures in this section.

To simplify fork service and to prevent the mixing of parts, the legs should be removed, serviced and installed individually.

Removal

NOTE
The Allen bolt at the base of the slider has been secured with Loctite. It is often very difficult to remove because the damper rod will turn inside the slider. It sometimes can be removed with an air impact driver. If you are unable to remove it, take the fork tubes to a dealer and have the screws removed.

1. If the fork assembly is going to be disassembled, perform the following:
   a. Have an assistant hold the front brake on, compress the front forks and hold them in that position.
   b. Using a 6 mm Allen wrench, slightly loosen the Allen bolt at the base of the slider. If the bolt is loosened too much, fork oil may start to drain out of the slider.

2. Remove the air valve cap and bleed off *all* air pressure by depressing the valve stem (A, **Figure 44**).

WARNING
Always bleed off all air pressure; failure to do so may cause personal injury when disassembling the fork assembly.

NOTE
Release the air pressure gradually. If released too fast, fork oil will spurt out with the air. Protect your eyes and clothing accordingly.

3. Remove the front wheel and brake caliper assembly as described in this chapter.

4. Remove the chrome cover caps. Remove the Allen bolts (**Figure 45**) securing the fork brace and remove the fork brace.

5. Loosen, but do not remove, the fork top cap bolts (B, **Figure 44**).

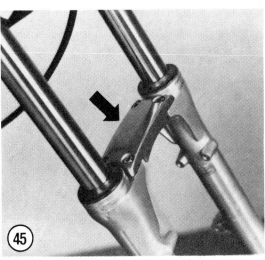

6. Remove the bolts securing the front fender (**Figure 46**) and remove the fender.

7. Loosen the upper and lower fork bridge bolts (**Figure 47**).

8. On Ascot models, perform the following:

    a. Remove the bolt securing the fork cover and remove the cover (**Figure 48**).

    b. In the next step, as the fork tube is removed catch the fork cover stay as it will fall off from the fork tube.

9. Remove the fork tube. It may be necessary to slightly rotate the fork tube while pulling it down and out.

Installation

1. On Ascot models, position the fork cover stay with the solid portion facing toward the inside. Place the stay between the upper and lower fork bridge.

2. Insert the fork tube up through the lower then the upper fork bridges (**Figure 49**).

3. Align the top of the fork tube with the top surface of the upper fork bridge.

4. Tighten the upper and lower fork bridge bolts loosely at this time—just tight enough to hold them in place.

5. Tighten the upper and lower fork bridge bolts to the torque specifications listed in **Table 1**.

6. Position the fork brace with the "F" mark and arrow (**Figure 50**) facing forward. If installed wrong the fender will not fit correctly.

7. Install the fork brace and tighten the bolts to the torque specification listed in **Table 1**. Install the trim caps into the bolt heads.

8. Install the front fender and tighten the bolts securely.

9. Install the front wheel and brake caliper assembly as described in this chapter.

10. Make sure the front wheel is off the ground and inflate the forks to 0-0.4 kg/cm² (0-6 psi). Do not

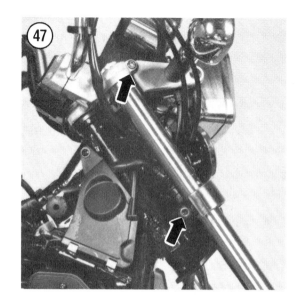

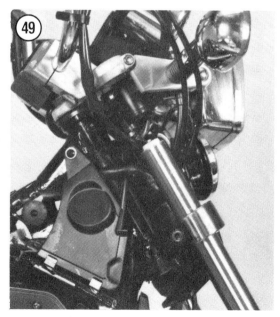

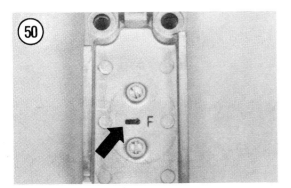

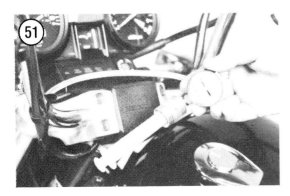

use compressed air, only use a small hand-operated air pump as shown in **Figure 51**.

WARNING
Never use any type of compressed gas as an explosion may be lethal. Never heat the fork assembly with a torch or place it near an open flame or extreme heat, as this will also result in an explosion.

CAUTION
Never exceed an air pressure of 43 psi (3.0 kg/cm²) as damage may occur to internal components of the fork assembly.

11. Take the bike off of the centerstand, apply the front brake and pump the forks several times. Recheck the air pressure and readjust if necessary.

Disassembly

Refer to **Figure 52** during the disassembly and assembly procedures.
1. Clamp the slider in a vise with soft jaws.
2. If not loosened during the fork removal sequence, loosen the Allen bolt and gasket from the base of the slider.

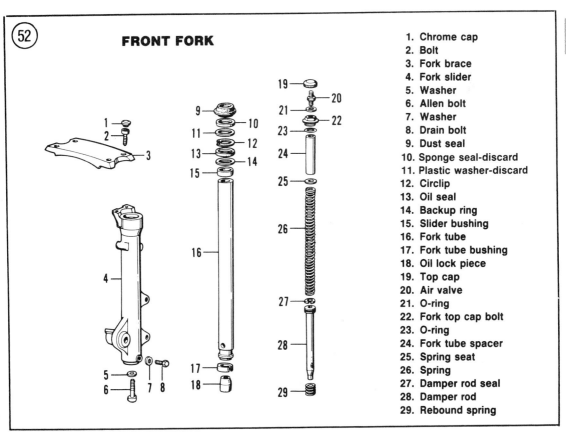

FRONT FORK

1. Chrome cap
2. Bolt
3. Fork brace
4. Fork slider
5. Washer
6. Allen bolt
7. Washer
8. Drain bolt
9. Dust seal
10. Sponge seal-discard
11. Plastic washer-discard
12. Circlip
13. Oil seal
14. Backup ring
15. Slider bushing
16. Fork tube
17. Fork tube bushing
18. Oil lock piece
19. Top cap
20. Air valve
21. O-ring
22. Fork top cap bolt
23. O-ring
24. Fork tube spacer
25. Spring seat
26. Spring
27. Damper rod seal
28. Damper rod
29. Rebound spring

NOTE
This bolt has been secured with Loctite and is often very difficult to remove because the damper rod will turn inside the slider. It sometimes can be removed with an air impact driver. If you are unable to remove it, take the fork tubes to a dealer and have the screws removed.

3. Remove the Allen bolt (**Figure 53**) at the base of the slider.

4. Hold the upper fork tube in a vise with soft jaws and loosen the fork top cap bolt (if it was not loosened during the fork removal sequence).

WARNING
Be careful when removing the fork top cap bolt as the spring is under pressure. Protect your eyes accordingly.

5. Remove the fork top cap bolt from the fork.

6. Remove the fork tube spacer, the spring seat and the fork spring.

7. Remove the fork from the vise, pour the fork oil out and discard it. Pump the fork several times by hand to expel most of the remaining oil.

NOTE
*The Honda factory has determined that the sponge seal may work its way down into the oil seal and give the appearance of a worn or leaking oil seal. Therefore do **not** reinstall the sponge seal and plastic washer under the dust seal during the assembly procedure. If you purchase a new seal kit that still has these 2 parts in it; discard them, they are not to be used.*

8. Remove the dust seal, sponge seal and the plastic washer. Discard the sponge seal and plastic washer as they are not to be reinstalled. These 2 parts were installed on the early 1983 production run of these models and then were eliminated on later 1983 production bikes. **Figure 52** shows these 2 parts and indicates that they should be discarded.

9. Using circlip pliers, remove the circlip from the slider.

10. Install the fork slider in a vise with soft jaws.

NOTE
On this type of fork, force is needed to remove the fork tube from the slider.

11. There is an interference fit between the bushing in the fork slider and the bushing on the fork tube. In order to remove the fork tube from the slider, pull hard on the fork tube using quick in and out strokes. Doing this will withdraw the bushing, backup ring and oil seal from the slider.

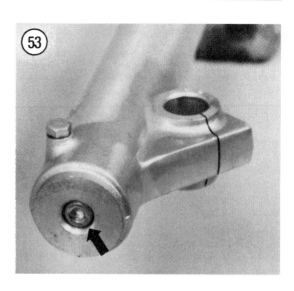

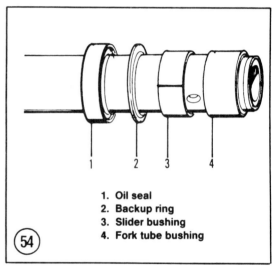

1. Oil seal
2. Backup ring
3. Slider bushing
4. Fork tube bushing

NOTE
It may be necessary to slightly heat the area on the slider around the oil seal prior to removal. Use a rag soaked in hot water; do not apply a flame directly to the fork slider.

12. Withdraw the fork tube from the slider.

NOTE
Do not remove the fork tube bushing unless it is going to be replaced. Inspect it as described in this chapter.

13. Turn the fork tube upside down and slide off the oil seal, backup ring and slider bushing from the fork tube (**Figure 54**).

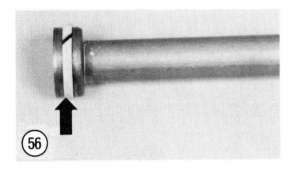

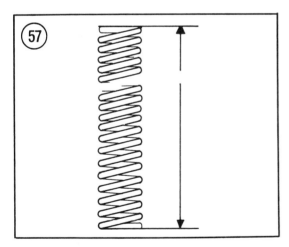

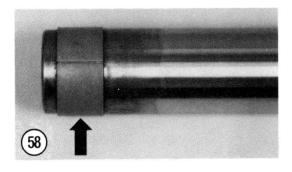

NOTE
Do not discard the slider bushing at this time. It will be used during the installation procedure.

14. Remove the oil lock piece, the damper rod and rebound spring.

15. Inspect the components as described in this chapter.

Inspection

1. Thoroughly clean all parts in solvent and dry them. Check the fork tube for signs of wear or scratches.

2. Check the damper rod for straightness. **Figure 55** shows one method. The rod should be replaced if the runout is 0.2 mm (0.008 in.) or greater.

3. Carefully check the damper rod and piston ring for wear or damage (**Figure 56**).

4. Check the upper fork tube for straightness. If bent or severely scratched, it should be replaced.

5. Check the lower slider for dents or exterior damage that may cause the upper fork tube to hang up during riding. Replace if necessary.

6. Measure the uncompressed length of the fork spring (not rebound spring) as shown in **Figure 57**. If the spring has sagged to the service limit dimensions listed in **Table 3** the spring must be replaced.

7. Inspect the slider and fork tube bushings (**Figure 58**). If either is scratched or scored they must be replaced. If the Teflon coating is worn off so that the copper base material is showing on approximately 3/4 of the total surface, the bushing must be replaced. Also check for distortion on the check points of the backup ring; replace as necessary. Refer to **Figure 59**.

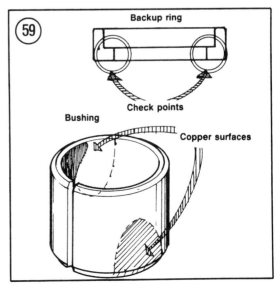

9

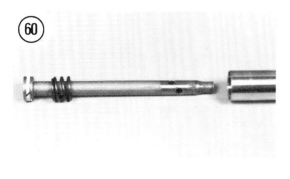

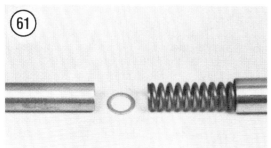

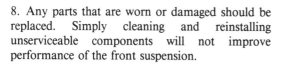

8. Any parts that are worn or damaged should be replaced. Simply cleaning and reinstalling unserviceable components will not improve performance of the front suspension.

Assembly

1. Coat all parts with fresh DEXRON automatic transmission fluid or fork oil prior to installation.
2. If removed, install a new fork tube bushing (**Figure 58**).
3. Install the rebound spring onto the damper rod and insert this assembly into the fork tube (**Figure 60**).
4. Temporarily install the fork spring, spring seat, the spacer (**Figure 61**) and fork top cap bolt. This will help hold the damper rod in place.
5. Install the oil lock piece onto the damper rod (**Figure 62**).
6. Install the upper fork assembly into the slider (**Figure 63**).
7. Slide the fork slider bushing down the fork tube and rest it on the slider.
8. Slide the fork slider backup ring (flange side up) down the fork tube and rest it on top of the fork slider bushing.
9. Place the old fork slider bushing on top of the backup ring. Drive the bushing into the fork slider with Honda special tool Fork Seal Driver (part No. 07947-4630100). Drive the bushing into place until it seats completely in the recess in the slider. Remove the installation tool and the old fork slider bushing.

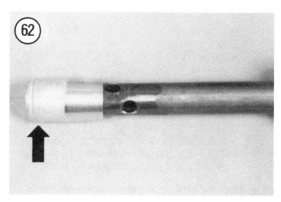

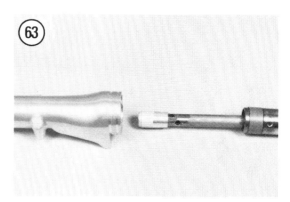

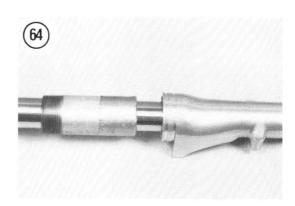

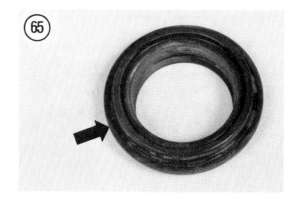

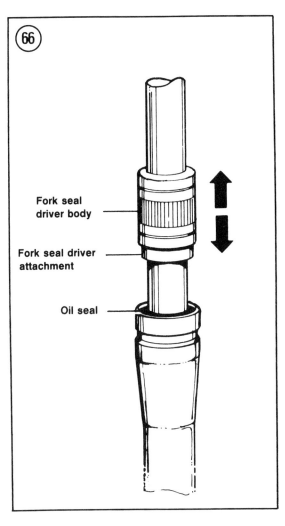

Fork seal driver body

Fork seal driver attachment

Oil seal

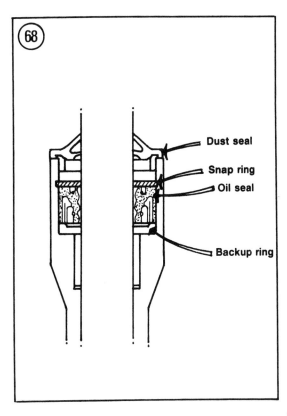

Dust seal

Snap ring

Oil seal

Backup ring

NOTE
*A piece of 2 in. galvanized pipe can also work as a tool. If both ends are threaded (a close nipple pipe fitting), wrap one end with duct tape (**Figure 64**) to prevent the threads from damaging the interior of the slider.*

10. Coat the new seal with DEXRON automatic transmission fluid. Position the seal with the marking facing upward (**Figure 65**) and slide it down onto the fork tube. Drive the seal into the slider with Honda special tool Fork Seal Driver (part No. 07947-4630100); refer to **Figure 66**. Drive the oil seal in until the groove in the slider can be seen above the top surface of the oil seal.

NOTE
The slider seal can be driven in with a homemade tool described in the NOTE following Step 9.

11. Install the circlip with the sharp side facing up. Make sure the circlip is completely seated in the groove in the fork slider (**Figure 67**).

NOTE
Figure 68 *shows the correct placement of all components installed in Step 12.*

12. Install the dust seal (**Figure 69**). Remember *do not* install the plastic washer and the sponge seal. Discard them if they are included in a new seal kit that you may have purchased. Refer to the Note regarding these items in the Disassembly procedure.

13. Make sure the gasket is on the Allen bolt (**Figure 72**).

14. Apply Loctite 242 to the threads of the Allen bolt prior to installation. Install it in the fork slider (**Figure 53**) and tighten to the torque specification listed in **Table 1**. If you are unable to tighten the bolt to the correct torque specification, finish tightening the bolt after the fork tube is reinstalled in the bike's frame.

15. Remove the fork top cap bolt, the fork tube spacer, the spring seat and the fork spring.

16. Fill the fork tube with the correct quantity of DEXRON automatic transmission fluid as listed in **Table 4**.

17. Install the fork spring with the closer wound coils toward the top end of the fork.

18. Install the fork seat and the fork tube spacer (**Figure 61**).

19. Inspect the O-ring seal (**Figure 71**) on the fork top cap bolt; replace if necessary.

20. Install the fork top cap bolt (**Figure 72**) while pushing down on the spring. Start the bolt slowly, don't cross thread it.

21. Place the slider in a vise with soft jaws and tighten the top fork cap bolt to the torque specification listed in **Table 1**.

22. Repeat for the other fork assembly.

23. Install the fork assemblies as described in this chapter.

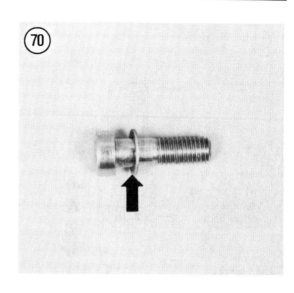

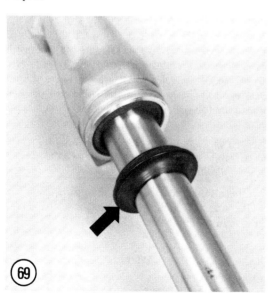

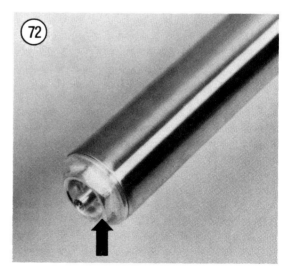

Table 1 FRONT SUSPENSION TORQUE SPECIFICATIONS

Item	N·m	ft.-lb.
Front axle	55-65	40-47
Front axle pinch bolt or clamp nuts	18-28	13-20
Caliper mounting bolts	30-40	22-29
Brake system union bolts	25-35	18-25
Brake disc bolts	35-40	25-29
Handlebar holder bolts	20-30	14-22
Fork bridge bolts		
Upper	9-13	7-9
Lower	45-55	33-40
Fork cap bolt	15-30	11-22
Fork brace Allen bolts	15-25	11-18
Fork slide Allen bolt	15-25	11-18
Steering stem nut	80-120	58-87

Table 2 TIRE INFLATION PRESSURE (COLD)

	Air pressure	
Tire size	Up to 200 lb. (890 kg)	Maximum load limit*
Front		
3.50S-18	28 psi (2.00 kg/cm^2)	28 psi (2.00 kg/cm^2)
Rear		
130/19-16	28 psi (2.00 kg/cm^2)	36 psi (2.50 kg/cm^2)

*Maximum load limit includes total weight of motorcycle with accessories, rider(s) and luggage.

Table 3 FRONT FORK SPRING LENGTH

	Standard	Service limit
VT500C		
1983-1984	456.2 mm (17.96 in.)	447 mm (17.6 in.)
1985-1986	443 mm (17.4 in.)	434 mm (17.1 in.)
VT500FT	475 mm (16.33 in.)	465.5 mm (18.33 in.)
VT500E	445.4 mm (17.53 in.)	436.4 mm (17.18 in.)

Table 4 FORK OIL CAPACITY

VT500FT Ascot*	390 cc (13.2 U.S. fl. oz.)
VT500C Shadow	
1983-1984	
Right-hand leg	440 cc (14.9 U.S. fl. oz.)
Left-hand leg	455 cc (15.4 U.S. fl. oz.)
1985-1986	
Left- and right-hand leg	442 cc (15.0 U.S. fl. oz.)
VT500E Euro Sport*	360 cc (12.7 Imp. fl. oz.)

*Capacity for each fork leg.

9

CHAPTER TEN

REAR SUSPENSION AND FINAL DRIVE

This chapter includes repair and replacement procedures for the rear wheel, rear suspension components and the final drive unit.

Power from the engine is transmitted to the rear wheel by a drive shaft and the final drive unit.

Tire changing and wheel balancing is covered in Chapter Nine.

Refer to **Table 1** for rear suspension torque specifications. **Table 1** and **Table 2** are located at the end of this chapter.

REAR WHEEL

Removal/Installation

1. Place the bike on the centerstand or block up the engine so that the rear wheel clears the ground.
2. Completely unscrew the rear brake adjusting nut (A, **Figure 1**).
3. Depress the brake pedal and remove the brake rod from the pivot joint in the brake arm. Remove the pivot joint from the brake arm and install the pivot joint and the adjusting nut onto the brake rod to avoid misplacing them.
4. To remove the brake torque link, perform the following:
   a. Remove the cotter pin from the bolt (B, **Figure 1**).
   b. Remove the bolt, nut and washer.
   c. Swing the brake arm down and out of the way.

5. Loosen the axle pinch bolt (A, **Figure 2**).
6. Remove the rear axle self-locking nut (**Figure 3**).
7. Insert a drift or screwdriver into the hole in the end of the rear axle and withdraw the axle (B, **Figure 2**) from the right-hand side.
8. Remove the license plate.
9. Slide the wheel to the right to disengage it from the hub drive splines and remove the wheel.
10. Don't lose the spacer on the right-hand side between the brake and the swing arm.

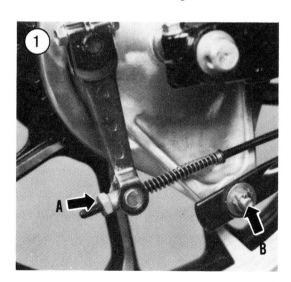

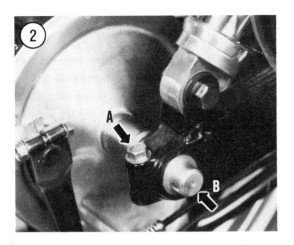

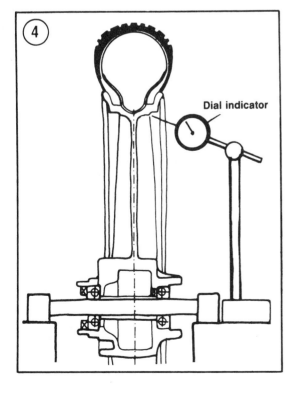

Inspection

Measure the axial and radial runout of the wheel with a dial indicator as shown in **Figure 4**. The maximum axial and radial runout is 2.0 mm (0.08 in.). If the runout exceeds this dimension, check the wheel bearing condition.

If the wheel bearings are okay, the wheel will have to be replaced, as it cannot be serviced. Inspect the wheel for signs of cracks, fractures, dents or bends. If it is damaged in any way, it must be replaced.

> *WARNING*
> *Do not try to repair any damage to an alloy wheel as it will result in an unsafe riding condition.*

Check axial runout as described under *Rear Hub Inspection* in this chapter.

Installation

1. The distance collar within the final drive unit may move out during axle and wheel removal. If so, push it back into place. If the distance collar falls out, reinstall it into the final drive unit with the narrow end in first (**Figure 5**).

> *NOTE*
> ***Figure 5*** *is shown with the final drive unit removed for clarity.*

2. Apply a light coat of grease (lithium based NLGI No. 2 grease with molybdenum disulfide) to the final driven flange spline and to the rear wheel ring gear (**Figure 6**).

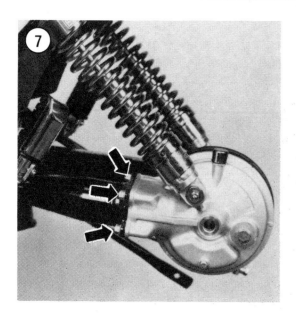

3. Loosen the final drive case nuts (**Figure 7**).

4. Position the rear wheel so that the splines of the final driven flange and the final drive align. Slowly move the wheel back and forth and push the wheel to the left until it completely seats.

5. Position the spacer (**Figure 8**) on the right-hand side between the brake and the swing arm.

6. Install the rear axle from the right-hand side and install the axle nut only finger-tight.

7. To install the brake torque link, perform the following:

   a. Swing the brake arm up and into position.

   b. Install the bolt from the backside and install the washer and nut. Tighten the bolt and nut to the torque specification listed in **Table 1**.

   c. Install a new cotter pin and bend the ends over completely.

8. Insert a drift into the hole in the axle to keep the axle from turning.

9. Tighten the rear axle nut to the torque specifications listed in **Table 1**.

10. Tighten the final drive gear case nuts, then the axle pinch bolt to the torque specifications listed in **Table 1**.

11. After the wheel is installed, completely rotate it and apply the brake several times to make sure it rotates freely and that the brakes work properly.

12. Adjust the rear brake free play as described in Chapter Three.

REAR HUB

Inspection

Inspect each wheel bearing prior to removing it from the wheel hub.

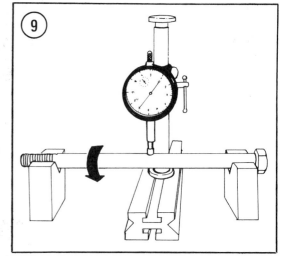

CAUTION
Do not remove the wheel bearings for inspection purposes as they will be damaged during the removal process. Remove wheel bearings only if they are to be replaced.

1. Perform Step 1 and Step 2 of *Disassembly* in this chapter.

2. Turn each bearing by hand. Make sure the bearings turn smoothly.

3. On non-sealed bearings, check the balls for evidence of wear, pitting or excessive heat (bluish tint). Replace the bearings if necessary; always replace as a complete set. When replacing the bearings, be sure to take your old bearings along to ensure a perfect matchup.

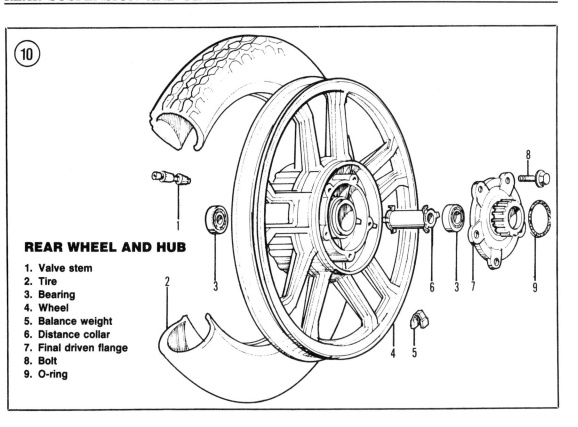

REAR WHEEL AND HUB

1. Valve stem
2. Tire
3. Bearing
4. Wheel
5. Balance weight
6. Distance collar
7. Final driven flange
8. Bolt
9. O-ring

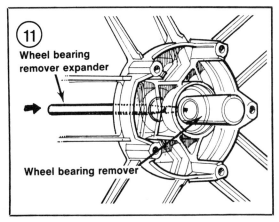

Wheel bearing remover expander

Wheel bearing remover

NOTE
Fully sealed bearings are available from many bearing specialty shops. Fully sealed bearings provide better protection from dirt and moisture that may get into the hub.

4. Check the axle for wear and straightness. Use V-blocks and a dial indicator as shown in **Figure 9**. If the runout is 0.2 mm (0.01 in.) or greater, the axle should be replaced.

5. Inspect the splines of the final driven flange. If any are damaged the flange must be replaced.

Disassembly

Refer to **Figure 10** for this procedure.

1. Remove the rear wheel as described in this chapter.

2. Remove the bolts securing the final driven flange and remove the flange (**Figure 6**).

3. Before proceeding further, inspect the wheel bearings as described in this chapter. If they must be replaced, proceed as follows.

4A. A special Honda tool set-up can be used to remove the wheel bearings as follows:

a. Install the 15 mm bearing remover (Honda part No. 07746-0050400) into the right-hand bearing.

b. Turn the wheel over (left-hand side up) on the workbench so the end of the bearing remover is touching the workbench surface.

c. From the left-hand side of the hub, install the bearing remover expander (Honda part No. 07746-050100) into the bearing remover. Using a hammer, tap the expander into the bearing remover with a hammer.

d. Stand the wheel up to a vertical position.

e. Tap on the end of the expander (**Figure 11**) and drive the right-hand bearing out of the hub. Remove the bearing and the distance collar.

f. Repeat for the left-hand bearing.

4B. If special tools are not available, perform the following:
   a. To remove the right- and left-hand bearings and distance collar, insert a soft aluminum or brass drift into one side of the hub.
   b. Push the distance collar over to one side and place the drift on the inner race of the lower bearing.
   c. Tap the bearing out of the hub with a hammer, working around the perimeter of the inner race.
   d. Repeat for the other bearing.
5. Clean the inside and the outside of the hub with solvent. Dry with compressed air.
6. Clean the inside and the outside of the final driven flange with solvent. Remove and discard the O-ring seal at the base of the splines. Dry with compressed air.

Assembly

1. On non-sealed bearings, pack the bearings with a good quality bearing grease. Work the grease in between the balls thoroughly; turn the bearing by hand a couple of times to make sure the grease is distributed evenly inside the bearing.
2. Blow any dirt or foreign matter out of the hub prior to installing the bearings.

> *CAUTION*
> *Install non-sealed bearings with the single sealed side facing outward. Tap the bearings squarely into place and tap on the outer race only. Use a socket (**Figure 12**) that matches the outer race diameter. Do not tap on the inner race or the bearing might be damaged. Be sure that the bearings are completely seated.*

3. Pack the hub with multipurpose grease.
4. Press the distance collar into the hub from the left-hand side.

> *CAUTION*
> *Install the standard bearings (they are sealed on one side only) with the sealed side facing out (**Figure 13**). Tap the bearings squarely into place and tap only on the outer race. Use a socket (**Figure 12**) that matches the outer race diameter. Do not tap on the inner race or the bearing will be damaged. Be sure to tap the bearings in until they seat completely.*

5. Install the right-hand bearing into the hub.
6. Install the left-hand bearing into the hub.
7. Install the final driven flange and bolts. Tighten the bolts to the torque specifications listed in **Table 1**.

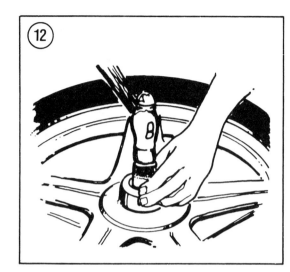

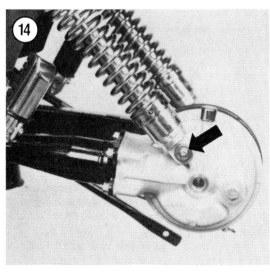

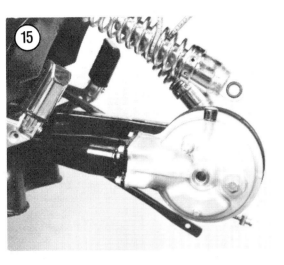

8. Install a new O-ring seal onto the base of the splines on the final driven flange.

9. Install the rear wheel as described in this chapter.

FINAL DRIVE UNIT AND DRIVE SHAFT

Removal

1. Drain the final drive unit oil as described in Chapter Three.

2. Remove the rear wheel as described in this chapter.

3. Remove the lower nut and washer (**Figure 14**) securing the left-hand shock absorber to the final drive unit. Pivot the shock absorber up and out of the way and secure it to the frame with a Bungee cord (**Figure 15**).

4. Remove the nuts and washers (**Figure 16**) securing the final drive unit to the swing arm.

5. Pull the final drive unit and drive shaft straight back until it is disengaged from the splines on the universal joint.

Disassembly/Inspection/ Assembly

The final drive unit requires a considerable number of special Honda tools for disassembly and assembly. The price of all of these tools could be more than the cost of most repairs or seal replacement by a dealer.

Figure 17 shows all of the internal components of the final drive unit.

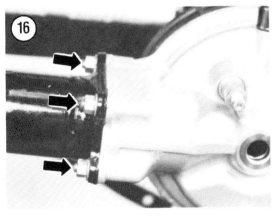

10

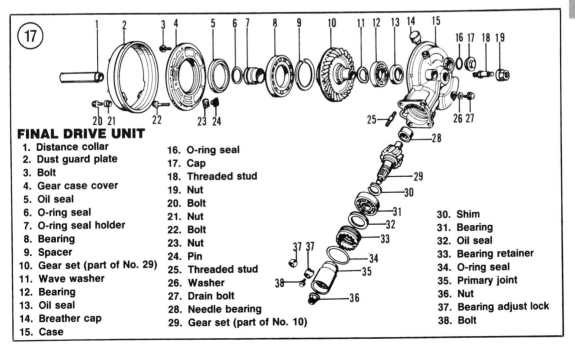

FINAL DRIVE UNIT

1. Distance collar
2. Dust guard plate
3. Bolt
4. Gear case cover
5. Oil seal
6. O-ring seal
7. O-ring seal holder
8. Bearing
9. Spacer
10. Gear set (part of No. 29)
11. Wave washer
12. Bearing
13. Oil seal
14. Breather cap
15. Case

16. O-ring seal
17. Cap
18. Threaded stud
19. Nut
20. Bolt
21. Nut
22. Bolt
23. Nut
24. Pin
25. Threaded stud
26. Washer
27. Drain bolt
28. Needle bearing
29. Gear set (part of No. 10)

30. Shim
31. Bearing
32. Oil seal
33. Bearing retainer
34. O-ring seal
35. Primary joint
36. Nut
37. Bearing adjust lock
38. Bolt

1. Using a circular motion, carefully pull the drive shaft from the final drive unit.

2. Check that the dust cover flange bolt (**Figure 18**) is in place and is tight.

3. Inspect the splines on the final driven ring gear (**Figure 19**). If they are damaged or worn the ring gear must be replaced.

NOTE
If these splines are damaged, also inspect the splines on the rear wheel final driven flange; it may also need to be replaced.

4. Inspect the splines on the final driven primary joint (A, **Figure 20**). If they are damaged or worn the primary joint must be replaced.

NOTE
If these splines are damaged, also inspect the splines on the drive shaft; it may also need to be replaced.

5. Make sure the bearing retainer adjust lock and bolt (B, **Figure 20**) are in place and tight.

6. Inspect the splines on the universal joint end of drive shaft (**Figure 21**). If they are damaged or worn, the drive shaft must be replaced.

NOTE
If these splines are damaged, also inspect the splines on the universal joint; it may also need to be replaced.

7. Inspect the splines on the final drive unit end of drive shaft (A, **Figure 22**). If they are damaged or worn, the drive shaft must be replaced.

NOTE
If these splines are damaged, also inspect the splines in the final drive unit; it may also need to be replaced.

8. Check the damper spring (B, **Figure 22**); replace if necessary.

9. Replace the oil seal (C, **Figure 22**) on the drive shaft. The oil seal must be replaced every time it is removed from the drive shaft.

10. Remove the stopper ring (D, **Figure 22**) from the groove in the end of the drive shaft splines. Discard the stopper ring.

11. Check that gear oil has not been leaking from either side of the unit (ring gear side or pinion joint side). If there are traces of oil leakage, take the unit to a dealer for oil seal replacement.

12. Make sure the damper spring (B, **Figure 22**) is installed in the end of the drive shaft.

13. Install a new stopper ring into the groove in the end of the drive shaft splines. Make sure it is correctly seated in the groove.

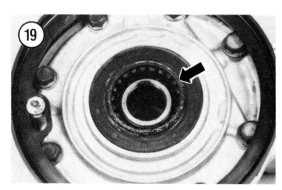

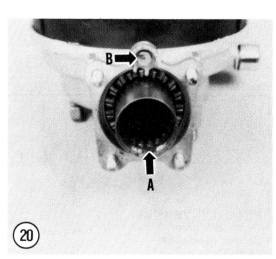

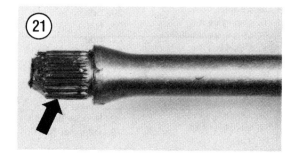

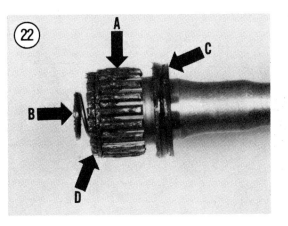

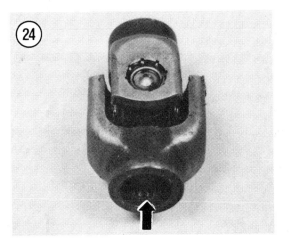

Installation

1. Apply a light coat of molybdenum disulfide grease (NGLI No. 2 grease) to the splines of the drive shaft and install the drive shaft into the final drive unit. Using a soft-faced mallet, tap on the end of the drive shaft to make sure the drive shaft is completely seated into the final drive unit splines.
2. Apply a light coat of molybdenum disulfide grease (NGLI No. 2 grease) to the final driven spline.

3. Install the final drive unit and drive shaft into the swing arm. It may be necessary to slightly rotate the final driven spline back and forth to align the splines of the drive shaft and the universal joint.
4. Install the final drive unit's washers and nuts only finger-tight at this time. Do not tighten the nuts until the rear wheel and rear axle are in place.
5. Install the rear wheel as described in this chapter.
6. Tighten the final drive unit nuts to the specifications listed in **Table 1**.
7. Install the shock absorber lower washer and nut and tighten to the torque specifications listed in **Table 1**.
8. Refill the final drive unit with the correct amount and type of gear oil. Refer to Chapter Three.

UNIVERSAL JOINT

Removal/Inspection/Installation

1. Remove the swing arm as described in this chapter.
2. Remove the universal joint from the engine output shaft.
3. Clean the universal joint in solvent and thoroughly dry with compressed air.
4. Inspect the universal joint pivot points for play (**Figure 23**). Rotate the joint in both directions. If there is noticeable side play the universal joint must be replaced.
5. Inspect the splines at each end of the univeral joint (**Figure 24**). If they are damaged or worn, the universal joint must be replaced.

NOTE
If these splines are damaged, also inspect the splines in the final drive unit and the engine output shaft; they may also need to be replaced.

6. Apply a light coat of molybdenum disulfide grease (NGLI No. 2 grease) to both splines.
7. Install the universal joint onto the engine output shaft.

SWING ARM

In time, the roller bearings will wear and will have to be replaced. The condition of the bearings can greatly affect handling performance and if worn parts are not replaced they can produce erratic and dangerous handling. Common symptoms are wheel hop, pulling to one side during acceleration and pulling to the other side during braking.

A Honda special tool is required for loosening and tightening of the pivot adjusting bolt locknut. The tool is the Swing Arm Pivot Locknut Wrench

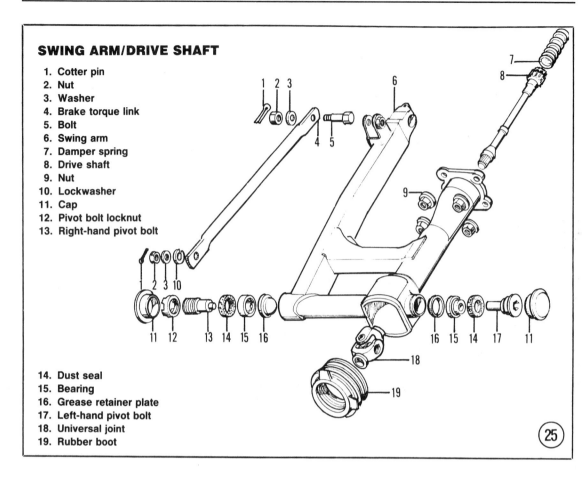

SWING ARM/DRIVE SHAFT

1. Cotter pin
2. Nut
3. Washer
4. Brake torque link
5. Bolt
6. Swing arm
7. Damper spring
8. Drive shaft
9. Nut
10. Lockwasher
11. Cap
12. Pivot bolt locknut
13. Right-hand pivot bolt

14. Dust seal
15. Bearing
16. Grease retainer plate
17. Left-hand pivot bolt
18. Universal joint
19. Rubber boot

(Honda part No. 07908-ME90000). This tool is required for proper and safe installation of the swing arm. If this locknut is not tightened to the correct torque specification it may allow the adjusting bolt to work loose. This could result in the swing arm working free from the right-hand side of the frame causing a serious accident.

Refer to **Figure 25** for these procedures.

Removal

1. Place the bike on the centerstand and remove the seat.
2. Remove the exhaust system (A, **Figure 26**) as described in Chapter Six.
3. Remove the rear wheel (B, **Figure 26**) as described in this chapter.
4. Remove the final drive unit and drive shaft (C, **Figure 26**) as described in this chapter.
5. Remove the lower mounting bolt and nut securing the right-hand shock absorber.

NOTE
It is not necessary to remove the shock absorber unit, just pivot the unit up and out of the way with a Bungee cord.

6. Grasp the rear end of the swing arm and try to move it from side to side in a horizontal arc. There should be no noticeable side play. If play is evident and the pivot adjusting bolt is tightened correctly, the bearings should be replaced.
7. Remove the cap (D, **Figure 26**) on both pivot bolts.

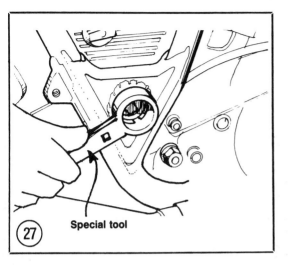

Special tool

(27)

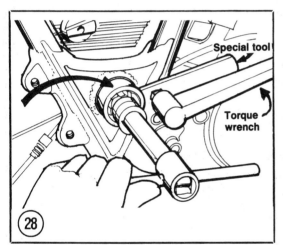

Special tool

Torque wrench

(28)

4. Apply a light coat of grease to the inner end of both the right- and left-hand pivot bolts. Install the right- and left-hand pivot bolts.

5. Make sure the swing arm is properly located in the frame and then tighten the left-hand pivot bolt to the torque specifications listed in **Table 1**.

6. Tighten the right-hand pivot bolt to 20 N•m (14 ft.-lb.), then loosen it and retighten it to the torque specification listed in **Table 1**.

7. Move the swing arm up and down several times to make sure all components are properly seated.

8. Retighten the right-hand pivot bolt to the correct torque specification.

9. On the right-hand side, perform the following:

   a. Hold onto the right-hand pivot bolt with a 10 mm Allen wrench to make sure the pivot bolt does not move while tightening the locknut.

   b. Use special tool, Swing Arm Pivot Locknut Wrench (Honda part No. 07908-ME90000) and torque wrench (**Figure 28**). Tighten the locknut to the torque specification listed in **Table 1**.

10. Install the final drive unit and drive shaft assembly as described in this chapter.

11. Attach the rubber boot onto the rear of the engine. Make sure it is correctly installed on both the engine and swing arm. This seal is necessary to keep out dirt and water.

12. Install the rear shock absorbers as described in this chapter.

13. Install the rear wheel as described in this chapter.

14. Install the exhaust system as described in Chapter Six.

10

8. Use the special tool, Swing Arm Pivot Locknut Wrench (Honda part No. 07908-ME90000), and loosen the right-hand pivot bolt locknut (**Figure 27**).

9. Use a 10 mm Allen wrench and remove the right-hand adjusting bolt.

10. Remove the left-hand pivot bolt.

11. Pull back on the swing arm, free it from the frame and remove it from the frame.

12. Leave the universal joint on the engine output shaft.

Installation

1. Make sure the universal joint is installed on the engine output shaft.

2. If removed, install the rubber boot on the drive shaft side of the swing arm with the "UP" mark facing up.

3. Position the swing arm into the mounting area of the frame. Align the holes in the swing arm with the holes in the frame.

Bearing Replacement

The swing arm is equipped with a roller bearing at each end. The inner race and roller bearing will come right out (no force needed) after the grease seal is removed. The bearing outer race is pressed in place and has to be removed with force. The race will get distorted when removed, so don't remove it unless the bearing assembly is going to be replaced.

The bearing outer race must be removed and installed with special tools that are available from a Honda dealer. The special tools are as follows:

   a. Bearing remover: Honda part No. 07936-3710200.

   b. Slide hammer handle: Honda part No. 07936-3710100.

   c. Slide hammer weight: Honda part No. 07936-3710200.

   d. Driver handle: Honda part No. 07749-00100000.

e. Bearing driver outer: Honda part No. 07746-0010200.

1. Remove the swing arm as described in this chapter.

2. Remove the dust seal and bearing assembly from each side of the swing arm.

3. Secure the swing arm in a vise with soft jaws.

NOTE
These special tools grab the outer race and then withdraw it from the swing arm with the use of a tool similar to a body shop slide hammer.

4. Remove the right-hand bearing race first (**Figure 29**) as follows:

a. Remove the attachment from the end of the bearing remover.

b. Slide the shaft of the bearing remover through the hole in the bearing race and install a 29 mm OD washer or equivalent attachment onto the end of the shaft.

c. Slide the weight on the hammer upward several times and remove the bearing race.

d. Remove the grease retainer plate and discard it.

5. Turn the swing arm over in the vise and repeat for the other end.

6. Thoroughly clean out the inside of the swing arm with solvent and dry with compressed air.

7. Apply a light coat of waterproof grease to all parts prior to installation.

8. Install a new grease retainer plate into the bearing receptacle.

NOTE
Either the right- or left-hand bearing race can be installed first.

9. To install the new roller bearing outer race place the bearing driver outer over the bearing race and drive the race into place with the driver handle and a hammer (**Figure 30**). Drive the race into place slowly and squarely. Make sure it is properly seated.

CAUTION
Never reinstall a bearing outer race that has been removed. During removal it becomes slightly damaged and is no longer true to alignment. If installed, it will damage the roller bearing assembly and create an unsafe riding condition.

10. Repeat Step 9 for the other bearing race.

11. Install a new roller bearing and dust seal on each end of the swing arm.

12. Install the swing arm as described in this chapter.

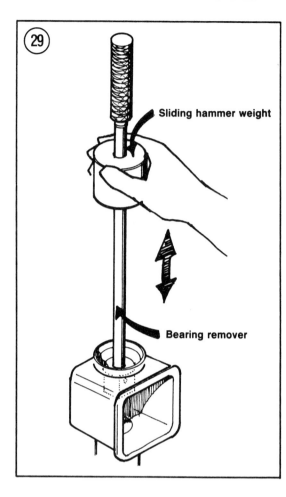

Sliding hammer weight

Bearing remover

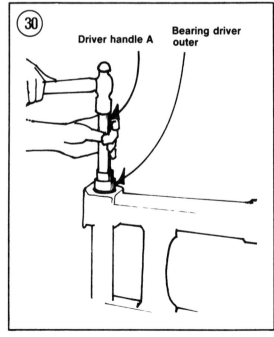

Driver handle A

Bearing driver outer

SHOCK ABSORBERS

The shock absorbers are spring controlled and hydraulically dampened. Spring preload can be adjusted by rotating the spring lower seat at the base of the spring (**Figure 31**) *clockwise to increase* preload and *counterclockwise to decrease* it.

NOTE
Use the wrench furnished in the factory tool kit.

Both cams must be indexed on the same detent. The shocks are sealed and cannot be rebuilt. Service is limited to removal and replacement of the hydraulic unit or the spring.

Removal/Installation

Removal and installation of the rear shocks is easier if done separately. The remaining unit will support the rear of the bike and maintain the correct relationship between the top and bottom shock mounts.

1. Place the bike on the centerstand and remove the seat.

NOTE
It is not necessary to remove the seat but it will protect the cover from the accidental slippage of a tool during removal and installation of the upper Allen bolt.

2. Adjust both shocks to their softest setting, *completely counterclockwise.*
3. On the left-hand side, remove the lower nut and washer and the upper Allen bolt (**Figure 32**).
4. On the right-hand side, remove the lower bolt and washer and the upper Allen bolt.
5. Pull the unit straight off the upper bolt and remove it.
6. Install by reversing these removal steps. Tighten the upper mounting nut and lower mounting bolt or nut to the torque specifications listed in **Table 1**.
7. Repeat for the other side.

Disassembly/Inspection/
Assembly

Refer to **Figure 33** for this procedure.

The shock is spring-controlled and hydraulically damped. The shock damper unit is sealed and cannot be serviced. Service is limited to removal and replacement of the damper unit and the spring.

The shock must be disassembled with the use of special tools that are available from a Honda dealer. They are described in this procedure.

WARNING
Without the proper tool, this procedure can be dangerous. The spring can fly loose, causing injury. For a small bench fee, a dealer can do the job for you.

1. Install the shock absorber in a compression tool (Honda part No. 07959-3290001) as shown in **Figure 34**.

NOTE
The shock compressor tool must be modified to safely accommodate this particular shock absorber. Two additional components have to be added to the basic compressor tool. Replace the base and guide of the compressor tool with a set of attachments (Honda part No. 07959-MB 1000). Also place a collar

10

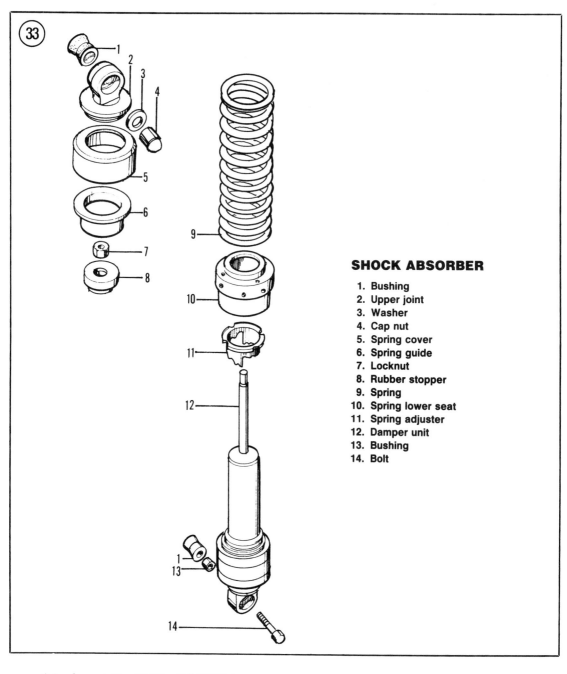

㉝

SHOCK ABSORBER

1. Bushing
2. Upper joint
3. Washer
4. Cap nut
5. Spring cover
6. Spring guide
7. Locknut
8. Rubber stopper
9. Spring
10. Spring lower seat
11. Spring adjuster
12. Damper unit
13. Bushing
14. Bolt

(Honda part No. 52486- 463-0000) in the shock absorber's lower joint prior to installing the shock absorber into the compressor tool.

2. Compress the spring just enough (approximately 30 mm) to gain access to the locknut under the upper joint.

3. Place the upper joint in a vise with soft jaws and loosen the locknut (**Figure 35**).

4. Completely unscrew the upper joint. This part may be difficult to break loose as Loctite Lock N' Seal was applied during assembly.

5. Release the spring tension and remove the shock from the compression tool.

6. Remove the spring cover, spring, spring lower seat and spring adjuster from the damper unit.

7. Measure the spring free length (**Figure 36**). The spring must be replaced if it has sagged to the service limit listed in **Table 2** or less.

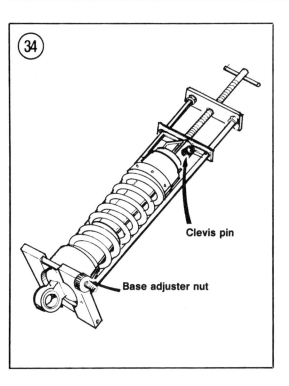

Clevis pin

Base adjuster nut

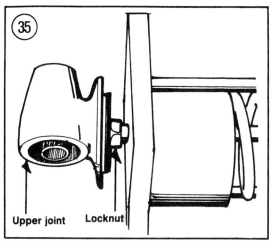

Upper joint   Locknut

8. Check the damper unit for leakage and make sure the damper rod is straight.

NOTE
The damper unit cannot be rebuilt; it must be replaced as a unit.

9. Inspect the rubber bushings in the upper and lower joints. Replace if necessary.
10. Inspect the rubber stopper. If it is worn or deteriorated, remove the locknut and slide off the rubber stopper. Replace with a new one.
11. Assembly is the reverse of these disassembly steps, noting the following.

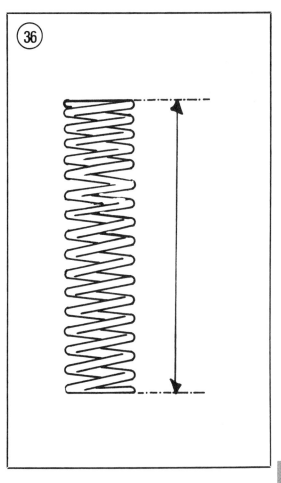

12. If the locknut was removed, apply Loctite Lock N' Seal to the threads of the damper rod prior to installing the locknut. Screw the locknut all the way down and tight against the end of the threads.
13. Apply Loctite Lock N' Seal to the threads of the damper rod prior to installing the upper joint. Screw the upper joint on all the way. Secure the upper joint in a vise with soft jaws and tighten the locknut along with the damper rod against the upper joint.

NOTE
The damper rod should rotate with the locknut when the locknut is tightened against the bottom surface of the upper joint.

NOTE
After the locknut is tightened completely the locknut must be against the bottom surface of the upper joint and against the end of the threads on the damper rod.

14. Align the upper spring seat with the upper joint when releasing the spring compressor tool.

Table 1 REAR SUSPENSION TORQUE SPECIFICATIONS

Item	N·m	ft.-lb.
Rear axle nut		
1985-1986 VT500C	80-100	58-72
All others	50-80	36-58
Rear axle pinch bolt	20-30	14-22
Shock absorber mounting nut and bolt	30-40	22-29
Brake torque link bolt	15-25	11-18
Final drive unit nuts	50-60	36-43
Swing arm		
Left-hand pivot bolt		
1985-1986 VT500C	60-80	43-58
All others	80-120	58-87
Right-hand pivot bolt	8-12	6-9
Pivot locknut	80-120	58-87

Table 2 REAR SHOCK ABSORBER SPRING FREE LENGTH

Item	Standard	Service limit
VT500C	249.7 mm (8.93 in.)	237 mm (9.3 in.)
VT500FT	263 mm (10.35 in.)	257.6 mm (10.14 in.)
VT500E	261.8 mm (10.31 in.)	256.8 mm (10.11 in.)

NOTE: If you own a VT500E, first check the Supplement at the back of the book for any additional service information.

CHAPTER ELEVEN

BRAKES

The brake system consists of a single disc on the front wheel and a drum brake on the rear.

Refer to **Table 1** for brake specifications and **Table 2** for torque specifications. **Table 1** and **Table 2** are located at the end of this chapter.

FRONT DISC BRAKE

The front disc brake is actuated by hydraulic fluid and is controlled by a hand lever on the master cylinder. As the brake pads wear, the brake fluid level drops in the reservoir and automatically adjusts for wear.

When working on hydraulic brake systems, it is necessary that the work area and all tools be absolutely clean. Any tiny particles of foreign matter and grit in the caliper assembly or the master cylinder can damage the components. Also, sharp tools must not be used inside the caliper or on the piston. If there is any doubt about your ability to correctly and safely carry out major service on the brake components, take the job to a dealer or brake specialist.

FRONT MASTER CYLINDER

Removal/Installation

1. Remove the rear view mirror (A, **Figure 1**) from the master cylinder.

> *CAUTION*
> *Cover the fuel tank and instrument cluster with a heavy cloth or plastic tarp to protect them from accidental brake fluid spills. Wash brake fluid off any painted or plated surfaces immediately, as it will destroy the finish. Use soapy water and rinse completely.*

2. Pull back the rubber boot (B, **Figure 1**) and remove the union bolt (**Figure 2**) securing the brake hose to the master cylinder. Remove the brake hose. Tie the end of the brake hose up and cover the end to prevent the entry of foreign matter.

3. Remove the clamping bolts (**Figure 3**) and clamp securing the master cylinder to the handlebar and remove the master cylinder.

11

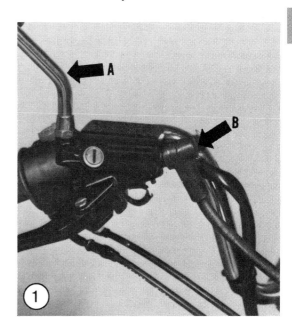

1

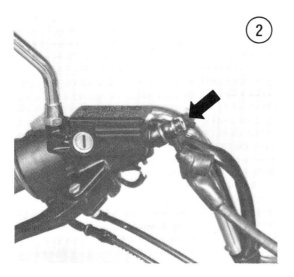

4. Install by reversing these removal steps, noting the following.

5. Install the clamp with the "UP" arrow (**Figure 4**) facing up. Align the face of the clamp with the punch mark on the handlebar (**Figure 5**). Tighten the upper bolt first, then the lower to the torque specification listed in **Table 2**.

6. Install the brake hose onto the master cylinder. Be sure to place a sealing washer on each side of the fitting and install the union bolt. Tighten the union bolt to the torque specifications listed in **Table 2**.

7. Bleed the brake as described in this chapter.

Disassembly

Refer to **Figure 6** for this procedure.

1. Remove the master cylinder as described in this chapter.

2. Remove the bolt and nut securing the brake lever and remove the lever.

3. Remove the screws securing the cover and remove the cover and diaphragm; pour out the brake fluid and discard it. *Never* reuse brake fluid.

4. Remove the rubber boot from the area where the hand lever actuates the internal piston assembly.

5. Using circlip pliers and remove the internal circlip from the body.

6. Remove the secondary cup and the piston assembly.

7. Remove the primary cup and spring.

8. Remove the brake light switch if necessary.

Inspection

1. Clean all parts in denatured alcohol or fresh brake fluid. Inspect the cylinder bore and piston contact surfaces for signs of wear and damage. If either part is less than perfect, replace it.

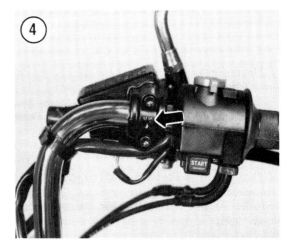

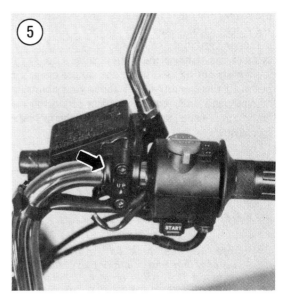

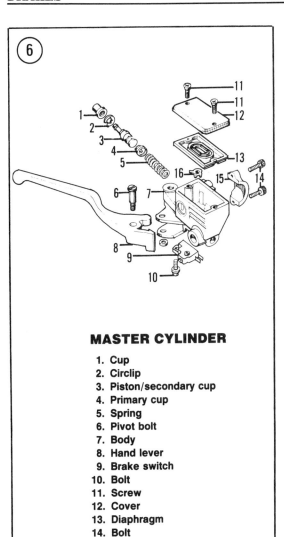

MASTER CYLINDER

1. Cup
2. Circlip
3. Piston/secondary cup
4. Primary cup
5. Spring
6. Pivot bolt
7. Body
8. Hand lever
9. Brake switch
10. Bolt
11. Screw
12. Cover
13. Diaphragm
14. Bolt
15. Clamp

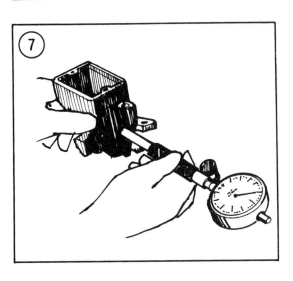

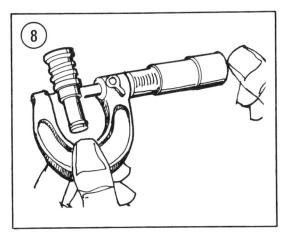

2. Check the end of the piston for wear caused by the hand lever. Replace if worn.

3. Replace the piston if the secondary cup requires replacement.

4. Inspect the pivot hole in the hand lever. If worn or elongated it must be replaced.

5. Make sure the passages in the bottom of the brake fluid reservoir are clear. Check the reservoir cap and diaphragm for damage and deterioration and replace as necessary.

6. Inspect the threads in the bore for the brake line.

7. Check the hand lever pivot lugs on the master cylinder body for cracks.

8. Measure the cylinder bore (**Figure 7**). Replace the master cylinder if the bore exceeds the specifications given in **Table 1**.

9. Measure the outside diameter of the piston as shown in **Figure 8** with a micrometer. Replace the piston assembly if it is less than the specifications given in **Table 1**.

Assembly

1. Soak the new cups in fresh brake fluid for at least 15 minutes to make them pliable. Coat the inside of the cylinder with fresh brake fluid prior to the assembly of parts.

CAUTION
When installing the piston assembly, do not allow the cups to turn inside out as they will be damaged and allow brake fluid leakage within the cylinder bore.

2. Install the spring, primary cup and piston assembly into the cylinder together. Install the spring with the tapered end facing toward the primary cup.

NOTE
Be sure to install the primary cup with the open end in first, toward the spring.

11

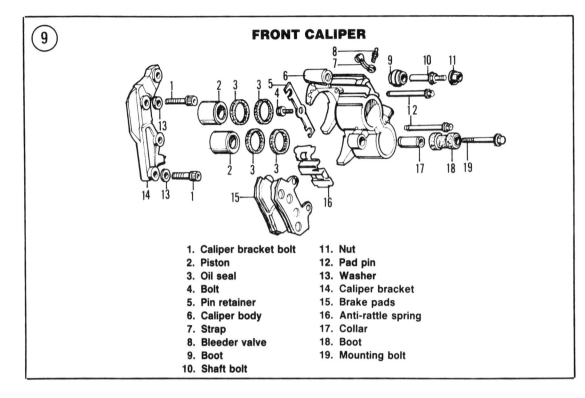

FRONT CALIPER

1. Caliper bracket bolt
2. Piston
3. Oil seal
4. Bolt
5. Pin retainer
6. Caliper body
7. Strap
8. Bleeder valve
9. Boot
10. Shaft bolt
11. Nut
12. Pad pin
13. Washer
14. Caliper bracket
15. Brake pads
16. Anti-rattle spring
17. Collar
18. Boot
19. Mounting bolt

3. Install the circlip and slide in the rubber boot.

4. Install the diaphragm and cover. Do not tighten the cover screws at this time as fluid will have to be added later when the system is bled.

5. Install the brake lever onto the master cylinder body.

6. If removed, install the brake light switch.

7. Install the master cylinder as described in this chapter.

FRONT BRAKE
PAD REPLACEMENT

There is no recommended mileage interval for changing the friction pads in the disc brake. Pad wear depends greatly on riding habits and conditions. The pads should be checked for wear every 6,400 km (4,000 miles) and replaced when the wear indicator reaches the edge of the brake disc. To maintain an even brake pressure on the disc always replace both pads in the caliper at the same time.

CAUTION
Watch the pads more closely when the wear line approaches the disc. On some pads the wear line is very close to the metal backing plate. If pad wear happens to be uneven for some reason the backing plate may come in contact with the disc and cause damage to the disc.

Refer to **Figure 9** for this procedure.

1. Remove the mounting bolt (A, **Figure 10**) and the caliper shaft bolt (B, **Figure 10**) securing the caliper assembly to the caliper bracket.

2. Pivot the caliper assembly up and off the disc and remove the caliper assembly.

3. Remove the bolt (A, **Figure 11**) securing the pad pin retainer to the caliper assembly and remove the pad pin retainer (B, **Figure 11**).

4. Remove both pad pins and both brake pads.

5. Clean the pad recess and the end of the pistons with a soft brush. Do not use solvent, a wire brush

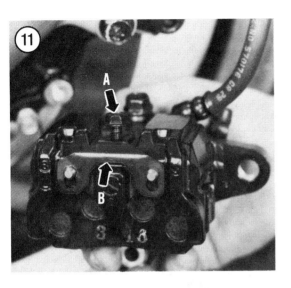

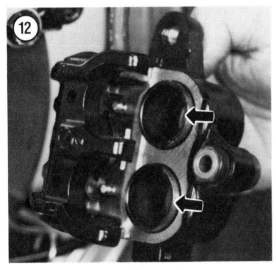

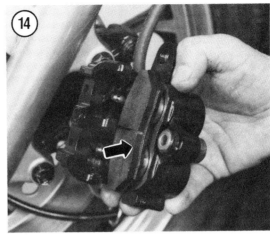

or any hard tool which would damage the cylinders or pistons.

6. Carefully remove any rust or corrosion from the disc.

7. Lightly coat the end of the pistons and the backs of the new pads (*not* the friction material) with disc brake lubricant.

> *NOTE*
> *When purchasing new pads, check with your dealer to make sure the friction compound of the new pad is compatible with the disc material. Remove any roughness from the backs of the new pads with a fine-cut file; blow them clean with compressed air.*

8. When new pads are installed in the caliper the master cylinder brake fluid level will rise as the caliper pistons are repositioned. Perform the following:

   a. Clean the top of the master cylinder of all dirt and foreign matter.

   b. Remove the cap and diaphragm from the master cylinder and slowly push the caliper pistons into the caliper. Constantly check the reservoir to make sure brake fluid does not overflow. Remove fluid, if necessary, prior to it overflowing.

   c. The pistons should move freely. If they don't and there is evidence of them sticking in the cylinder, the caliper should be removed and serviced as described in this chapter.

9. Push the caliper pistons in all the way (**Figure 12**) to allow room for the new pads.

10. Install the anti-rattle spring as shown in **Figure 13**.

11. Install the outboard pad (**Figure 14**) and partially install the pins through that pad.

12. Install the inboard pad (**Figure 15**).

13. Push the pins (**Figure 16**) all the way through.

14. Install the pad pin retainer onto the ends of the pins. Push the pin retainer down and make sure it seats completely on the groove in each pin.

15. Install the pad pin retaining bolt (A, **Figure 11**).

16. Carefully install the caliper assembly onto the disc. Be careful not to damage the leading edge of the pads during installation.

17. Lubricate the caliper upper pivot bolt and pivot boot on the caliper bracket with silicone grease.

18. Install the caliper mounting bolt and caliper shaft bolt. Tighten both bolts to torque specifications listed in **Table 2**.

19. Place wood blocks under the engine or frame so that the front wheel is off the ground. Spin the front wheel and activate the brake lever as many times as it takes to refill the cylinder in the caliper and correctly locate the pads.

20. Refill the master cylinder reservoir, if necessary, to maintain the correct fluid level. Install the diaphragm and top cap.

> *WARNING*
> *Use brake fluid from a sealed container clearly marked DOT 3. Other types may vaporize and cause brake failure. Always use the same brand name; do not intermix as many brands are not compatible. Do not intermix silicone based (DOT 5) brake fluid as it can cause brake component damage leading to brake system failure.*

> *WARNING*
> *Do not ride the motorcycle until you are sure the brakes are operating correctly with full hydraulic advantage. If necessary, bleed the brake as described in this chapter.*

21. Bed the pads in gradually for the first 80 km (50 miles) by using only light pressure as much as possible. Immediate hard application will glaze the new friction pads and greatly reduce the effectiveness of the brake.

FRONT CALIPER

Removal/Installation

Refer to **Figure 9** for this procedure.

It is not necessary to remove the front wheel in order to remove the caliper assembly.

> *CAUTION*
> *Do not spill any brake fluid on the painted portion of the front wheel. Wash any spilled brake fluid immediately, as it will destroy the finish. Use soapy water and rinse completely.*

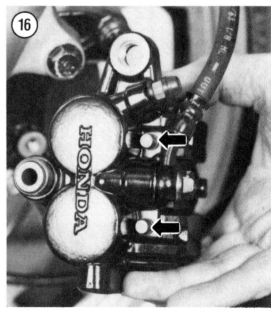

1. Place a container under the brake line at the caliper. Remove the union bolt and sealing washers (A, **Figure 17**) securing the brake line to the caliper assembly. Remove the brake line and let the brake fluid drain out into the container. Dispose of this brake fluid—never reuse brake fluid. To prevent the entry of moisture and dirt, cap the end of the brake line and tie the loose end up to the forks.

2. Loosen the caliper mounting bolt (B, **Figure 17**) and caliper shaft bolt (C, **Figure 17**) gradually in

several steps. Push on the caliper while loosening the bolts to push the pistons back into the caliper.

3. Remove the caliper mounting bolt (B, **Figure 17**) and caliper shaft bolt (C, **Figure 17**). Pivot the caliper assembly up and off the disc and remove the caliper assembly.

4. Lubricate the caliper upper pivot bolt and pivot boot with silicone grease.

5. Install by reversing these removal steps, noting the following.

6. Carefully install the caliper assembly onto the disc. Be careful not to damage the leading edge of the pads during installation.

7. Tighten the caliper mounting bolt and caliper shaft bolt to the torque specifications listed in **Table 2**.

8. Install the brake hose, with a sealing washer on each side of the fitting, onto the caliper. Install the union bolt and tighten to the torque specifications listed in **Table 2**.

9. Bleed the brake as described in this chapter.

> *WARNING*
> *Do not ride the motorcycle until you are sure that the brakes are operating properly.*

Rebuilding

If the caliper leaks, the caliper should be rebuilt. If the pistons stick in the cylinders, indicating severe wear or galling, the entire unit should be replaced. Rebuilding a leaky caliper requires special tools and experience.

Caliper service should be entrusted to a dealer, motorcycle repair shop or brake specialist. Considerable money can be saved by removing the caliper yourself and taking it in for repair.

FRONT BRAKE HOSE REPLACEMENT

There is no factory-recommended replacement interval but it is a good idea to replace the brake hose every four years or when it shows signs of cracking or damage.

Refer to **Figure 18** for this procedure.

> *CAUTION*
> *Cover the front wheel, fender and fuel tank with a heavy cloth or plastic tarp to protect it from accidental spilling of brake fluid. Wash brake fluid off of any painted or plated surface immediately, as it will destroy the finish. Use soapy water and rinse completely.*

1. Place a container under the brake hose at the caliper. Remove the union bolt and sealing washers

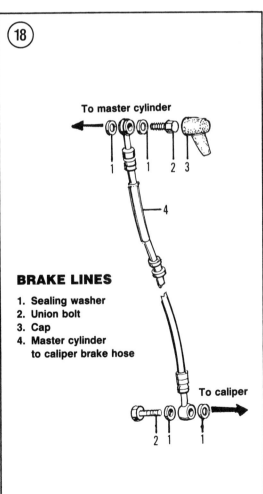

BRAKE LINES

1. Sealing washer
2. Union bolt
3. Cap
4. Master cylinder to caliper brake hose

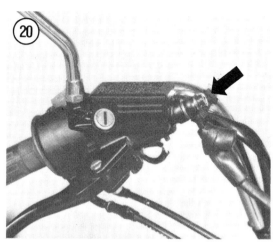

(**Figure 19**) securing the brake hose fitting to the caliper assembly.

2. Remove brake hose from the clip on the fork leg. Remove the brake hose and let the brake fluid drain out into the container. To prevent the entry of moisture and dirt, plug the brake hose inlet in the caliper.

> *WARNING*
> *Dispose of this brake fluid—never reuse brake fluid. Contaminated brake fluid can cause brake failure.*

3. Remove the union bolt (**Figure 20**) securing the brake hose to the master cylinder and remove the hose and the sealing washers.

4. Install new hoses, sealing washers and union bolts in the reverse order of removal. Be sure to install new sealing washers in the correct positions; refer to **Figure 18**.

5. Tighten all union bolts to torque specifications listed in **Table 2**.

6. Refill the master cylinder with fresh brake fluid clearly marked DOT 3 only. Bleed the brake as described in this chapter.

> *WARNING*
> *Use brake fluid from a sealed container clearly marked DOT 3. Other types may vaporize and cause brake failure. Always use the same brand name; do not intermix as many brands are not compatible. Do not intermix silicone based (DOT 5) brake fluid as it can cause brake component damage leading to brake system failure.*

> *WARNING*
> *Do not ride the motorcycle until you are sure that the brakes are operating properly.*

FRONT BRAKE DISC

Removal/Installation

1. Remove the front wheel as described in Chapter Nine.

> *NOTE*
> *Place a piece of wood or vinyl tube in the caliper in place of the disc. This way, if the brake lever is inadvertently squeezed, the pistons will not be forced out of the cylinders. If this does happen, the caliper might have to be disassembled to reseat the pistons and the system will have to be bled. By using the wood or vinyl tube, bleeding the system is not necessary when installing the wheel.*

> *CAUTION*
> *Do not set the wheel down on the disc surface, as it may get scratched or warped. Set the wheel on 2 blocks of wood (*Figure 21*).*

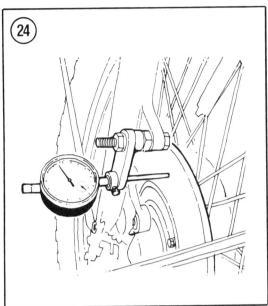

2. Remove the speedometer housing from the left-hand side and the spacer from the right-hand side.

3. Remove the Allen bolts (**Figure 22**) securing the brake disc to the hub and remove the disc.

4. Remove the damping shim located between the wheel hub and the disc.

5. Install by reversing these removal steps, noting the following.

6. Install the damping shim between the wheel hub and the disc.

7. Tighten the disc mounting Allen bolts to the torque specifications listed in **Table 2**.

Inspection

It is not necessary to remove the disc from the wheel to inspect it. Small marks on the disc are not important, but radial scratches deep enough to snag a fingernail reduce braking effectiveness and increase brake pad wear. If these grooves are found, the disc should be replaced.

1. Measure the thickness of the disc at several locations around the disc with a micrometer or vernier caliper (**Figure 23**). The disc must be replaced if the thickness, in any area, is less than that specified in **Table 1**.

2. Make sure the disc bolts are tight prior to running this check. Check the disc runout with a dial indicator as shown in **Figure 24**. Slowly rotate the wheel and watch the dial indicator. On all models, if the runout exceeds that listed in **Table 1** the disc must be replaced.

3. Clean the disc of any rust or corrosion and wipe clean with lacquer thinner. Never use an oil based solvent that may leave an oil residue on the disc.

BLEEDING THE SYSTEM

This procedure is not necessary unless the brakes feel spongy, there has been a leak in the system, a component has been replaced or the brake fluid has been replaced.

1. Remove the dust cap from the brake bleed valve.

11

2. Connect a length of clear tubing to the bleed valve on the caliper (**Figure 25**).

3. Place the other end of the tube into a clean container.

4. Fill the container with enough fresh brake fluid to keep the end submerged. The tube should be long enough so that a loop can be made higher than the bleed valve to prevent air from being drawn into the caliper during bleeding.

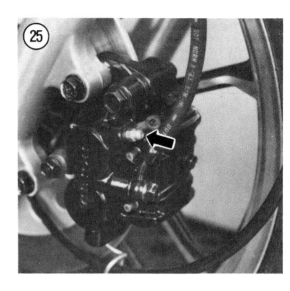

> *CAUTION*
> *Cover the fuel tank and instrument cluster with a heavy cloth or plastic tarp to protect it from the accidental spilling of brake fluid. Wash brake fluid off of any painted or plated surface immediately, as it will destroy the finish.*

5. Clean the cover of the master cylinder of all dirt and foreign matter. Remove the screws securing the top cover and remove the cover and diaphragm. Fill the reservoir almost to the top lip; insert the diaphragm and the cover loosely. Leave the cover in place during this procedure to prevent the entry of dirt.

> *WARNING*
> *Use brake fluid from a sealed container clearly marked DOT 3. Other types may vaporize and cause brake failure. Always use the same brand name; do not intermix as many brands are not compatible. Do not intermix (DOT 5) silicone based brake fluid as it can cause brake component damage leading to brake system failure.*

6. Insert a 20 mm (3/4 in.) spacer between the handlebar grip and the brake lever. This will prevent over-travel of the piston within the master cylinder.

7. Slowly apply the brake lever several times. Hold the lever in the applied position.

8. Open the bleed valve about one-half turn. Allow the lever to travel to its limit against the installed spacer. When this limit is reached, tighten the bleed screw.

9. As the fluid enters the system, the level will drop in the reservoir. Maintain the level at about 3/8 inch from the top of the reservoir to prevent air from being drawn into the system.

10. Continue to pump the lever and fill the reservoir until the fluid emerging from the hose is completely free of bubbles.

> *NOTE*
> *Do not allow the reservoir to empty during the bleeding operation or more air will enter the system. If this occurs, the entire procedure must be repeated.*

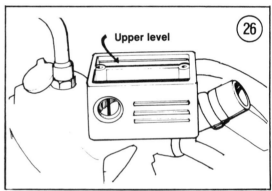

Upper level

11. Hold the lever in, tighten the bleed valve, remove the bleed tube and install the bleed valve dust cap.

12. If necessary, add fluid to correct the level in the reservoir. It should be to the upper level line (**Figure 26**).

13. Install the reservoir cover and tighten the screws.

14. Remove the spacer from the brake lever (installed in Step 6). Test the feel of the brake lever. It should be firm and should offer the same resistance each time it's operated. If it feels spongy, it is likely that there still is air in the system and it must be bled again. When all air has been bled from the system and the fluid level is correct in the reservoir, double-check for leaks and tighten all the fittings and connections.

> *WARNING*
> *Before riding the motorcycle, make certain that the brakes are operating correctly by operating the lever several times.*

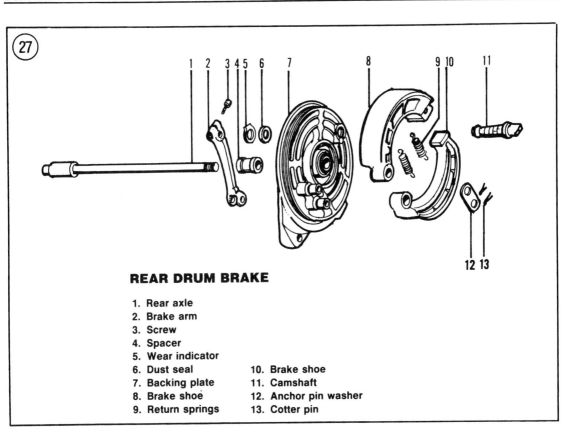

REAR DRUM BRAKE

1. Rear axle
2. Brake arm
3. Screw
4. Spacer
5. Wear indicator
6. Dust seal
7. Backing plate
8. Brake shoe
9. Return springs
10. Brake shoe
11. Camshaft
12. Anchor pin washer
13. Cotter pin

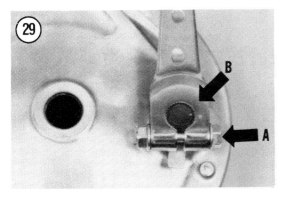

REAR DRUM BRAKE

Pushing down on the brake foot pedal pulls the rod which in turn rotates the camshaft. This forces the brake shoes out into contact with the brake drum.

Pedal free play must be maintained to minimize brake drag and premature brake wear and maximize braking effectiveness. Refer to Chapter Three for complete brake adjustment procedures.

Disassembly

Refer to **Figure 27** for this procedure.

1. Remove the rear wheel as described in Chapter Ten.
2. Pull the brake assembly straight up and out of the brake drum.
3. Remove the cotter pin and washer from the brake backing plate (**Figure 28**).
4. Remove the bolt and nut (A, **Figure 29**) securing the brake arm and remove the brake arm, wear indicator and dust seal. Withdraw the camshaft from the backing plate.
5. Using needlenose pliers remove the return spring (next to the camshaft) from the brake linings. Remove the other return spring in the same manner.

11

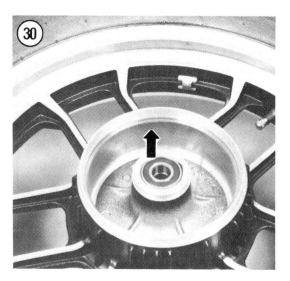

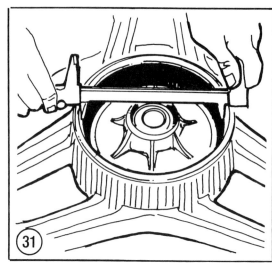

Inspection

1. Thoroughly clean and dry all parts except the brake linings.

2. Check the contact surface of the drum (**Figure 30**) for scoring. If there are grooves deep enough to snag your fingernail, the drum should be reground.

3. Measure the inside diameter of the brake drum with vernier calipers (**Figure 31**). If the measurement is greater than the service limit listed in **Table 1** the rear wheel must be replaced (the brake drum is an integral part of the wheel).

4. If the drum can be turned and still stay within the maximum service limit diameter, have the drum turned. If the drum is turned new linings will have to be installed and they must be arced to conform to the new drum contour.

5. Measure the brake linings with a vernier caliper (**Figure 32**). They should be replaced if the lining portion is worn to the service limit dimensions or less. Refer to specifications in **Table 1**.

6. Inspect the linings for imbedded foreign material. Dirt can be removed with a stiff wire brush. Check for any traces of oil or grease; if they are contaminated they must be replaced.

7. Inspect the cam lobe and pivot pin area of the backing plate (**Figure 33**) for wear or corrosion. Minor roughness can be removed with fine emery cloth.

8. Inspect the brake shoe return springs for wear. If they are stretched, they will not fully retract the brake shoes. Replace as necessary.

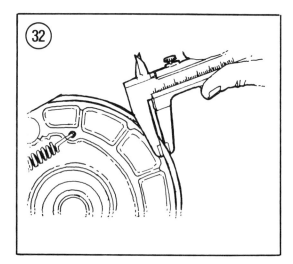

Assembly

1. Grease the camshaft with a light coat of molybdenum disulfide grease. Install the cam into the backing plate from the backside (**Figure 34**).

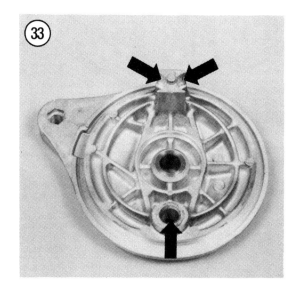

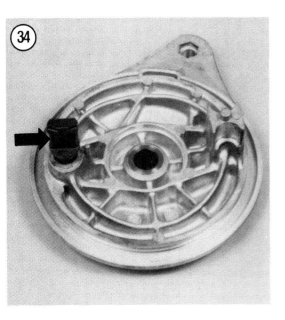

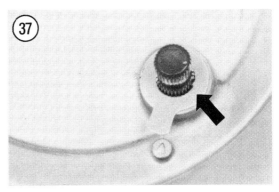

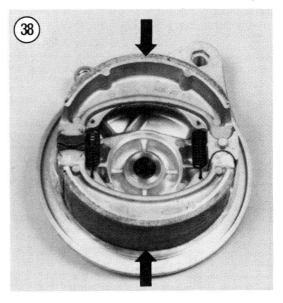

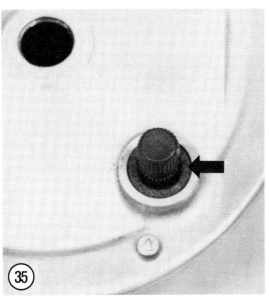

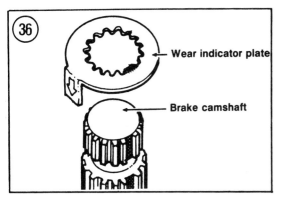

Wear indicator plate

Brake camshaft

2. From the outside of the backing plate install the dust seal (**Figure 35**).

3. Align the wear indicator to the camshaft as shown in **Figure 36** and push it down all the way to the backing plate (**Figure 37**).

4. When installing the brake arm onto the camshaft, be sure to align the dimples on the two parts (B, **Figure 29**). Tighten the bolt and nut to the torque specification listed in **Table 2**.

5. Grease the camshaft and pivot post with a light coat of molybdenum disulfide grease; avoid getting any grease on the brake backing plate where the brake linings may come in contact with it.

6. Hold the brake shoes in a "V" formation with the return springs attached and snap them into place on the brake backing plate. Make sure they are firmly seated on it (**Figure 38**). Install the lockwasher and a new cotter pin. Bend the ends over completely.

7. Install the brake panel assembly into the brake drum.

11

8. Install the rear wheel as described in Chapter Ten.

9. Adjust the rear brake as described in Chapter Three.

REAR BRAKE PEDAL

Removal/Installation

Refer to **Figure 39** for this procedure.

1. Completely unscrew the adjustment nut (**Figure 40**) on the brake rod.

2. Push down on the brake pedal and remove the brake rod from the pivot joint in the brake arm. Install the pivot joint onto the brake rod and reinstall the adjustment nut to avoid losing any small parts.

3. Disconnect the brake light switch return spring and the brake pedal return spring from the brake lever.

4. Remove the bolt and nut (**Figure 41**) securing the brake lever to the pivot shaft. Remove the brake pedal.

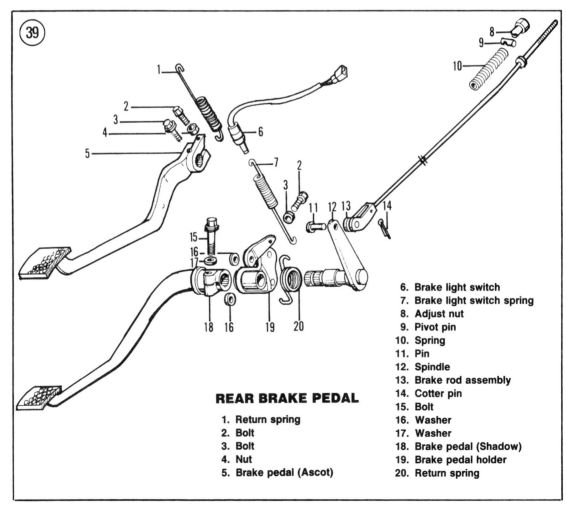

REAR BRAKE PEDAL

1. Return spring
2. Bolt
3. Bolt
4. Nut
5. Brake pedal (Ascot)
6. Brake light switch
7. Brake light switch spring
8. Adjust nut
9. Pivot pin
10. Spring
11. Pin
12. Spindle
13. Brake rod assembly
14. Cotter pin
15. Bolt
16. Washer
17. Washer
18. Brake pedal (Shadow)
19. Brake pedal holder
20. Return spring

5. Remove the cotter pin and pivot pin securing the brake rod to the pivot shaft arm.

6. Disconnect the return spring from the pivot shaft arm.

7A. On VT500C models, remove the bolts securing the pivot shaft holder and remove the holder and the pivot shaft arm.

7B. On VT500FT models, remove the pivot shaft arm from the frame.

8. Install by reversing these removal steps, noting the following.

9. Apply a light coat of multipurpose grease to all pivot areas prior to installing any components.

10. Install the brake pedal. Align the punch marks on the brake pedal and the brake pivot shaft.

Table 1 BRAKE SPECIFICATIONS

Item	Specifications	Wear limit
Master cylinder		
Cylinder bore ID	15.870-15.913 mm (0.6248-0.6265 in.)	15.93 mm (0.627 in.)
Piston OD	15.827-15.854 mm (0.6231-0.6242 in.)	15.82 mm (0.623 in.)
Front caliper		
Cylinder bore ID	30.148-30.280 mm (1.1901-1.1921 in.)	30.290 mm (1.1925 in.)
Piston OD	30.230-30.280 mm (1.1902-1.1913 in.)	30.140 mm (1.187 in.)
Front brake disc thickness	4.8-5.2 mm 0.19-0.20 in.	4.0 mm (0.16 in.)
Disc runout	—	0.3 mm (0.12 in.)
Rear brake drum ID	160.0-160.3 mm (6.30-6.31 in.)	161 mm (6.34 in.)
Rear brake shoe thickness	4.9-5.0 mm (0.19-0.20 in.)	2.0 mm (0.08 in.

Table 2 BRAKE TORQUE SPECIFICATIONS

Item	N•m	ft.-lb.
Brake hose union bolts	25-35	18-25
Front master cylinder cover screws	1-2	0.7-0.9
Rear master cylinder mounting bolts	10-14	7-10
Caliper shaft bolt	25-30	18-22
Caliper mounting bolt	20-25	14-18
Caliper bracket mounting bolts	30-40	22-29
Brake disc mounting bolts	35-40	25-29
Rear brake torque link bolt	15-25	11-18
Rear brake arm bolt	24-30	17-22

11

CHAPTER TWELVE

FRAME AND REPAINTING

This chapter includes replacement procedures for components attached to the frame that are not covered in the rest of the book.

This chapter also describes procedures for completely stripping the frame. Recommendations are provided for repainting the stripped frame.

KICKSTAND (SIDESTAND)

Removal/Installation

1. Place a wood block(s) under the frame to support the bike securely.
2. Raise the kickstand and disconnect the return spring (A, **Figure 1**) from the pin on the frame with Vise Grips.
3. From under the frame, remove the bolt and nut (B, **Figure 1**) and remove the kickstand from the frame.
4. Install by reversing these removal steps. Apply a light coat of multipurpose grease to the pivot surfaces of the frame tab and the kickstand yoke prior to installation.

CENTERSTAND

Removal/Installation

1. Place a wood block(s) under the frame to hold the bike securely in place.

CAUTION
Figure 2 *is shown with the centerstand in the lowered position for clarity. The*

centerstand must be in the raised position for spring removal to relieve the tension on the return spring.

2. Raise the centerstand and use Vise Grip pliers to unhook the return spring (A, **Figure 2**) from the centerstand.
3. Unscrew the bolt (B, **Figure 2**) on each side securing the centerstand to the frame.
4. Remove the centerstand from the frame.
5. Remove the pivot collar from each pivot area on the centerstand.
6. Install by reversing these removal steps, noting the following.

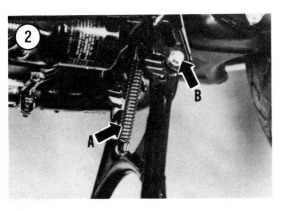

7. Apply multipurpose grease to the pivot collars and to the pivot areas of the centerstand where the pivot collars rides.

8. Tighten the bolts securely.

FOOTPEGS

Replacement

Remove the cotter pin and washer securing the footpeg to the bracket on the frame. Remove the pivot pin (**Figure 3**) and footpeg.

Make sure the spring is in good condition and not broken. Replace as necessary.

Lubricate the pivot point and pivot pin prior to installation. Install a new cotter pin and bend the ends over completely.

To remove the entire footpeg assembly, remove the bolts securing the assembly to the crankcase and remove the assembly.

SEAT

Removal/Installation (Ascot)

1. Remove both side covers.
2. Remove the bolt (**Figure 4**) on each side.
3. Remove the seat.
4. Install by reversing these removal steps.

Removal/Installation (Shadow)

1. Remove the screw (**Figure 5**) securing the small storage container and remove the container.
2. Remove the bolts (**Figure 6**) securing the seat at the rear.
3. Pull the rear of the seat up and pull toward the rear to disengage the seat from the front locator. Remove the seat.
4. Install by reversing these removal steps.

12

REAR FENDER

Removal/Installation (Ascot)

1. Remove both side covers and the seat.
2. Remove the bolts securing the upper rear cowl.
3. Remove the bolts securing the internal hand grips and remove both hand grips.
4. Remove the bolt and washer on each side and the nuts on the top of the front portion of the lower rear cowl and license plate holder.
5. Remove the nuts on the top of the forward fender section.
6. Remove the lower rear cowl.
7. Lift up on the forward fender section and remove the spacers on the studs located on the rear fender section.
8. Remove the forward and rear fender sections.
9. Install by reversing these removal steps.

Removal/Installation (Shadow)

1. Remove both side covers and the seat.
2. Remove the bolts securing the upper portion of the grab rail and remove the grab rail (A, **Figure 7**).
3. Disconnect the electrical connectors to both rear turn signals.
4. Remove the nuts and bolts securing the lower portion of the grab rail (B, **Figure 7**) on each side and remove both grab rails.
5. Remove the upper and lower rear fender sections from the frame.
6. Remove the forward section of the rear fender.
7. Install by reversing these removal steps.

FRAME

The frame does not require routine maintenance. However, it should be inspected immediately after any accident or spill.

Component Removal/Installation

1. Remove the seat, side cover panels and fuel tank.
2. Remove the engine as described in Chapter Four.
3. Remove the front wheel, steering head and front forks as described in Chapter Nine.
4. Remove the rear wheel, shock absorber and swing arm as described in Chapter Ten.
5. Remove the battery as described in Chapter Three.
6. Remove the wiring harness.
7. Remove the kickstand and footpegs as described in this chapter.
8. Remove the centerstand as described in this chapter.

9. Remove the steering head races from the steering head tube as described in Chapter Nine.
10. Inspect the frame for bends, cracks or other damage, especially around welded joints and areas that are rusted.
11. Assemble by reversing these removal steps.

Stripping and Painting

Remove all components from the frame. Thoroughly strip off all old paint. The best way is to have it sandblasted down to bare metal. If this is not possible, you can use a liquid paint remover and steel wool and a fine, hard wire brush.

CAUTION
Some of the fenders, side covers, frame covers and air box are molded plastic. If you wish to change the color of these parts, consult an automotive paint supplier for the proper procedure. Do not use any liquid paint remover on these components as it will damage the surface. The color is an integral part of some of these components and cannot be removed.

When the frame is down to bare metal, have it inspected for hairline and internal cracks. Magnaflux is the most common and complete process.

Make sure that the primer is compatible with the type of paint you are going to use for the finish color. Spray on one or two coats of primer as smoothly as possible. Let it dry thoroughly and use a fine grade of wet sandpaper (400-600 grit) to remove any flaws. Carefully wipe the surface clean and then spray a couple of coats of the final color. Use either lacquer or enamel base paint and follow the manufacturer's instructions.

A shop specializing in painting will probably do the best job. However, you can do a surprisingly good job with a good grade of spray paint. Spend a few extra dollars and get a good grade of paint as it will make a difference in how well it looks and how long it will stand up. It's a good idea to shake the can and make sure the ball inside the can is loose when you purchase the can of paint. Shake the can as long as is stated on the can. Then immerse the can *upright* in a pot or bucket of *warm water* (not hot—not over 120° F).

WARNING
*Higher temperatures could cause the can to burst. Do **not** place the can in direct contact with any flame or heat source.*

Leave the can in the water for several minutes. When thoroughly warmed, shake the can again and spray the frame. Be sure to get into all the crevices where there may be rust problems. Several light mist coats are better than one heavy coat. Spray painting is best done in temperatures of 70-80° F (21-26° C); any temperature above or below this will cause problems.

After the final coat has dried completely, at least 48 hours, any overspray or orange peel may be removed with a *light* application of Dupont rubbing compound (red color) and finished with Dupont polishing compound (white color). Be careful not to rub too hard or you will go through the finish.

Finish off with a couple coats of good wax prior to reassembling all the components.

It's a good idea to keep the frame touched up with fresh paint if any minor rust spots or scratches appear.

12

SUPPLEMENT

ADDITIONAL UK INFORMATION

The following supplement provides procedures unique to the 1983-1988 VT500E Euro Sport models. All other service procedures are identical to the U.S. models.

The chapter headings in this supplement correspond to those in the main body of this book. If a procedure is not included in the supplement, follow the procedure in the main body of this book.

CHAPTER SIX

FUEL AND EXHAUST SYSTEMS

EXHAUST SYSTEM

The VT500E exhaust system resembles that of the other models except that it does not have an inter-connecting power chamber mounted transversely before the two mufflers. The mufflers are of the tapering megaphone type.

Removal/Installation

Refer to **Figure 1** for this procedure.
1. Place the bike on the centerstand.
2. Remove the nuts securing the exhaust pipe flange to the front cylinder head and loosen the clamp bolt on the front exhaust pipe mounting clamp. Remove the front exhaust pipe.
3. Remove the nuts securing the exhaust pipe flange to the rear cylinder head and loosen the left muffler clamp bolt.
4. Remove the mounting bolts from the right and left mufflers, and remove the right muffler. Remove the left muffler and the rear exhaust pipe assembly.

NOTE
If difficult to remove, spray some WD-40 on the clamping bolts to help loosen the muffler joints.

5. Inspect the gaskets at all joints and replace if necessary.
6. Be sure to install a new gasket in the exhaust port of both cylinder heads.
7. Apply a light coating of multipurpose grease to the cross-over joints between the two mufflers. This will make connecting them much easier.
8. Install the assembly into position and install all bolts and nuts only finger-tight until the exhaust flange nuts and washers are installed and securely tightened. This will minimize an exhaust leak at the cylinder heads.
9. Tighten all bolts and nuts to the torque specifications listed in **Table 2** of the main body.
10. After installation is complete, make sure there are no exhaust leaks.

13

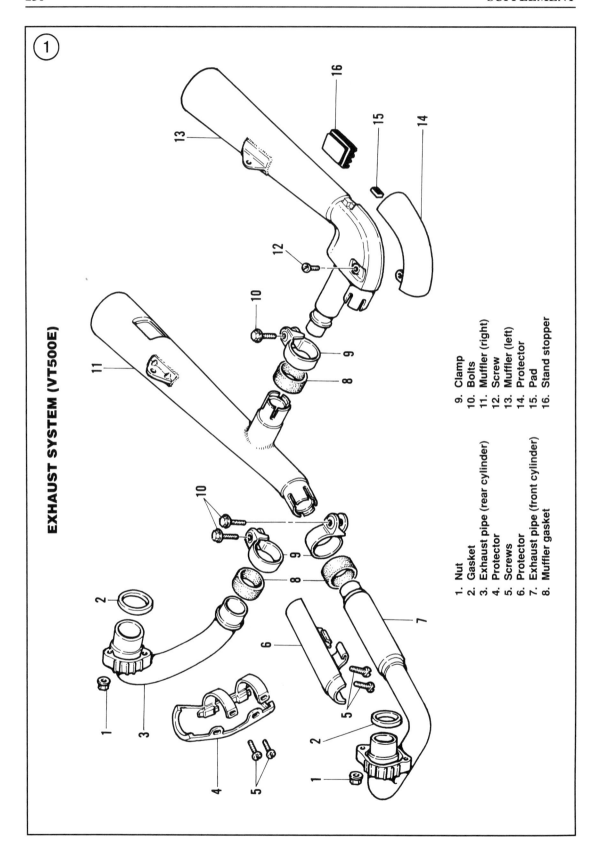

EXHAUST SYSTEM (VT500E)

1. Nut
2. Gasket
3. Exhaust pipe (rear cylinder)
4. Protector
5. Screws
6. Protector
7. Exhaust pipe (front cylinder)
8. Muffler gasket
9. Clamp
10. Bolts
11. Muffler (right)
12. Screw
13. Muffler (left)
14. Protector
15. Pad
16. Stand stopper

CHAPTER NINE

FRONT SUSPENSION AND STEERING

The VT500 Euro Sport models imported into the UK have a different front fork assembly and are fitted with Comstar wheels. The front wheel is fitted with a single inboard, ventilated disc brake. The following instructions and references to **Figure 2** and **Figure 3** should be observed for removal and installation of the front wheel.

FRONT WHEEL

Removal

1. Place the bike on the centerstand or place wood blocks under the engine and frame to support it securely with the front wheel off the ground.
2. Remove the speedometer cable set screw and pull the speedometer cable from the speedometer gearbox.
3. Remove the three set screws that retain the disc shroud.
4. Loosen the nuts securing the right-hand axle clamp at the bottom of the fork slider. Unscrew and remove the axle shaft.
5. Let the wheel drop, then maneuver the disc cover, caliper assembly and brake disc out of position together.
6. Tie the brake assembly to the front fork so that it is not left suspended by the brake hose.

NOTE
Insert a piece of vinyl tubing or wood into the caliper in place of the brake disc. That way if the brake lever is inadvertently squeezed, the pistons will not be forced out of the caliper cylinders. If this does happen, the caliper may have to be disassembled to reseat the pistons and the system will have to be bled. By using the tubing or wood, bleeding the

brake is not necessary when installing the wheel.

7. Pull the wheel forward to remove it from the fork sliders.

CAUTION
Do not lay the wheel on the disc surface as it may otherwise get scratched or become warped. If necessary, suspend the disc by resting the wheel on two wooden blocks.

Installation

1. Make sure the axle bearing surfaces of the fork slider and axle are free from burrs and nicks. Also check the condition of the threads on the studs and nuts that secure the right-hand axle clamp.
2. Remove the vinyl tubing or piece of wood from the brake caliper.
3. Position the wheel between the fork sliders and replace the brake disc, caliper assembly and the disc cover. Make sure the grooves of the disc are aligned with the brake disc springs.
4. Align the slot in the brake caliper assembly with the protruding stop on the left-hand fork slider.
5. Install the right-hand axle clamp loosely, with the arrow mark facing forward.
6. Replace and tighten the axle shaft to 55-65 N•m (40-47 ft.-lb.).
7. Tighten the axle clamp nuts, starting with the forward facing nut to 18-25 N•m (13-18 ft.-lb.).
8. Replace and tighten the three set screws that retain the disc shroud.
9. Slowly rotate the wheel and install the speedometer cable. Replace and tighten the set screw.
10. After the wheel is completely installed, rotate it several times and apply the front brake a couple of times to make sure the wheel rotates freely and that the brake pads are against the disc correctly.

13

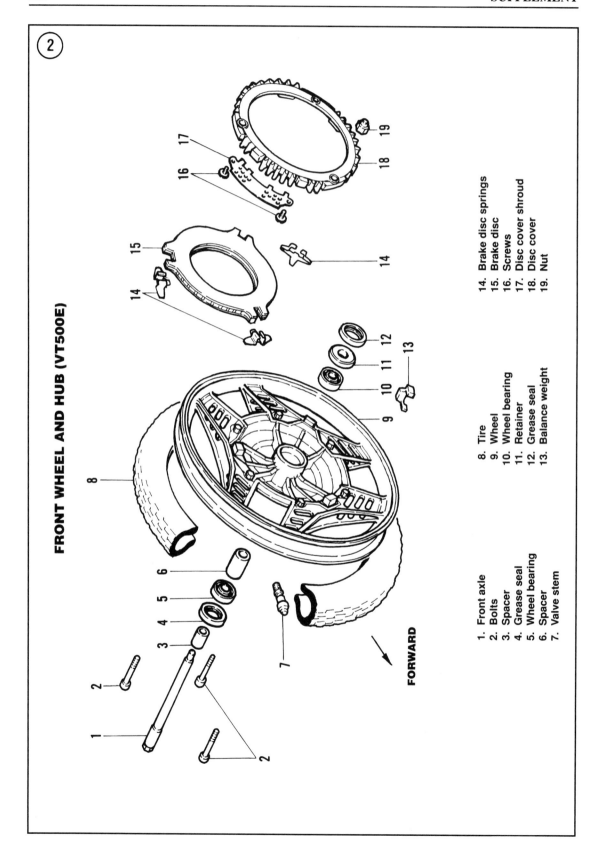

FRONT WHEEL AND HUB (VT500E)

FORWARD

1. Front axle
2. Bolts
3. Spacer
4. Grease seal
5. Wheel bearing
6. Spacer
7. Valve stem
8. Tire
9. Wheel
10. Wheel bearing
11. Retainer
12. Grease seal
13. Balance weight
14. Brake disc springs
15. Brake disc
16. Screws
17. Disc cover shroud
18. Disc cover
19. Nut

FRONT CALIPER AND BRACKET (VT500E)

FORWARD

1. Circlip
2. Speedometer gear
3. Washers
4. Screws
5. Brake disc shroud
6. Caliper bracket
7. Indicator
8. Pin bolt
9. Shims
10. Screw
11. Speedometer cable holder
12. Bolt
13. Pin bolt
14. O-ring
15. Spacer
16. Antirattle spring
17. Brake pad
18. Brake pad
19. Piston
20. Dust seal
21. Piston seal
22. Boot
23. Caliper
24. Cap
25. Bleeder screw
26. Locating bolt

13

CHAPTER ELEVEN

BRAKES

FRONT BRAKE PAD REPLACEMENT

Refer to **Figure 3**.

1. Remove the speedometer cable set screw and pull the speedometer cable from the speedometer gearbox.

2. Remove the three set screws that retain the disc shroud and maneuver it clear of the brake.

3. Unscrew the pad locating bolt and push the brake caliper against the disc so that the pistons are forced back into their housings to give the maximum amount of clearance.

> *CAUTION*
> *Clean the top of the master cylinder of all dirt and foreign matter. Remove the cap and diaphragm from the master cylinder and constantly check the reservoir to make sure the brake fluid does not overflow as the pistons are forced back into their housings. Remove fluid, if necessary, prior to it overflowing. Brake fluid will destroy any paint finish on which it is spilled. Wash any spilled brake fluid immediately, using soapy water, and rinse completely.*

4. Lift out the brake pads.

5. The pistons should move freely. If they don't and there is evidence of them sticking in the cylinder, the caliper should be removed and serviced as described in this chapter.

6. Clean the pad recess and the end of the pistons with a soft brush. Do not use solvent, a wire brush or any hard tool which would damage the cylinders or pistons.

7. Carefully remove any rust or corrosion from the disc.

8. Lightly coat the end of the pistons and the back of the new pads (not the friction material) with disc brake lubricant.

> *NOTE*
> *When purchasing new pads, check with your dealer to make sure the friction compound is compatible with the disc*

material. Remove any roughness from the backs of the new pads with a fine-cut file; blow them clean with compressed air.

9. Push the caliper pistons in all the way, to allow room for the new pads.

10. Install the antirattle spring and check that the shims are in position.

11. Install the pads, making sure they locate correctly.

12. Apply silicone grease to the pad locating bolt, then install and securely tighten the bolt.

13. Replace and tighten the three set screws that retain the disc shroud.

14. Replace the speedometer drive cable and retain it with the set screw.

15. Place the machine on the centerstand or place wooden blocks under the engine and frame to support it securely with the front wheel off the ground. Spin the front wheel and activate the brake lever as many times as it takes to refill the cylinders in the caliper and correctly locate the pads.

16. Refill the master cylinder reservoir, if necessary, to maintain the correct fluid level. Install the diaphragm and top cap.

> *WARNING*
> *Use brake fluid from a sealed container clearly marked DOT 3. Other types may vaporize and cause brake failure. Always use the same brand name; do not intermix as many brands are not compatible. Do not intermix silicone-based (DOT 5) brake fluid as it can cause brake component damage leading to brake system failure.*

> *WARNING*
> *Do not ride the motorcycle until you are sure the brakes are operating correctly with full hydraulic advantage. If necessary, bleed the brake system as described in the main body.*

FRONT CALIPER

Removal/Installation

Refer to **Figure 3**.

1. Remove the front wheel as described in this supplement.

2. Remove the union bolt and sealing washers securing the brake line to the caliper. Remove the brake line and let the brake fluid drain out into a container. Properly dispose of this brake fluid. To prevent the entry of moisture or dirt, cap the end of the brake line and tie the loose end to the fork slider.

3. Remove the brake disc from the disc cover and caliper assembly.

4. Unscrew the pad locating bolt and remove the brake pads.

5. Pull the caliper assembly out of the caliper bracket.

6. Install by reversing the above procedure while noting the following.

7. Carefully install the brake disc, taking care not to damage the leading edge of the pads.

8. Apply silicone grease to the pad locating bolt, then install and securely tighten the bolt.

9. Install the brake hose on the caliper, with a sealing washer on each side of the union. Install the union bolt and tighten to 25-35 N•m (18-25 ft.-lb.).

10. Bleed the brake as described in the main body.

WARNING
Do not ride the motorcycle until you are
sure the brakes are operating properly.

Rebuilding

If the caliper leaks, it should be rebuilt. If the pistons stick in the cylinders, indicating severe wear or galling, the entire unit should be replaced. Rebuilding a leaky caliper requires special tools and experience. Caliper service should be entrusted to a dealer, motorcycle repair shop or brake specialist. Considerable money can be saved by removing the caliper yourself and taking it in for repair.

13

INDEX

14

14

1983 VT500FT Ascot
1983-1988 VT500E Euro Sport*

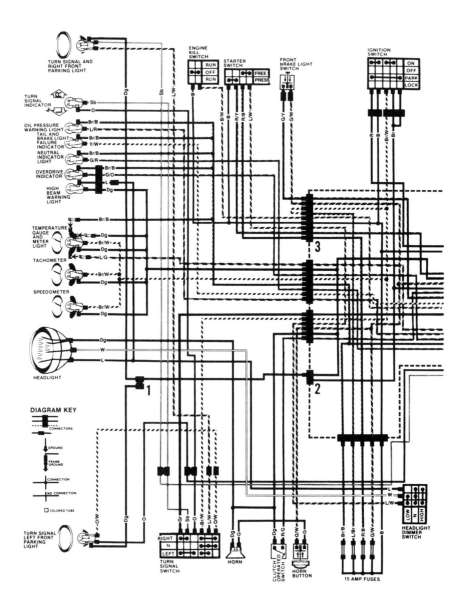

*VT500E models are equipped with a position light. A green wire connects at location 1 and routes to the position light in the headlight assembly. A brown wire runs from the position light to location 2. Parking lights are not used in front turn signals. VT500E models are equipped with a manual control light switch. Red/black wire at location 3 is routed to light switch assembly. Red/black and blue/white wires in starter switch are not used.

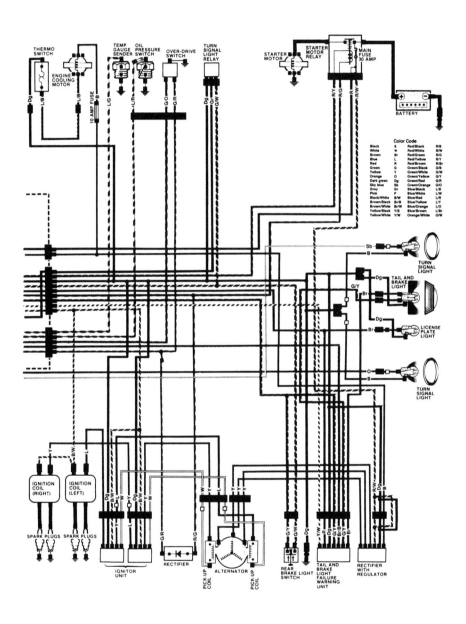

15

1983 VT500C Shadow

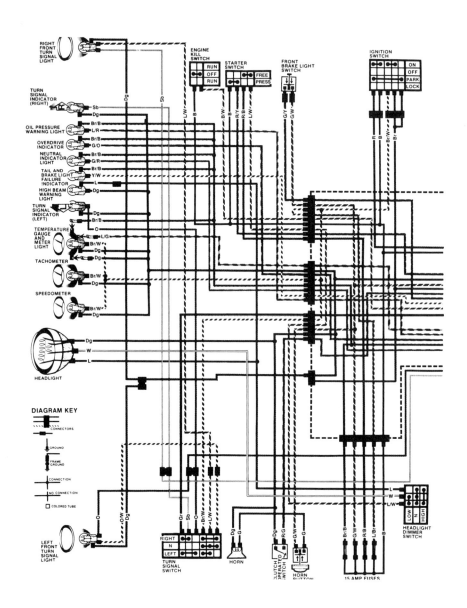

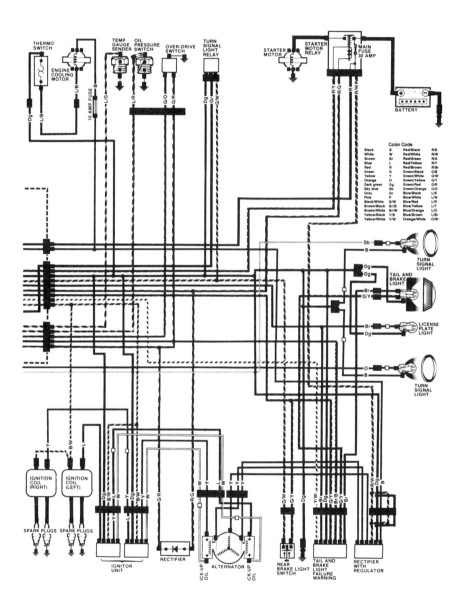

1984 VT500FT Ascot

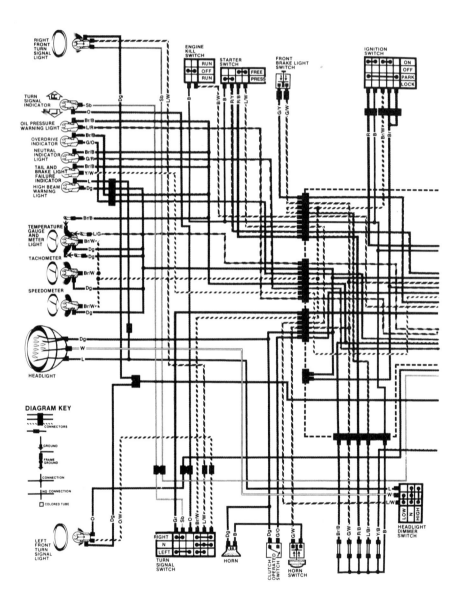

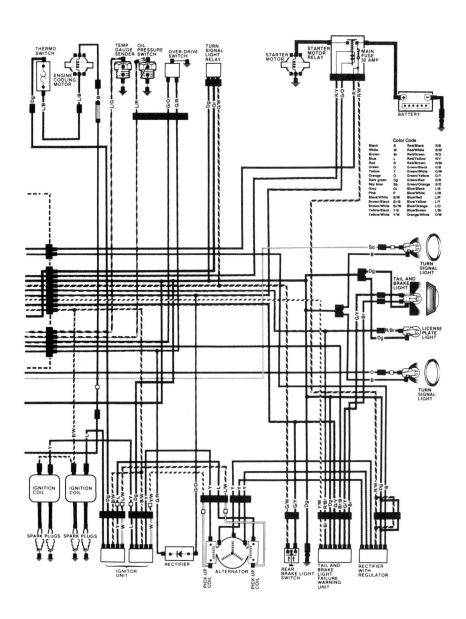

1984 VT500C Shadow

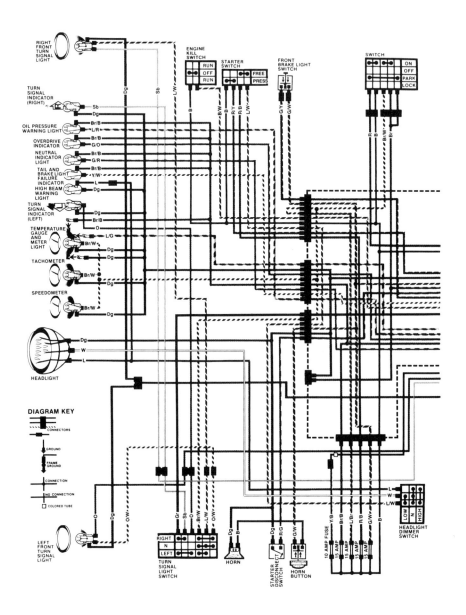

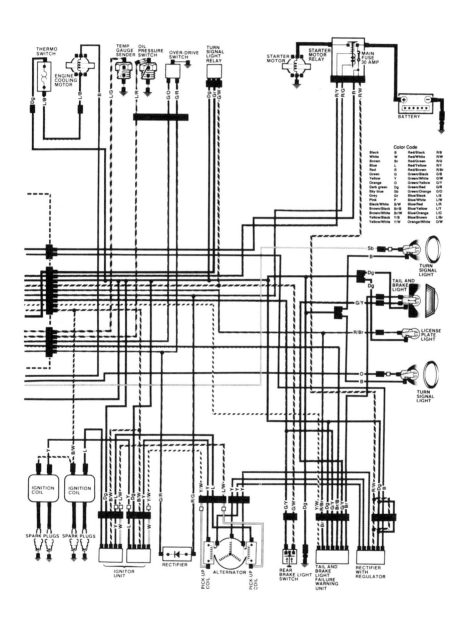

1985 VT500C

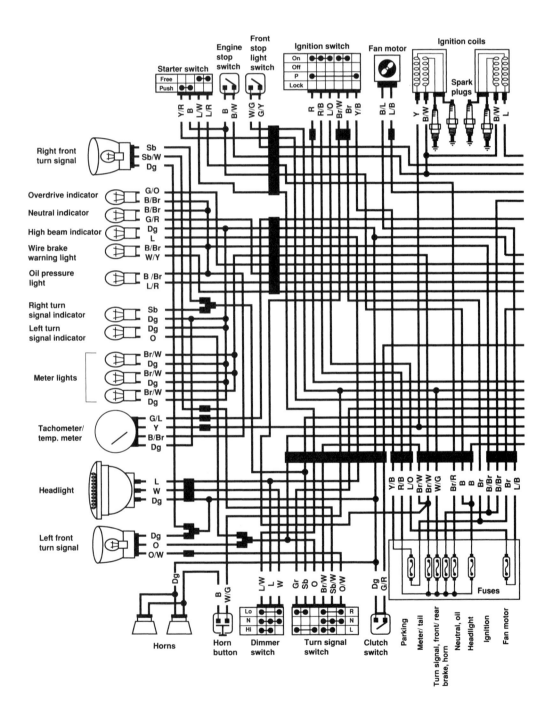

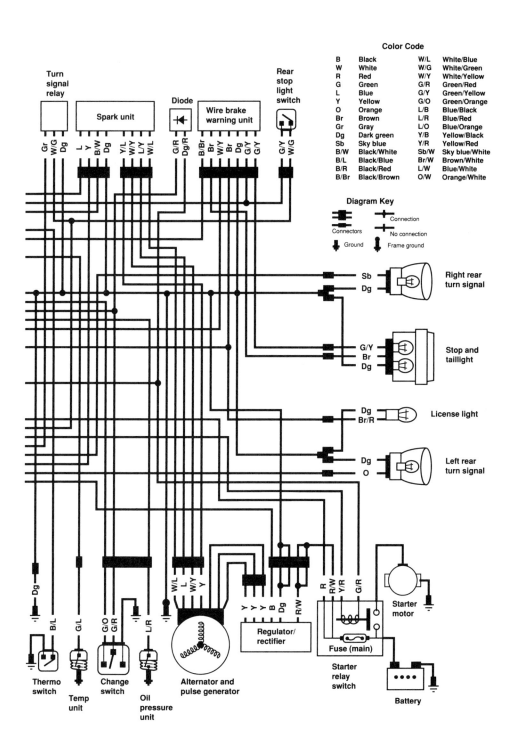

Color Code

B	Black	W/L	White/Blue
W	White	W/G	White/Green
R	Red	W/Y	White/Yellow
G	Green	G/R	Green/Red
L	Blue	G/Y	Green/Yellow
Y	Yellow	G/O	Green/Orange
O	Orange	L/B	Blue/Black
Br	Brown	L/R	Blue/Red
Gr	Gray	L/O	Blue/Orange
Dg	Dark green	Y/B	Yellow/Black
Sb	Sky blue	Y/R	Yellow/Red
B/W	Black/White	Sb/W	Sky blue/White
B/L	Black/Blue	Br/W	Brown/White
B/R	Black/Red	L/W	Blue/White
B/Br	Black/Brown	O/W	Orange/White

15

1986 VT500C

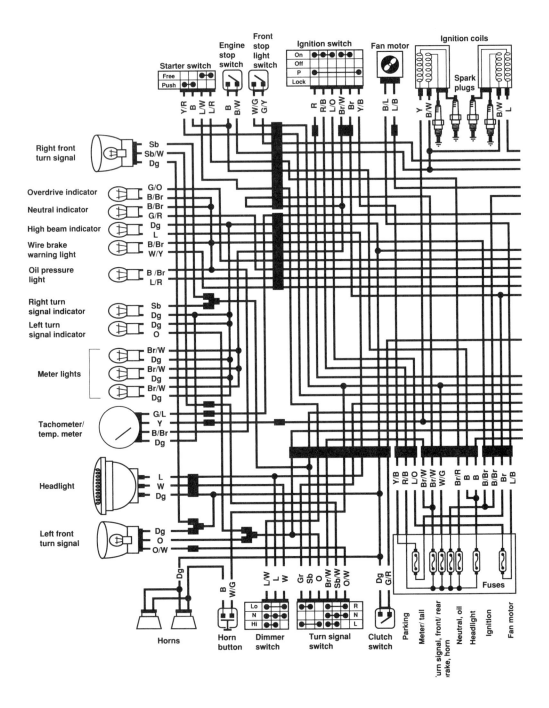

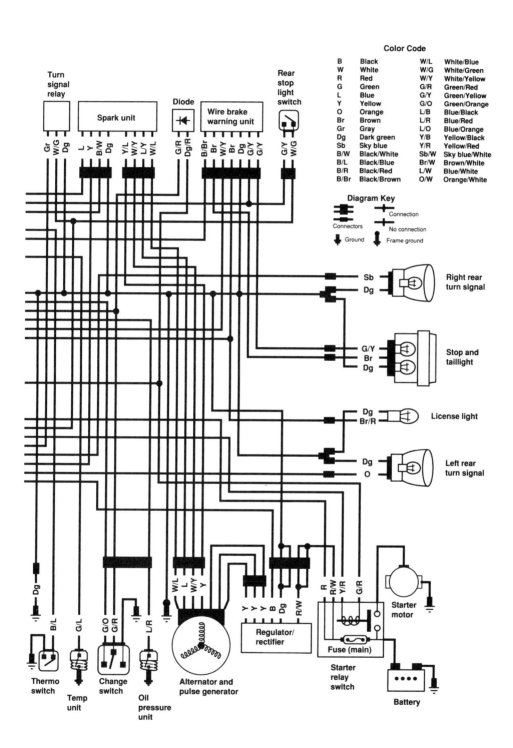

Color Code

B	Black	W/L	White/Blue
W	White	W/G	White/Green
R	Red	W/Y	White/Yellow
G	Green	G/R	Green/Red
L	Blue	G/Y	Green/Yellow
Y	Yellow	G/O	Green/Orange
O	Orange	L/B	Blue/Black
Br	Brown	L/R	Blue/Red
Gr	Gray	L/O	Blue/Orange
Dg	Dark green	Y/B	Yellow/Black
Sb	Sky blue	Y/R	Yellow/Red
B/W	Black/White	Sb/W	Sky blue/White
B/L	Black/Blue	Br/W	Brown/White
B/R	Black/Red	L/W	Blue/White
B/Br	Black/Brown	O/W	Orange/White

Diagram Key

Connectors

Connection

No connection

Ground

Frame ground

15

NOTES

MAINTENANCE LOG

Date	Miles	Type of Service

Check out *clymer.com* for our full line of powersport repair manuals.

BMW

M308	500 & 600 CC Twins, 55-69
M309	F650, 1994-2000
M500-3	BMW K-Series, 85-97
M501	K1200RS, GT & LT, 98-05
M502-3	BMW R50/5-R100GS PD, 70-96
M503-3	R850, R1100, R1150 and R1200C, 93-05

HARLEY-DAVIDSON

M419	Sportsters, 59-85
M429-5	XL/XLH Sportster, 86-03
M427-1	XL Sportster, 04-06
M418	Panheads, 48-65
M420	Shovelheads,66-84
M421-3	FLS/FXS Evolution,84-99
M423-2	FLS/FXS Twin Cam, 00-05
M422-3	FLH/FLT/FXR Evolution, 84-99
M430-4	FLH/FLT Twin Cam, 99-05
M424-2	FXD Evolution, 91-98
M425-3	FXD Twin Cam, 99-05
M426	V-Rod, 02-07

HONDA

ATVs

M316	Odyssey FL250, 77-84
M311	ATC, TRX & Fourtrax 70-125, 70-87
M433	Fourtrax 90, 93-00
M326	ATC185 & 200, 80-86
M347	ATC200X & Fourtrax 200SX, 86-88
M455	ATC250 & Fourtrax 200/250, 84-87
M342	ATC250R, 81-84
M348	TRX250R/Fourtrax 250R & ATC250R, 85-89
M456-3	TRX250X 87-92; TRX300EX 93-04
M215	TRX250EX, 01-05
M446-3	TRX250 Recon & Recon ES, 97-07
M346-3	TRX300/Fourtrax 300 & TRX300FW/Fourtrax 4x4, 88-00
M200-2	TRX350 Rancher, 00-06
M459-3	TRX400 Foreman 95-03
M454-3	TRX400EX 99-05
M205	TRX450 Foreman, 98-04
M210	TRX500 Rubicon, 01-04

Singles

M310-13	50-110cc OHC Singles, 65-99
M319-2	XR50R, CRF50F, XR70R & CRF70F, 97-05
M315	100-350cc OHC, 69-82
M317	Elsinore, 125-250cc, 73-80
M442	CR60-125R Pro-Link, 81-88
M431-2	CR80R, 89-95, CR125R, 89-91
M435	CR80R, 96-02
M457-2	CR125R & CR250R, 92-97
M464	CR125R, 1998-2002
M443	CR250R-500R Pro-Link, 81-87
M432-3	CR250R, 88-91 & CR500R, 88-01
M437	CR250R, 97-01
M352	CRF250R, CRF250X, CRF450R & CRF450X, 02-05
M312-13	XL/XR75-100, 75-03
M318-4	XL/XR/TLR 125-200, 79-03
M328-4	XL/XR250, 78-00; XL/XR350R 83-85; XR200R, 84-85; XR250L, 91-96
M320-2	XR400R, 96-04
M339-8	XL/XR 500-600, 79-90
M221	XR600R & XR650L, 91-07

Twins

M321	125-200cc Twins, 65-78
M322	250-360cc Twins, 64-74
M323	250-360cc Twins, 74-77
M324-5	Twinstar, Rebel 250 & Nighthawk 250, 78-03
M334	400-450cc Twins, 78-87
M333	450 & 500cc Twins, 65-76
M335	CX & GL500/650, 78-83
M344	VT500, 83-88
M313	VT700 & 750, 83-87
M314-3	VT750 Shadow (chain drive), 98-06
M440	VT1100C Shadow , 85-96
M460-4	VT1100 Series, 95-07

Fours

M332	CB350-550, SOHC, 71-78
M345	CB550 & 650, 83-85
M336	CB650,79-82
M341	CB750 SOHC, 69-78
M337	CB750 DOHC, 79-82
M436	CB750 Nighthawk, 91-93 & 95-99
M325	CB900, 1000 & 1100, 80-83
M439	Hurricane 600, 87-90
M441-2	CBR600F2 & F3, 91-98
M445-2	CBR600F4, 99-06
M220	CBR600RR, 03-06
M434-2	CBR900RR Fireblade, 93-99
M329	500cc V-Fours, 84-86
M438	VFR800 Interceptor, 98-00
M349	700-1000 Interceptor, 83-85
M458-2	VFR700F-750F, 86-97
M327	700-1100cc V-Fours, 82-88
M340	GL1000 & 1100, 75-83
M504	GL1200, 84-87
M508	ST1100/Pan European, 90-02

Sixes

M505	GL1500 Gold Wing, 88-92
M506-2	GL1500 Gold Wing, 93-00
M507-2	GL1800 Gold Wing, 01-05
M462-2	GL1500C Valkyrie, 97-03

KAWASAKI

ATVs

M465-2	Bayou KLF220 & KLF250, 88-03
M466-4	Bayou KLF300, 86-04
M467	Bayou KLF400, 93-99
M470	KEF300 Lakota, 95-99
M385-2	Mojave KSF250, 87-04

Singles

M350-9	Rotary Valve 80-350cc, 66-01
M444-2	KX60, 83-02; KX80 83-90
M448	KX80/85/100, 89-03
M351	KDX200, 83-88
M447-3	KX125 & KX250, 82-91 KX500, 83-04
M472-2	KX125, 92-00
M473-2	KX250, 92-00
M474-2	KLR650, 87-06

Twins

M355	KZ400, KZ/Z440, EN450 & EN500, 74-95
M360-3	EX500, GPZ500S, Ninja 500 R, 87-02
M356-5	Vulcan 700 & 750, 85-06
M354-2	Vulcan 800 & Vulcan 800 Classic, 95-04
M357-2	Vulcan 1500, 87-99
M471-3	Vulcan 1500, 96-08

Fours

M449	KZ500/550 & ZX550, 79-85
M450	KZ, Z & ZX750, 80-85
M358	KZ650, 77-83
M359-3	Z & KZ 900-1000cc, 73-81
M451-3	KZ, ZX & ZN 1000 &1100cc, 81-02
M452-3	ZX500 & Ninja ZX600, 85-97
M453-3	Ninja ZX900-1100 84-01
M468-2	Ninja ZX-6, 90-04
M469	ZX-7 Ninja, 91-98
M453-3	Ninja ZX900, ZX1000 & ZX1100, 84-01
M409	Concours, 86-04

POLARIS

ATVs

M496	3-, 4- and 6-Wheel Models w/250-425cc Engines, 85-95
M362	Magnum and Big Boss, 96-98
M363	Scrambler 500, 4X4 97-00
M365-2	Sportsman/Xplorer, 96-03

SUZUKI

ATVs

M381	ALT/LT 125 & 185, 83-87
M475	LT230 & LT250, 85-90
M380-2	LT250R Quad Racer, 85-92
M270	LT-Z400, 03-07
M343	LTF500F Quadrunner, 98-00
M483-2	King Quad/ Quad Runner 250, 87-98

Singles

M371	RM50-400 Twin Shock, 75-81
M369	125-400cc 64-81
M379	RM125-500 Single Shock, 81-88
M476	DR250-350, 90-94
M477	DR-Z400, 00-06
M384-3	LS650 Savage, 86-04
M386	RM80-250, 89-95
M400	RM125, 96-00
M401	RM250, 96-02

Twins

M372	GS400-450 Chain Drive, 77-87
M481-5	VS700-800 Intruder, 85-07
M260	Volusia/Boulevard C50, 01-06
M482-2	VS1400 Intruder, 87-03
M261	LC/VL1500 & C90, 98-07
M484-3	GS500E Twins, 89-02
M361	SV650, 1999-2002

Triple

M368	380-750cc, 72-77

Fours

M373	GS550, 77-86
M364	GS650, 81-83
M370	GS750, 77-82
M376	GS850-1100 Shaft Drive, 79-84
M378	GS1100 Chain Drive, 80-81
M383-3	Katana 600, 88-96 GSX-R750-1100, 86-87
M331	GSX-R600, 97-00
M264	GSX-R600, 01-05
M478-2	GSX-R750, 88-92 GSX750F Katana, 89-96
M485	GSX-R750, 96-99
M377	GSX-R1000, 01-04
M265	GSX1300R, 99-07
M338	GSF600 Bandit, 95-00
M353	GSF1200 Bandit, 96-03

YAMAHA

ATVs

M499	YFM80 Badger, 85-88 & 92-01
M394	YTM200, 250 & YFM200, 83-86
M488-5	Blaster, 88-05
M489-2	Timberwolf, 89-00
M487-5	Warrior, 87-04
M486-6	Banshee, 87-06
M490-3	Moto-4 & Big Bear, 87-04
M493	Kodiak, 93-98
M280-2	Raptor 660R, 01-05
M285	Grizzly 660, 02-07

Singles

M492-2	PW50 & PW80, BW80 Big Wheel 80, 81-02
M410	80-175 Piston Port, 68-76
M415	250-400 Piston Port, 68-76
M412	DT & MX 100-400, 77-83
M414	IT125-490, 76-86
M393	YZ50-80 Monoshock, 78-90
M413	YZ100-490 Monoshock, 76-84
M390	YZ125-250, 85-87 YZ490, 85-90
M391	YZ125-250, 88-93 WR250Z, 91-93
M497-2	YZ125, 94-01
M498	YZ250, 94-98 WR250Z, 94-97
M406	YZ250F & WR250F, 01-03
M491-2	YZ400F, YZ426F, WR400F WR426F, 98-02
M417	XT125-250, 80-84
M480-3	XT/TT 350, 85-00
M405	XT/TT 500, 76-81
M416	XT/TT 600, 83-89

Twins

M403	650cc, 70-82
M395-10	XV535-1100 Virago, 81-03
M495-5	V-Star 650, 98-07
M281-3	V-Star 1100, 99-07
M282	Road Star, 99-05

Triple

M404	XS750 & 850, 77-81

Fours

M387	XJ550, XJ600 & FJ600, 81-92
M494	XJ600 Seca II/Diversion, 92-98
M388	YX600 Radian & FZ600, 86-90
M396	FZR600, 89-93
M392	FZ700-750 & Fazer, 85-87
M411	XS1100, 78-81
M397	FJ1100 & 1200, 84-93
M375	V-Max, 85-03
M374	Royal Star, 96-03
M461	YZF-R6, 99-04
M398	YZF-R1, 98-03
M399	FZ1, 01-05

VINTAGE MOTORCYCLES

Clymer® Collection Series

M330	Vintage British Street Bikes, BSA, 500–650cc Unit Twins; Norton, 750 & 850cc Commandos; Triumph, 500-750cc Twins
M300	Vintage Dirt Bikes, V. 1 Bultaco, 125-370cc Singles; Montesa, 123-360cc Singles; Ossa, 125-250cc Singles
M301	Vintage Dirt Bikes, V. 2 CZ, 125-400cc Singles; Husqvarna, 125-450cc Singles; Maico, 250-501cc Singles; Hodaka, 90-125cc Singles
M305	Vintage Japanese Street Bikes Honda, 250 & 305cc Twins; Kawasaki, 250-750cc Triples; Kawasaki, 900 & 1000cc Fours